SEX IN JAPAN'S GLOBALIZATION, 1870–1930: PROSTITUTES, EMIGRATION AND NATION-BUILDING

Perspectives in Economic and Social History

Series Editors: *Andrew August*
Robert E. Wright

Titles in this Series

1 Migrants and Urban Change: Newcomers to Antwerp, 1760–1860
Anne Winter

2 Female Entrepreneurs in Nineteenth-Century Russia
Galina Ulianova

3 Barriers to Competition: The Evolution of the Debate
Ana Rosado Cubero

4 Rural Unwed Mothers: An American Experience, 1870–1950
Mazie Hough

5 English Catholics and the Education of the Poor, 1847–1902
Eric G. Tenbus

6 The World of Carolus Clusius: Natural History in the Making, 1550–1610
Florike Egmond

7 The Determinants of Entrepreneurship: Leadership, Culture, Institutions
José L. García-Ruiz and Pierangelo Toninelli (eds)

8 London Clerical Workers, 1880–1914: Development of the Labour Market
Michael Heller

9 The Decline of Jute: Managing Industrial Change
Jim Tomlinson, Carlo Morelli and Valerie Wright

10 Mining and the State in Brazilian Development
Gail D. Triner

11 Global Trade and Commercial Networks: Eighteenth-Century Diamond Merchants
Tijl Vanneste

12 The Clothing Trade in Provincial England, 1800–1850
Alison Toplis

Forthcoming Titles

Financing India's Imperial Railways, 1875–1914
Stuart Sweeney

Energy, Trade and Finance in Asia: A Political and Economic Analysis
Justin Dargin and Tai Wei Lim

Welfare and Old Age in Europe and North America: The Development of Social Insurance
Bernard Harris (ed.)

SEX IN JAPAN'S GLOBALIZATION, 1870–1930: PROSTITUTES, EMIGRATION AND NATION-BUILDING

BY

Bill Mihalopoulos

Routledge
Taylor & Francis Group
LONDON AND NEW YORK

First published 2011 by Pickering & Chatto (Publishers) Limited

Published 2016 by Routledge
2 Park Square, Milton Park, Abingdon, Oxfordshire OX14 4RN
711 Third Avenue, New York, NY 10017, USA

First issued in paperback 2015

Routledge is an imprint of the Taylor & Francis Group, an informa business

BRITISH LIBRARY CATALOGUING IN PUBLICATION DATA

Mihalopoulos, Bill.
Sex in Japan's globalization, 1870–1930: prostitutes, emigration and nation building. – (Perspectives in economic and social history)
1. Women peasants – Japan – History – 19th century. 2. Women peasants – Japan – History – 20th century. 3. Prostitution – Japan – History – 19th century. 4. Prostitution – Japan – History – 20th century.
I. Title II. Series
305.4'89624'0952-dc22

ISBN-13: 978-1-138-66164-6 (pbk)
ISBN-13: 978-1-8489-3201-2 (hbk)

Typeset by Pickering & Chatto (Publishers) Limited

CONTENTS

Acknowledgements ix
Note on Japanese Names xi

Introduction: In the Beginning was the Prostitute 1
1 Another Japan: Sex and Women's Work 15
2 Creating the Archive: The Power of the Pen 37
3 Sexuality and Class: Prostitution and the Japanese Woman's Christian Temperance Union 61
4 Sex as Progress: Fukuzawa Yukichi on Trade and Overseas Prostitution 83
5 Disciplining Globalizing: The Colonial Singapore Example 105
Conclusion: Globalization and the Poor 125

Notes 135
Works Cited 163
Index 175

To Gregorios, Timotheos and Sophia

ACKNOWLEDGEMENTS

I would like to take the opportunity to express my gratitude to the many people who have helped over the years. My undying thanks go to the friendship of Stephen Vlastos, Peter Williams and Graham Burchell and their belief: in the project and me. The manuscript would be a deadly dull affair if it wasn't for their input, insight and clarity. I also would like to express my gratitude to Harry Harootunian. It was a privilege to work with Harry. He is also one of the most generous individuals I have met. Although he has never read any of this work, I am beholden to John Kelly whose influence, like Harry's, is quietly found on nearly every page. My gratitude also goes to Stafan Zetterholm and Arima Manabu. It was my pleasure to work and learn alongside them.

I owe a pound of flesh to all my friends who have had the misfortune of putting up with me whilst I was trying to turn an unruly archive into something resembling a coherent narrative. I owe John Whalen-Bridge and Chris Nelson the first two pounds for camaraderie and humour. Another in line is Lynette Zeitz, who has been there right from the start. My endless thanks go to Hayashi Keita, Kinaga Katsuya, Moriyama Atsushi and the indefatigable Shimizu Hajime who, during my stay in Fukuoka, nurtured and domesticated me. Last, but not least, my deepest gratitude to the people from Kyushu University *kokushi gakka* who put up with me graciously even when I bugged them to help me read the difficult bits of *monjo*.

I am indebted to Yagishita Hiroko for all her friendship and help in demystifying the Japanese Diplomatic Record Office. My thanks also go to Rumi Yasutake, Elyssa Fasion (whom I hope to meet one day), Sheldon Garon, Sylvia Cannizzaro (ditto), Christopher Gerteis, Jan Bardsley and George Bacca, who generously read the complete manuscript, and to Dominique Ruhlmann for her last-minute help with editorial queries.

I would like to express my thanks to the Northeast Asia Council of the Association for Asian for bestowing on me a Short-Term Research Travel to Japan Grant in summer 2008. The grant was incredibly helpful in allowing me do the necessary archival work to finish the book.

The following articles have been reprinted in revised form with permission:

Bill Mihalopoulos, '"Ousting the 'Prostitute": Retelling the Story of the *Karayuki-san*', *postcolonial studies*, 4:3 (September 2001), pp. 169–87.

Bill Mihalopoulos, 'Mediating the Good Life: Prostitution and the Japanese Woman's Christian Temperance Union, 1880s–1920s', *Gender and History*, 21:1 (2009), pp. 19–38.

NOTE ON JAPANESE NAMES

All Japanese names are given with surnames first, as is customary in Japanese usage. The exception is individuals of Japanese ancestry living abroad and whose English works have been cited. Macrons have been omitted in place names for well-known regions such as Kyushu and cities such as Tokyo or Osaka when they appear in the text, organizations and as places of publication.

INTRODUCTION: IN THE BEGINNING WAS THE PROSTITUTE

Sex in Japan's Globalization deals with poor Japanese peasant women who migrated overseas and worked as sex labourers. The core subject matter of the book is a historical study of the gendered and class impact of Japan's first encounter with globalization that began in the 1860s. The women who worked in overseas brothels, I argue, must be first understood as peasants unchained from the land by Meiji land and tax policies, who become 'free labour' searching for work in the colonial cities of Asia. The integration of Japanese women into the global workforce involved a series of activities not normally associated with work – the fixing of cultural standards of ideal womanhood and, strategically, public opinion.

At the heart of the monograph lies a structural contradiction inherent in the efforts of Meiji Japan to incorporate itself into a global economy. The book traces two moves of government. Japanese peasants were offered to the global market by government-sponsored migration to work the plantations of Hawaii and Australia as 'free labourers' from the mid-1880s. Simultaneously, the Japanese government attempted to implement laws to prevent Japanese women going abroad and 'making do' as itinerate vagrants and prostitutes. This double move was driven by two contradictory ends. One aim was the quest for 'freedom' crystallized around government efforts to promote Japanese trade and industry in a global economy and to secure the 'free' movement of Japanese labourers to places of work abroad in the face of race restrictions placed on coloured labourers in North America, colonial Australia and Dutch East Indies to name a few locations. The other governmental aim was 'restrictions', which coalesced around administrative endeavours to demarcate acceptable and unacceptable forms of work that the Japanese could pursue abroad: a peasant woman could accept work as a cook or domestic servant but not as a sex worker.

The originality of this research is its sceptical scrutiny of the widespread tendency in Japanese historiography to see modernization as the downward diffusion of patterns of domesticity and womanhood from the former samurai strata to the rest of Japanese society. The source of this scepticism is important. To argue that modern Japanese womanhood was obtained by a singular route, constructed on the basis of a general doctrine such as 'good wife and wise mother' (*ryōsai kenbo*), which was diffused across classes by example and the force of ideology, in effect effaces the multiplicity of experience born out of class, age and place. An aim of this monograph is to address this silencing effect by dramatizing how contemporary claims made about overseas prostitution by a large and ideologically disparate body of interested parties pre-empted the voices of the poor while simultaneously concealing the exploitation and agency of women working as overseas prostitutes.

Methodology

Our present understanding of these women is as *karayuki-san* – Japanese women who went to work as prostitutes, mainly in South-East Asia, but also in places such as Siberia, Manchuria, China, the South Pacific, Australian colonies and the North American north-west after the Meiji Restoration (1868). However, the history of the term *karayuki-san* reveals a very different picture. The noun *karayuki-san* has its origins in Kyushu's north-west region.[1] Although the initial derivation and application is unclear, after the Meiji Restoration the noun *karayuki-san* was one of many used in north-west Kyushu to denote migrants of both sexes who left to find work abroad.[2] *Kara*, in this context, referred to the general body of land that awaited the migrants once they traversed the seas that separated Kyushu from the Asian continent. By the turn of the century, however, the definition of *karayuki-san* had come to refer generally to women who left north-west Kyushu to work in brothels overseas.[3] During the Taisho period (1912–26) the term underwent a further change in meaning, coming to connote the considerable number of women who left Kyushu to engage in work at various locations in the Pacific, especially South-East Asia. The majority of young women went to work in house-brothels, specifically established to service the carnal needs of the large number of male labourers relocated to the region to work the mines and plantations of the new colonies. Consequently, *kara* became more specialized in meaning. Instead of referring to an undifferentiated body of land overseas, it became a category denoting the Pacific basin region and, in particular, South-East Asia.

After the Pacific War, the category *karayuki-san* underwent yet another change in definition. In 1959, there appeared two academic pieces of research concerning the *karayuki-san*. These were *Jinshin baibai – kaigai dekasegi onna* (*White Slave Trade*)[4] by Mori Katsumi, and a chapter entitled 'Amakusa onna' ('Amakusa Women') in the first volume of the series *Nihon zankoku monogatari* (*Narratives of Atrocities in Japan*) subtitled *Mazushiki hitobito no mure* (*The Masses of the Poor*), and edited by Shimonaka Kunihiko, a pupil of the famous Japanese folklorist Origukuchi Shinobu.[5] Both of these works present the women of the Amakusa Islands who left to work overseas as a product of chronic poverty, demographic pressures, a local tradition of out-migration, and their consequent familiarity with the possibilities and practices of leaving the island to seek opportunities on the nearby Asian mainland.

The shifts in the definitions of what the women represented cue us to two points of observation that are underplayed in our contemporary understanding of them. First, the island women were part of a larger disenfranchised peasant migrant group that followed new routes of exchange and commerce arising from the opening of the Japanese economy in the 1860s to unrestricted trade with foreign merchants. Second, as suggested by their mobility, the women's labour in sex work was determined by the flow of colonial capital into East and South-East Asia, and the relocation of indigenous peoples to supply the sinew and sweat for the extraction of wealth. The background to the displacement of large numbers of Japanese women to the major ports of ocean trade in East and South-East Asia was the carving up of the region by European colonial powers into distinct geopolitical domains. Colonial-ruled port towns, indispensable sites for the defence and security of European imperial strategies and possessions, developed in tandem with the promotion of medium- to large-scale industry. Coeval with the development of industries was the creation of a proletariat made of newly arrived, single male labourers mostly from south China and southern India. The overseas Japanese sex trade emerged alongside the large-scale displacement of at least 12 million 'Asiatic' male labourers who, more often than not, were its main source of clientele.[6] There is, however, an underlying shared commonality in all of the different definitions of where the women migrated and the nature of their work. In areas of Kyushu where the classification *karayuki-san* circulated prior to the Second World War, the women were recognized as playing an important role in the maintenance, survival and material development of the local community they left behind. The monies sent or brought back by these women kept farms and families from going under.[7]

It is important to recognize that the term *karayuki-san* had its origins in the areas of Kyushu where these people were born and raised. *Karayuki-san* as a term did not have universal use, but was confined to certain areas of Kyushu. Contemporaneous Japanese who had dealings with, or an interest in, the migration of the rural poor abroad, but who did not come from the same region or cultural background as the women – people such as journalists, consular staff, Christian philanthropists, merchants – labelled the women in different terms: *mikkōfu* (female stowaway(s)), *kaigai shūgyōfu* (disreputable woman abroad) or *rōshigun* (group of young women). Under the rubric of these classifications, all of which began circulating in popular press in the 1880s and early 1890s, the conduct and existence of the Japanese women engaged in sex work abroad was used as an index of Japan's relation to the European colonial powers in Asia and to other Asian countries, especially China and Korea.

For example, *kaigai shūgyōfu* was a classification based on an understanding of the women as a symptom of Japan's lack of progress towards the centre of world civilization, formulated around a linear evolutionary perspective of progress, where Western civilization was the pinnacle of history. Etymologically, *shūgyōfu* was a compound made up of three characters. The first character *shū* can also be read as *minikui*, which has the meanings 'unsightly', 'ignominious' or 'base'. The second character *gyō* is also read as *waza*, and means 'occupation', 'livelihood' and 'work'. The last character *fu* can be read as *onna*, and stands for 'woman'. We can see from its etymology that *shūgyōfu* was tied to an idea of culture in terms of the ability to discern how to conduct oneself appropriately according to one's place in society at all times. *Shūgyōfu* was the gendered connation of the incorrigible, a subspecies on the fringes of Japanese society who lacked the intrinsic human capacity to understand right from wrong, shameful from virtuous.

Japanese Christians used *shūgyōfu* to designate the women they aimed to save from the shame of their occupation and to draw attention to the ignominious stain such women made on the Japanese flag by displaying their wretched existence to the rest of the world. Japanese consuls also saw the women's behaviour as detrimental to the standing of the Japanese nation in relation to other countries. They used the term *shūgyōfu* to emphasize for Tokyo the abominable behaviour of Japanese women, raucously and indiscriminately soliciting men in the streets and alleyways of foreign cities.

The term *mikkōfu* originated in the early to mid-1880s for an illegality that had nothing to do with prostitution. *Mikkōfu*, literally 'women who travel secretly onboard ship', referred to women who travelled abroad without going through the proper administrative procedures, and without the approval of the Japanese state. The term denoted a gendered migrant labour force, albeit recognizable by her marginalized utility in a foreign land, and the limited, badly paid work, which sometimes meant employment as beggar and prostitute. In contrast, the term *rōshigun*, which started circulating in the 1890s, was comparatively favourable, connoting that Japan profited from the heroism of the women who eked out an existence, in an often hostile environment, abroad. The term *rōshigun*, a colloquialism derived from the noun *jōshigun* (Amazonian troops), referred to the peasant army organized and led by Princess Ping Yang, daughter of Gaozu, the founder of the Tang Dynasty. *Rōshigun* was used widely in the media, and grafted reports of Japanese women working as prostitutes abroad to Japanese imperial sentiments advocating northward expansion on the Asian continent. The noun *rōshigun* echoed a past heroism and successful moment of empire-building. Akin to Princess Ping Yang, who raised and commanded the army that secured an empire, Japanese women residing and working abroad were the advance guard of Japanese interests and presence on the Asian continent.[8]

Interest in overseas Japanese sex workers at the turn of the twentieth century resurfaced in the early 1970s, when an intense debate unfolded in Japan around the question of how history can help make sense of contemporary Japanese identity in light of Japan's rapidly changing position within Asia. One source of contention was the long, protracted conflict in Indochina. During the Vietnam War, Japan served as a base from which the US military could carry out its operations, including the manufacture of napalm and bombs, and the use of airfields for bombing raids on Vietnam, Laos and Cambodia.[9] Many Japanese regarded the incorporation of their country in the Vietnam War as unconstitutional, a violation of the political will of the Japanese people, who formally banned war as a sovereign right in Article Nine.

Another point of contention was Japanese economic penetration in Asia. Under the US umbrella, the Japanese economy grew at an astonishing rate in the 1960s. Many Japanese, however, were critical of the type of economic development promoted in Japan, which emphasized the export of commodities to a less economically developed South-East Asia, thereby imposing a structurally unequal relationship between Japan and the rest of Asia. Many critics of export-led development were concerned that this latest economic trend was the spectre of Japan's imperial past coming back to haunt the present.[10] The Imperial Army may no longer have been marching through South-East Asia, but the conduct of Japanese business remained the same as it was during the war in terms of the underlying assumptions of superiority and right to dominate. The behaviour that seemingly epitomized this best was the audacity of all-male Japanese tour groups, organized and paid for by Japanese business for the 'rest and recreation' (*ian ryokō*) of their employees, which around 1970 began frequenting South Korea, Taiwan and Thailand for cheap sex.[11]

In the context of Japan's problematic relationship with the rest of Asia, critics of Japanese economic expansion began to search history to find references to the possibility of Japan becoming other than a dominator. One example unearthed was the rediscovery of Japanese women who, from the late 1870s, went overseas to work in brothels generally for use by non-Japanese men. It was two feminist writers, Yamazaki Tomoko and Morisaki Kazue, who brought the history of these Japanese women to the attention of large audiences. Historically, the semi-fictional accounts of the women by Yamazaki and Morisaki are important in several ways. First, their texts successfully introduced to a large audience a new political and intellectual framework, which sought to address the questions of gender inequality and the effects of the subordinate position of women in their relations with men. They also successfully used a new set of techniques and assumptions to reidentify the *karayuki-san*. The works of Morisaki and Yamazaki were persuasive precisely because they were semi-fictional rather than historical. They were able to draw the attention of their non-academic/popular audiences to the plight of the *karayuki-san* and to the oppression of women in general, because they presented the lives of the *karayuki-san* as a story of human interest, rather than historical interest. Yamazaki and Morisaki were successful in addressing the silencing of women in history, because they claimed their writings were 'realistic' representations or unfettered 'expressions' of the individuality of the women they based their narratives on. Just as importantly, both writers initiated new ways of constructing what is thinkable about women's issues, which greatly influenced all subsequent works on the gendered emigration of the rural poor, including this monograph.

Yamazaki and Morisaki's use of new representational techniques in narrating the history of the *karayuki-san* relied heavily on their claim to present the authentic experience of the women. Through the technique of universal narrator's 'voice', these authors positioned themselves as the spokespersons for the women. Yamazaki, as a woman, appropriated a position of privilege over male scholars. She argued that only a woman is in a position to address and empathize with the women who led lives abroad. Men, associated by their gender with the clients who bought the women's bodies for demeaning sexual purposes, are unable to unlock the stories hidden deep in the hearts of the women. On the other hand, she asserted, sympathetic fellow women are in a position of solidarity from which to ask about their experiences, what sexual intercourse was like under these conditions, and, more importantly, to understand the psychological motives that drove the women into life as an overseas sex worker.[12] In the case of Morisaki, it was her intimate, first-hand experience and knowledge of such women, together with the shared experience of having spent a portion of her life outside of Japan that enabled her to reproduce faithfully the details and psychology of the women for her Japanese-born, non-Kyushu audience.[13] Yamazaki also ascribed to the women who became overseas sex workers the symbolic status as 'the collective expression of the agony of Japanese women repressed under the double yoke of sex and class', and as the starting point for the search for an alternative style of existence.[14]

There are similarities between the pre-war Amakusa/Shimabara-derived usage of the term *karayuki-san* and its resurrected form in the early 1970s. Both present the towns, villages and inhabitants of the region as profiting from the women's labour overseas through the return of monies. However, there is a major difference. In the 1970s, the term *karayuki-san* was synonymous with the social problem of prostitution. Despite her sympathetic representations, Yamazaki in particular demarcated the *karayuki-san* as deviations from a particular norm. In in one of her later works Yamazaki states that:

> [In my first work] *Sandakan No. 8 Brothel*, the heroine Saki leads the typical life of a street-walker after she is sent abroad by Japanese white slavers ... The Saki in real life is shrivelled up, hopelessly impoverished and adopts a pragmatic philosophy of resignation that enables her to go on living ... In any event, all the *karayuki-san* I have known are losers. Another writer on the subject, Morisaki Kazue, agrees with me.[15]

The net effect is that the rural poor portrayed as the *karayuki-san* are subjected to representations as a 'peripheral identity' ('shrivelled up, hopelessly impoverished', 'street-walker') which, in turn, becomes the explanation for why the women were unable to fulfil themselves as mothers, workers, household heads, lovers or active agents in their local communities. Moreover, as the texts moralize and blame 'society' for this state of affairs, *karayuki-san* becomes a term that imprisons the women in their identity as prostitutes, and as a separate class of women. Moreover, the emphasis on sexual wrongs done to the *karayuki-san* indicates the impulse of the authors to demarcate the women's sexuality. The result is a retrospective policing of their conduct. The popular representations of Yamazaki and Morisaki impose a standardizing social code on the rural poor that stresses female adolescent dependency, the norm in present-day Japan.

The 1970s reassessment, furthermore, does not connect peasant women to any concrete social/historical formation, nor does it offer a description and analysis of their activities and social relations. The cathartic emphasis on the tragedy of the individual emotionally purges and closes the issue. The stress on victimization implicitly reproduces the notion of the women's passivity. The sentimental moralism and the prurient details undercut effective social criticism. The close moral focus on the purportedly passive, innocent female victims and individual evil men draws attention away from Japan's first encounter with globalization. Yamazaki and Morisaki erase the calculations made by the rural poor to leave Japan based on the rising expectations of jobs, coupled with the messages of wealth and luxury found abroad, and replace them with stories of the destitute, the undesirable and victimhood. The historical foundations of the female migration and sex work as integral factors within the wider context of nation-building, labour migration and the agency of dispossessed Japanese peasant women within a colonial world economy are left unexamined.

Laura María Agustín in her critique of anti-trafficking crusades of the twenty-first century argues that one of the greatest challenges faced in researching and writing on the sex trade is the risk of reducing the women's lives to deviance, victimization or violence. Agustín's concern is not theoretical speculation. She worked along the US–Mexican border with Mexican asylum-seekers in the 1990s. She supplemented this experience with research documenting how non-governmental organization (NGO) activities in Chile, Argentina, Brazil, Mexico, the Caribbean and Spain compartmentalize different sections of the labour market. Bordering on the absurd, Agustín found many NGOs depend on figures produced by the CIA for their statistics on the number of women caught in human trafficking, even though the CIA does not divulge its research methods.[16]

Agustín notes that other researchers work to rescue women because they think that no woman would voluntarily want to work in the sex industry. Such researchers automatically label migrant sex workers as 'trafficked persons'. The Coalition Against Trafficking in Women, whose founder and main spokesperson is Kathy Barry – author of *Female Sexual Slavery*, a book that equates prostitution with slavery – argues that most female sex workers are victims of trafficking.[17] Agustín's concern is that the anti-trafficking crusades spurred by the good intentions of white, middle-class feminists harm the very people they are trying to save. NGOs such as the Coalition Against Trafficking in Women make the efforts of migrant women to leave home, find work and to make the most of their lives in difficult and often merciless circumstances that much harder.

Agustín's research on prostitution is based on a politics of radical equality which I share.[18] Neither of us is blind to the exploitation faced by women engaged in sex work. The novelty our research shares is a sensitivity to the uneven relations of power inherent in the way philanthropic organizations, universities, NGOs and governments build a consensus on how to tackle and overcome prostitution. The asymmetry in power relations between sex workers and NGOs and government agencies involved in research and programmes aimed at 'rescuing' women from prostitution centres on the question of visibility. Namely, who has the authority to see and tell others about the character of prostitution? Individuals and institutions who take it upon themselves to diagnose, teach, categorize and overcome prostitution presuppose a relationship of superiority because of their position to teach the sex worker what they cannot know or do about their exploitation. Agustín attempts to circumnavigate this asymmetrical power relation by turning sex workers, who are the objection of intervention, into the subject of action. She does this by an act of dis-identification. Through her many interviews with sex workers, Agustín shows that migrant sex workers exceed the identity of 'victim' by making visible and legitimate what is denied: the women know what they are doing and can give a good reason for it.

Unfortunately for this research, the archive does not provide access to a history of Japanese overseas prostitution where the women speak about their own lives from their own embodied perspective. Instead, the archive is the collective response of those who supervise, monitor and police them. For example, this research relies heavily on the scores of files of varying thickness housed in the Japanese Diplomatic Record Office, Azabudai, Tokyo, under the major classification 'Juridical Administration and Police' (*shihō oyobi keisatsu*), subheading 'Matters of Police: Procedures and Regulations' (*keisatsu jikō: torishimari oyobi shobun*). These files are concerned with the relocation of Japanese women abroad and the impropriety and illegality (*fuseigyō*) of their work. The files are devoid of any sympathy for the women. The documents are not neutral inscriptions or innocent observations. On the contrary, they constitute a partisan, administrative interest in identifying and naming the daily routines of the women as a symptom of a wider social malaise facing Japan's quest for autonomy and national security. The women became an object of record because the subjects that wanted to know – the consul, the harbour police, lawmakers and administrators – were not concerned with the subjective reality of the women, but with how to intervene and shape their lives.

This unease about the logic that organizes the files housed in the Diplomatic Record Office does not stem from the idea that all histories are written from a particular perspective, but from the awareness of a productive element in the writing of the documents. The documents produce an identity, way of speaking, situation, assigned place and life station to rural poor women who migrate abroad. The archive is a mode of subjectivation; the meeting point between a social perspective that configures what the women mean, their position in society and the practices implemented to prevent and manage rural women emigrating abroad. The archive does more than record. It creates a public opinion by organizing and judging the content of women's life under the rubric of 'unsightly women'. For lack of a better term, the archive has an audio-visual function. The act of inscription gave the women a visibility and, at the same time, provided the vocabulary and rationale to understand and evaluate their existence. The idea of the women as a subject targeted by political intervention emerged hand-in-hand with the invention of the categories that defined them.

My research traverses the terrain opened up by the courageous work of Fujime Yuki. In her *Sei no Rekishigaku* (1997), Fujime shows how 'mainstream Japanese feminists' have done little to help women involved in prostitution, and have limited the possibilities of their agency because they have worked from a prohibitionist framework built around middle-class concerns. Fujime brilliantly shows that middle-class advocates and prohibitionists of licensed prostitution in Japan, both men and women, called upon extensive state power to intervene in the formerly private terrain of sexual relations and reproduction. The implications of her empirical findings were not lost on Fujime. She astutely points out that the first generation of middle-class activists saw the abolition of all forms of prostitution as a moral and social responsibility. Their social exposés on the exploitive, coercive nature of patriarchy and tradition were a critique of the current situation; a call to action for the Japanese people to live to higher ideals, and a demand for the state to established fixed agendas and programmes of action to help materialize higher values and ideals across the body politic of the Japanese nation. Fujime finds these accounts problematic because the abolitionist middle class was blind to its complicity in amplifying state control and, ironically, in its own repression. Fujime's position is that post-war feminists emulated the same prejudice as the pre-war abolitionists with dreadful consequences for sex workers. Namely, the emphasis continued to fall on eradicating prostitution and criminalizing sex work, leaving women engaged in the sex industry open to greater sexual violence and exploitation.

As a way to avoid the problem of rearticulating the same prejudices and values embedded in previous discussions of overseas Japanese sex workers, I take my cues from the work of Michel Foucault and his concept of problematization. Foucault identifies two sides to the exercise of power. On the one hand, there is the specific form of *representation*, namely the 'know-how'-cum-'understanding' formed out of practice that enables a problem to be addressed and offers certain solutions for handling the problem.[19] Thus, for Foucault, the responses to a problem do not present us with solutions, but are instead a practical space in which new styles of reason are put into effect. As such, a 'problem' has a history in that it will elicit several responses over time – 'unsightly women', 'stowaway', 'heroic advance guard of Japanese expansion' and, more recently, 'powerless victim'.[20]

On the other hand, the representation is not neutral; it also actively circumscribes forms of *intervention*. Problematization in the context of this research focuses on situating the institutional and social investments that call into question the conduct and way of life of rural poor women who sought sex work abroad with the aim of changing their lives. The behaviour of these women, constructed as a problem, is the effect of a practice that is inseparable from that problem. The values attached to the conduct of these women as 'overseas prostitutes' are created by complex interconnections of historical processes crystallized around Japanese efforts to become a modern nation-state rather than by collective moral sensibilities pertaining to prostitution. What exists in reality is the conduct of the women, the relation of their conduct to society, and the way their conduct has been identified as worthy of government intervention.[21] The historical investigation of the 'problematization' of Japanese women engaged directly or indirectly in sex work abroad involves identifying the relation between individuals and the political order from the angle of the different processes by which the women were objectified as certain kinds of subjects to be targeted by political power.

Modernization: The Politics of Governmental Problem-Solving

This research contributes to the study of global cultures by exploring the nexus of nation-building, labour migration and the agency of dispossessed Japanese peasant women within a colonial world economy. *Sex in Japan's Globalization* also deals directly with the wider question of how gender hierarchies and political economy entwined and developed in Japan during the pre-war period. Karl Marx noted how the fifteenth-century enclosure laws in England led peasants without adequate property to leave the land in search of work. The displaced peasants, 'dragged outside of their accustomed mode of life', did not immediately adapt to the new circumstances. Many turned into 'beggars, robbers, and vagabonds, partly by inclination, in most cases under the force of circumstances'. The tragedy of the disenfranchised was to be 'chastised for their enforced transformation into vagabonds and paupers', and treated as '"voluntary" criminals'.[22]

The flow of Japanese sex workers abroad from the 1870s is also a story about peasants unchained from the land who become 'free labour'. Most of the chapters of this monograph pertain to why such women *should* be the target of government intervention because of what they signified within the historical context in which they appeared; that is to say, the often contradictory yet causal relationship between Japan's quest to modernize and the effects of globalization on the Japanese state and society. *Sex in Japan's Globalization* analyses the plethora of issues raised by rural, poor Japanese women who migrated overseas and worked in the sex trade. This analysis works on three complementary levels. The first level examines how the moral label of 'prostitute' became affixed to the women who went abroad in order to leave rural poverty behind. The second level investigates how the women became a target of state intervention. The third offers a diagnosis of the moral judgements that accompanied evaluations of Japanese women engaging in sex work abroad, and the social hierarchies produced as an effect of such values in action.

Chapter 1 explains the movement of young Japanese women into sex work abroad as a spontaneous reaction by the rural poor to the radical social restructuring unfolding in Japan from 1870s onward that coincided with the relocation of capital and labour in South-East Asia. The focus falls on the layered contingencies that led to young Japanese women working abroad as sex labourers. The increased mobility made possible by Japan's incorporation into a money economy gave the rural poor of western Japan economic and social autonomy. The primacy of Kyushu coal in the Asian coal market, the Amakusa Islands labour migration patterns and the central role Amakusa women played in maintaining the household economy formed the necessary contingent conditions to allow poor Japanese peasant women to migrate abroad. The chapter offers a picture of rural poor emigration *before* it was encoded into value judgements concerning the sense of the shame women were supposed to feel for undertaking sex work to live. The aim is to present a 'disqualified knowledge' written out of narratives of nation-building that gave meaning to the everyday life of women in their village communities. The appeal to 'disqualified knowledge' is a strategic manoeuvre to sidestep representations, whether imposed by the state or the historiography of the *karayuki-san*, which confront the women with charges of shame that serve the interest of others.

Chapter 2 is inspired by the important essay 'Making Up People' by Ian Hacking.[23] In this essay, Hacking argues that policies based on an assumption create the conditions that produce behaviour conforming to that assumption. In short, there is a self-fulfilling predisposition built into the collection of data-cum-information, which acts as a feedback loop, so that the expectation of an action increases the probability of that action's being registered. The focus of the chapter is on how the systematic restructuring of bureaucratic knowledge was instrumental in transforming Meiji sensibilities regarding the sex life of the poor. Sex and bureaucracy are considered opposite forces, but bureaucrats redefined peasant women finding work abroad, who had been understood as filial daughters, making them into 'unsightly women abroad'. The looping effect or self-fulfilling prophecy here should be clear: it's almost a cliché to say that naming the women as 'unsightly women abroad' tends to create the reality in which others respond to the women as such, since their conduct proves the bureaucratic perspective.

Chapters 3 and 4 focus on the public discourses that emerged around Japanese women engaging in prostitution abroad in the late 1880s and early 1890s. What is significant is how public discourse framed the biological, economic and social conditions of reproduction with the need to change the behaviour, opinions and mental habits of the public. Chapter 3 examines the ambiguous relationship between the Japanese Woman's Christian Temperance Union (JWCTU) and Japanese women engaged in sexual labour abroad. The JWCTU's construction of prostitution as evil effectively transformed the relationship between prostitution and the family into a key socio-political issue. In the name of promoting liberty and rights of women in their relations with men, the JWCTU radically changed the way the family was conceptualized. The group challenged the existing view that the patriarchal management of family was the model of good government, using extramarital sex as a political issue to strengthen the position of the legal wife in the household as opposed to the concubine and prostitute. In the 1910s, the JWCTU changed the family to an instrument of government by employing corrective morality as a means of eradicating all forms of extramarital sex in Japan, basing its moral reform agenda on the importance of premarital chastity, strict monogamy and the obligation to work for the good of the nation. These types of philanthropic activities gave its members access to public life, but at the expense of lower-class women whose sexuality did not conform to their sensibilities.

Chapter 4 focuses on a series of articles by Fukuzawa Yukichi on the *positive* relationship between emigration of Japanese prostitutes abroad, Japanese commercial and territorial expansion, and the strength of the nation. The articles are significant as Fukuzawa is the most researched historical persona who advocated progress following Western models of education and family organization. In newspaper articles written in 1896, Fukuzawa argued for tolerating Japanese women going abroad to work as prostitutes as it met the objective of progress: namely, to increase the Japanese state's forces to compete with European powers on equal footing. The movement of rural poor women abroad, for Fukuzawa, pointed to a specific field of naturalness in the physics of progress that emerges from the spontaneous association of people, which is a necessary correlate of the state. The gist of Fukuzawa's argument is that scientific knowledge on the natural processes of association that accompany progress is indispensible to good government. Consequently, effective government has to become more than prohibitions and regulations. For Japan to achieve equality with the West and to turn itself into an industrialized, militarily powerful modern nation-state, the state has the responsibility to manage and advance the physics of progress.

Chapter 5 shifts focus to the English colony of Singapore. The problem of how to regulate Japanese sex labourers in Singapore was solved in the early 1920s through an arrangement worked out by the consul with a new form of Japanese migrant settling in the area – middle-class employees of the big trading houses of Japan. Japanese banks and *zaibatsu* firms consolidated their positions in South-East Asia, particularly in Singapore, at the outbreak of the First World War. The new Japanese migrant was professional, middle class and eager to affirm his or her social status. Working side by side with the local Japanese consuls, this new species of Japanese migrant devised ways to regulate and constrain the activities of Japanese women engaged in sex work. The newly arrived migrants actively cooperated with the consuls to turn the habits and values of their class into the general disposition of all Japanese subjects residing in South-East Asia, irrespective of class or regional background. The regulatory devices aimed at controlling the sexuality of Japanese women came into place at the moment that economic relations began to evolve in Japanese communities in South-East Asia towards the social integration and normalization of the workforce around the interests of Japanese banks and the *zaibatsu* firms. This development did not eradicate all acts of prostitution by Japanese women in Singapore, however. Rather, these acts of prostitution were integrated into the Japanese community. The clientele of Japanese sex workers changed from predominately non-Japanese to exclusively Japanese after the First World War. As long as the acts of prostitution were discreet and under the supervision of the Japanese community, a general policy of tolerance was followed.

1 ANOTHER JAPAN: SEX AND WOMEN'S WORK

Karayuki san

(literally 'one who goes to China', i.e., abroad). Japanese women who went to work as prostitutes in such places as Siberia, Manchuria, China, Southeast Asia, the South Pacific, India, and even America and Africa after the Meiji Restoration of 1868. While *karayuki-san* came from all parts of Japan, the majority were natives of western Kyushu, particularly the impoverished Amakusa area, where the term originated. Their exact number is unknown, but it may have been as many as 100,000. Girls in early adolescence were either sold by their parents or unwittingly signed themselves over to procurers (*zegen*), who then sold them to overseas brothels, where they worked as maids until they could become prostitutes in their mid-teens. Conditions were such that most women died before the age of 30. Nevertheless, many of them retained feelings of filial piety and loyalty to Japan, sending money home to support their former households and donating money to Japan in times of war.

Kodansha Encyclopedia of Japan

In the summer of 1968, Yamazaki Tomoko drew upon her family's meagre savings to travel to the Amakusa Islands in western Kyushu. Her travel was crucial to her exposé about the island women 'who had been sent far away' and 'forced to sell their bodies in distant lands'. Yamazaki hoped that during her three-week stay on the Amakusa Islands she would encounter such women, 'crawling through the dirt', living in miserable poverty, and would hear their life-stories, which would reveal the true experience of lower-class Japanese women during Japan's transition from an agrarian society to the major industrial and military power in Asia.[1]

Providence smiled on Yamazaki. Early in the first week of her stay in Amakusa, she had a chance encounter with a local elderly woman, Osaki, who had left the islands at the age of ten to work in Sandakan, North Borneo, and later worked as a prostitute in one of the Japanese brothels. Osaki's life history became the core of Yamazaki's prize-winning non-fiction novel *Sandakan hachiban shōkan* (1972), a biting depiction of the chronic poverty and the social pathology of patriarchy, which called on women from western Kyushu, specifically the Amakusa Islands and the Shimabara Peninsula, to make unimaginable sacrifices for the sake of family.[2] Yamazaki rendered the life-story of Osaki as a metonymy for the 'agony of Japanese women repressed under the yoke of sex and class'.

> It has been common women who have been oppressed as the subordinate of capital and men in the hundred years of modern Japanese history. Amongst the common women, it is the prostitute whose lot has been the cruellest. And amongst prostitutes, if we take the presence of the *karayuki-san* as being the women whose lives expressly held no promise of salvation then, in this sense, we can allow ourselves to regard them as the 'starting point' (*genten*) for all Japanese women.[3]

For Yamazaki, Osaki's story presaged modern Japanese sexual relations, where women are subject to appropriation by men. In fact the novel was so successful in addressing the problem of the repression faced by Japanese women that a considerable number of the exploited themselves, bar hostesses, to name only one occupational group, formed study groups to read and discuss the novel in terms of the significance of the *karayuki-san* for contemporary Japanese women.[4]

What does it mean to claim that Osaki's life-story is the 'starting point' (*genten*) for all Japanese women?[5] For one, it encodes women such as Osaki into an essentialist identity: the forcible violation of Osaki becomes the essence of her sex. The stress on victimization implicitly reproduces the notion of the *karayuki-san*'s passivity. Moreover, for 'patriarchy' to operate in the way assumed by Yamazaki, the abuse of women is foredoomed in hetrosexual relations. Male–female relations are understood as based on a natural antagonism: males are sexually active and aggressors while females are sexually passive and victims.[6] Yamazaki states in one of her later works that

> [In my first work] *Sandakan No. 8 Brothel*, the heroine Saki leads the typical life of a street-walker after she is sent abroad by Japanese white slavers ... The Saki in real life is shrivelled up, hopelessly impoverished and adopts a pragmatic philosophy of resignation that enables her to go on living ... In any event, all the *karayuki-san* I have known are losers.[7]

The net effect is that rural poor women such as Osaki become pathologized, as products of chronic poverty and social-historical constraints, which led to conduct radically different from what is asserted as the dominant norm of femininity. Embedded in Yamazaki's moralizing narrative on the sexual wrongs done to Osaki is an unconscious demarcation of the behaviour of the poor. The result is a retrospective policing of Osaki's conduct, whereby Yamazaki imposes a standardizing social code on Osaki that stresses female adolescent dependency, the norm in present-day Japan.

This chapter takes its cue from the exciting work on transnational labour flows, prostitution and globalization by Neferti Tadir. In her research on globalization and the feminization of the Filipina labour force in the 1980s, Tadir argues that in the analysis of transnational forms of prostitution the focus falls on exchange. In such explanations, women become objects dispossessed of agency by men: the 'necessary passivity of the exchanged goods' indicates 'the completeness of their objectification'.[8] The tendency to reduce the identity of women engaged in sex work to victim is also prevalent in the historiography of overseas Japanese prostitution. The women are seen as prostituted by others (predominately men) because of patriarchy and tradition subsumed by the Japanese state for imperial ambition and by the transformational power of capitalism to turn the bodies of Japanese women into commodities with exchange value in the colonial world market.[9] Tadir ingeniously points out that the women's agency becomes visible when we focus on the activity of the women from the perspective of their 'socially learned skills of accommodation, adaptation, and coping'.[10] That is to say, embedded in existing cultural practices are strategies and local values of affirmation that are life-enhancing – productive – rather than modes of domination. For Tadir, culture, mediated activity that requires forms of social cooperation, is full of self-constitutive potential that offers women the conditions of possibility to free themselves from poverty, prescribed gendered roles and familial obligations, and allows us to see the truth of Marx's statement that 'labour is absolute poverty as object, on one side, and is, on the other side, the general possibility of wealth as subject and as activity'.[11]

This chapter takes up Tadir's challenge to write the history of poor rural women leaving western Kyushu without reducing their lives to one of abject domination and exploitation. The task at hand is complicated. How does one convey knowledge of little-understood value systems and the fulfilment sought by rural poor women in western Kyushu at the end of the nineteenth century to an academic audience in the early twenty-first century that more or less sees prostitution as resulting from male domination and poverty, and which effectively robs women of their humanity? To that effect, the focus of the chapter will fall on a whole series of local, economic and cultural practices, long disqualified and forgotten. The aim is to describe the strategies that the rural poor drew upon as they adapted to the rapid social and economic changes occurring in Japan from the early 1870s, and the local social institutions, practices and knowledges that informed the decision by young women to gamble with migrating overseas to engage in sex work.

On a 'macroscopic' level, the women's ability to travel overseas was made possible when Kyushu coal emerged as the dominant energy source in East and South-East Asia. Ports such as Nagasaki, Kuchinotsu and Moji were junction points where the different contingencies that enabled Kyushu women to travel abroad met: the global energy market in coal, sea travel by steamship, and the local, socially prescribed practices of labour and migration. Around these port towns, a complex and informal network of social relations emerged that informed and redistributed – in terms of work, economic and cultural possibilities – strategies for life overseas as a means of survival, maintenance and material gain. On a 'microscopic' level, finding work overseas was a practical solution to particular problems of life faced by the women themselves and by their immediate communities. The suggestion here is twofold. First, in the case of rural north-west Kyushu at least, contemporary sexual mores differed greatly from those present in Japan today. Second, the gender relations of the rural communities the women originated from were in direct conflict with the diffusion of new techniques of government aimed at redefining the relationships between men and women under the rubric of 'modernization' and social progress.

Historically, the migration of Kyushu rural women to Singapore and Hong Kong to engage in sex work presented the greatest difficulty for the Japanese government, not in terms of numbers – more Japanese women worked as prostitutes on the Asian mainland – but in terms of visibility and the inability of Japanese authorities to find ways of curbing their movement.[12] A communiqué sent by Ōga Kamekichi, Japanese consular in Singapore, to Tokyo in September 1902 gives a glimpse into a transient Japanese female population migrating to South-East Asia looking for work. In his communiqué, Ōga informs the foreign minister that William Evans, head of the Chinese protectorate, paid a visit to tell him of the rapid increase in the number of young Japanese women arriving in Singapore. According to Evans, in the past eight months twenty to thirty young Japanese women had alighted from every ship coming from Japan, looking for work. Most of the women had fallen into 'pitiable circumstances'. They were burdened with a $500–600 debt to local brothel owners who had paid for their passage in advance, and were compelled to work as licensed prostitutes for four to five years to redeem money owed. At that time, Evans's office had registered 618 Japanese women to work in the 83 licensed Japanese-run brothels in Singapore. Of these, 458 of the women were new arrivals, having landed in Singapore in the last eight months. Moreover, from the registry, the Chinese protectorate could tell that a majority of the women came from western Kyushu: 107 women from Nagasaki prefecture and 96 from Kumamoto prefecture.[13]

Coal and Gendered Labour Networks: Nagasaki, Hong Kong and Singapore

As Evans indicated, a large percentage of the women migrating informally from Japan to the Straits Settlements were from Nagasaki and Kumamoto prefectures. The following sections address two questions: what historical contingency drew the women to the British colonial ports of Hong Kong and Singapore, and why were a majority of the women from western Kyushu?

Colonial Singapore and Hong Kong

In the latter half of the nineteenth century, Singapore and Hong Kong became important for British trade routes and military might between Europe, South-East Asia, and North-East Asia. The centre of the Straits Settlements, a flourishing British colony established in 1867, Singapore became a prized open commercial port (no import or export duty) after the opening of the Suez Canal in 1869, which made the distant regions of Asia more accessible to European trade. The result was rapid growth in the European, Indian and Eastern trade to Singapore as shipping costs become economical. By the end of the nineteenth century, European and American banking houses and shipping companies had established offices in Singapore, which was important as a hub for the entire region of South-East Asia. The rest of the colony became a significant site for plantations in rubber, sugar, coffee, tapioca and rice. Hong Kong too was a prized British mercantile and trading colony. Established in 1840, Hong Kong offered British interests a secure commercial foothold in the China Sea. Both ports were also the major centres for a British military presence in the Pacific, operating as outposts for the British army and as major coaling stations for the British navy.[14]

The evolution of Singapore and Hong Kong from mosquito-infested swamps and barren rocks to British centres of commerce and rule could not have happened, however, without the presence of a new social group: a proletariat made up of single, male labourers mostly from south China and India. This new class of migrant labourer, the so-called coolie, provided the muscle and sinew to construct the roads, wharves, godowns and buildings that made Singapore and Hong Kong into functional military and commercial centres. Migrant labourers from India and China also supplied the energy that kept the flow of goods circulating freely from dock to ship, and from ship to dock, in both ports.

Well into the twentieth century, young, single men comprised around 90 per cent of the labouring population in Singapore. The ratio of men to women in the port was 10:1 in 1900. The disproportion between men and women was not as acute in Hong Kong; the 1872 census showed a ratio of 5:1 among white colonialists and 7:2 among the Chinese population.[15] The concentration of a large, single male population at Singapore and Hong Kong encouraged the introduction of working-class houses of prostitution. These brothels introduced a culture of male pleasure that differed greatly from the codified areas of the East Asian city set aside for sexual encounters. Traditionally, the pleasure quarters of East Asian cities were spaces of gratification *and* sociality. Men could go as often as they wanted, usually in the company of friends, walk about, meet other acquaintances, eat, drink, discuss and, if they felt like it, take their pleasure. In contrast, the British authorities in Hong Kong and Singapore negated the sociability of the brothel and attempted to sanitize spaces of public sex. The colonial authorities licensed the brothels, registered the women working there, and introduced hygiene regimes with the aim of preventing the squalor of temporary dwellings and the venereal disease epidemics that followed unregulated prostitution.[16] The rules of registration also attempted to bring bourgeois domestic order into the brothel. Inside the brothel, the madam was given the function of social matron. She was required to have her eye on everything, and to exert discipline by directing the personal hygiene, movements and time of the women working in her house.[17] As a further hygiene precaution, the colonial masters of both Singapore and Hong Kong confined brothels to certain designated localities, with separate districts catering to Europeans and non-Europeans. The purpose of this segregation was to prevent the diseases and infections of the menial 'Asiatic' labourers from being communicated to Europeans.[18]

Japanese and Chinese brothel owners aligned with the British colonial authorities to negate the sociability of the brothel. It was in the interest of the brothel keeper to restrict all contact between women and clients to casual and quick encounters, to stop lasting relationships from developing. Intimate relationships held the risk that the women would abscond from the brothel with the help of the client-turned-lover. There was also an added economic incentive. Quick sexual interludes between the women and their clients meant that the women took more men per day, and thus more profit for the proprietor of the brothel. The main frustration faced by the single, male, migrant labourer was the lack of opportunity to establish lasting relations with a woman and start a household.[19]

Nagasaki, Kuchinotsu, Coal and Migration Routes

Nagasaki was one of the largest urban centres in Japan during the Tokugawa period. Its size and prosperity were due to the monopoly it held over official trade between Edo and other kingdoms/countries. From 1698 the *Nagasaki kaisho* (Nagasaki Meeting Place), a semi-official merchant organization, controlled the flow of nearly all goods brought by Chinese and Dutch traders to Japan; it was also responsible for overseeing the foreign exchange in gold and silver and the financial administration of the city. The majority of people who lived in Nagasaki were involved in some kind of craft or trade. They made their living around the shogunate administrators and large numbers of foreign and Japanese merchants who resided in the city. The commercial base of the city is best indicated by the fact that the residents of Nagasaki paid their taxes to the shogunate in fixed monetary sums (*unjo*) rather than in kind.

Nagasaki's commodity trade economy and higher standard of living attracted migrant labourers from other areas of Kyushu. Local history studies have identified a tradition of men and women migrating to the city from the adjacent Shimabara Peninsula and Amakusa Islands as early as the eighteenth century.[20] The prevalent form of migration was the *nenki bōkō* or term service type. In the case of women, the work taken up in Nagasaki was largely domestic, in such capacities as household servants or child carers.[21] The opening of Nagasaki port to all international trade in 1858/9 transformed the traditional migration routes between the Amakusa Islands, Shimabara Peninsula and Nagasaki.

From the 1850s onward, innovations in marine technology in the form of steam-driven ships and the expansion of land and submarine telegraphic communications firmly incorporated Japan into the European-based networks of power and exchange.[22] The Tokugawa authorities signed commercial treaties under duress with the United States, the Netherlands, Russia, Britain and France in 1858. As a result, the ports of Kanagawa, Nagasaki and Hakodate were opened to foreign trade. Trading privileges were extended to foreign merchants in 1863 to include the ports of Niigata, Hyogo and the cities of Edo and Osaka. The increase in steamers calling to ports in Japan also saw the demand for coal soar.[23] Encouraged by the demand for coal by energy-hungry steamers, the Japanese government investigated ways in which Kyushu coal mines could be exploited for nation-building.[24] The Meiji government invested heavily in the development of the Takashima and Miike mines in western Kyushu on the calculation that coal exports were a favourable way of obtaining badly needed foreign exchange.

Geographic location played a key role in the Japanese government's success in integrating Japanese coal into the Asian coal market. Kyushu coalmines were favourably located along the major maritime routes in East Asia. Low cost, labour-intensive coal mines and low freight rates gave Kyushu-mined coal a competitive edge over other imported coals from Australia and Wales. By the mid-1870s Kyushu coal controlled close to 60 per cent of the Shanghai coal market. The dominance of Kyushu coal exports spread southward in the next twenty years, gaining the greatest share of the Hong Kong coal market in the mid-1880s and the Singapore market by 1893–4.

The dominance of Kyushu coal in the East Asian markets saw Nagasaki become the coal-exporting centre of Japan between 1867 and 1880. During this period around 97 per cent of all coal exported from Japan was from the Takashima mine, five nautical miles from Nagasaki. The mined coal was transported to Nagasaki in a row of 60–80 barges towed by a small tug steamer.[25] In 1878, the volume of Kyushu coal exports increased with the establishment of Kuchinotsu, situated at the tip of the Shimabara Peninsula, as a special coal-exporting port for coal extracted from the Miike mines in Ōmuta, Fukuoka prefecture, and the Arao mines, Kumamoto prefecture. In 1880, coal from the Miike mines began to be shipped directly from Kuchinotsu for sale in Hong Kong. By the mid-1880s, Miike coal replaced Takashima coal as the major energy source available on the Hong Kong market. As a result, Kuchinotsu, along with Nagasaki, emerged as one of the major coal-export ports in East Asia. During this period of Kyushu dominance in the Asian coal market, it was common practice by companies such as Jardine, Matheson & Co., Butterfield & Swire and the China Merchant Steam Navigation Company to call on Nagasaki or Kuchinotsu and carry coal to Hong Kong or Singapore when they could not find any suitable return cargo.[26]

Nagasaki and Kuchinotsu maintained their status as the major coal-export centres until the mid-1890s. At that juncture, there was a shift from Nagasaki and

Kuchinotsu to Moji and Wakamatsu in north-east Kyushu, due to a combination of historical factors. The Chikuhō coalmines in north-west Fukuoka prefecture suddenly became profitable when developments in coal utilization widened the market for lower grades of coal. Heavy investment by Mitsubishi mechanized some of the better mines in the Chikuhō area and increased output tremendously. By 1897 the Chikuhō mines were producing 50 per cent of Japanese coal exports. Domestic politics also contributed to the shift of exporting coal from south-west Kyushu to the north-east part of the island. The abolition of the export duty on coal in 1888,[27] the establishment of Moji as a special export port in 1889 and the completion of a railway between the Chikuhō mines and Moji in 1893 all contributed to the relocation of the major coal-export ports in Kyushu.[28]

The export of coal from the ports of Nagasaki, Kuchinotsu and Moji provided the rural poor of western Kyushu with the means to seek work abroad. Informal practices of migration sprouted in tandem with the development of the coal industry in Kyushu. For example, the opening of Kuchinotsu as a special coal-exporting port in 1878, unlocked new possibilities for migration overseas. Miike mines in Fukuoka transported their coal by rail and sea to Kuchinotsu for export to Hong Kong and Singapore. The development of regional transport modes such as railways and harbours attracted people from neighbouring villages to the port with the intent of travelling abroad to escape the poverty that surrounded them. Local Kuchinotsu lore often refers to frequent outbreaks of fires in the hills surrounding the harbour when it was a major coal-exporting port. It is said that people purposely set the fires, diverting the attention of the harbour police so that they could secretly board the coal ships anchored in the harbour.[29] Miyagawa Kyūjirō, vice-consul at Hong Kong, made a direct correlation between Kuchinotsu, the number of Japanese women informally leaving Kyushu and the increase in the number of Japanese prostitutes in Hong Kong. In a missive sent to Tokyo in 1890, Miyagawa states that from the intelligence gathered, it is his humble opinion that: 'The increase in the flow of foreign ships entering and leaving recently opened special export ports such as Kuchinotsu and Karatsu for the purpose of exporting coal, has also increased the opportunity [for women] to slip secretly abroad'.[30]

The same opportunities for overseas travel were available in Nagasaki. The linkage between Kyushu coal exports and Nagasaki as the starting point for rural poor women to migrate informally abroad is visible in the following example. In early February 1894, the British owned SS *Macduff* laid anchor in Hong Kong. Forewarned by the governor of Nagasaki, the Japanese consul requested the local colonial authorities to organize an inspection of the vessel for thirty Japanese women allegedly hidden onboard. An extensive search by the Hong Kong harbour authorities revealed thirty-eight stowaways: six men and thirty-four women. In his statement to the marine magistrate and master attendant,

Edward Porter, the master of the SS *Macduff*, confessed to having personally taken ten women and three men on board once the ship had left the harbour of Kuchinotsu:

> [A]fter we had got out of the Harbour, one of the men came and said to me he had a boat outside with some girls in it. Would I pick them up? I said yes! We passed close by the boat and stopped and picked them up. The men had arranged to pay $30.00 each for the passage.[31]

The women and the procurers used stealth to go aboard to evade the numerous measures the Japanese government implemented to prevent them from leaving Japan or taking work abroad.

Japanese consuls also attempted to place controls on the women's movements. In 1885 Minami Sadatsuke, Japanese consul for Hong Kong, came to an informal agreement with the Hong Kong register general to restrict the number of Japanese women working in registered public brothels to fifty-two women at one time.[32] The Japanese consul and colonial authorities had an informal agreement that when a Japanese woman put in an application to work as a licensed prostitute, the general register's office would notify Minami, who in turn, would summon the woman to his office. During their meeting, the consul would instruct the woman that she was unable to register as a prostitute and that the best course of action would be to return home. The consul would then proceed to ascertain if the woman had any legal guardian present in Hong Kong so that they could be informed of her circumstances and she could be returned to their care. In cases where the woman interviewed had no legal guardian, and lacked money for a return fare to Japan, Minami placed her temporarily in the Wanchai Lock hospital, while he tried to identify family members in Japan who would pay repatriation expenses.[33] The expenses became the liability of the household head, who was legally responsible for all other members of the family.[34] However, by 1887 it became agonizingly obvious to successive Japanese consuls in Hong Kong that placing a ceiling on the number of Japanese women working as licensed prostitutes was not having the desired effect of stemming the number of them arriving at the port looking for work. The Japanese consuls noticed that the Hong Kong colonial authorities were reluctant to intercept and search ships unless they were almost certain that they would find women hidden aboard. The colonial authorities did not want to obstruct the movement of ships entering and leaving the harbour unless necessary.[35] Moreover, unless Japanese women stowaways came forward and stated that they were brought to Hong Kong against their will, the register general would not take any action to repatriate them to Japan.[36] The Japanese consul also lacked the cooperation of the majority of Japanese residing in the port in stopping Japanese women alighting in Hong

Kong. The Japanese-run inns, restaurants and taverns relied on the flow of Japanese women coming through the port for their livelihood.[37]

Commercial Shipping

Ships departing from Kyushu carrying coal from the Takashima and Miike mines and bound for city ports in South-East Asia were not the only means of travel available to Japanese women. By the turn of the century, the increase in postal, passage and cargo services between Japan and the rest of the world had generated new migratory routes. In his petition dated 15 September 1892, requesting the expulsion of Japanese prostitutes from Thursday Island, Sasaki Shigetoshi, a former samurai and community leader of the Japanese labourers on the same island, informed the Japanese foreign ministry that Japanese men and women connected with prostitution

> manage to board foreign vessels that call on the ports of Nagasaki, Kuchinotsu, Karatsu, Shimonoseki and Kobe. Many of these unseemly women [*shūgyōfu*] and their intermediates often board a pilot boat and intercept and board the foreign vessels, particularly the ships that service the area between Kobe and Shimonoseki, such as the French Mail [Société des Messageries Maritimes].[38]

With the expansion of shipping routes from Japan to South-East Asia, the means by which the women migrated overseas also changed. It was common to see groups of young Japanese women travelling in the third-class section of Japanese ships en route abroad.[39] Tanaka Tokichi, the Japanese consul in Singapore, attests to this fact in a report sent to Tokyo in 1906. In May–June of the same year, with the assistance of the local colonial authorities, Tanaka investigated the means by which women travelled to Singapore. From his findings, Tanaka concluded that over one thousand women had made their way to Singapore in the last year with the aim of working as prostitutes, an average of around twenty arrivals per week. In his report, Tanaka summarizes the main routes and means used by rural poor women to reach Singapore:

> 1) The method where women secretly board steamships entering and leaving such ports as Moji and Kuchinotsu, and cross either to Hong Kong or Singapore.
> 2) Instances when women buy a ticket [of travel] at Moji, passing inspection by the Harbour and Marine Police and come to Hong Kong and Singapore.
> 3) The procedure where women buy a ticket at Kobe for travel to Shanghai, and just before berthing in Shanghai, they buy a further ticket for Singapore.

Tanaka goes on to substantiate the content of his findings. The first method of transporting women to Singapore had been the most prevalent. Recently, however, there had been a decline in this type of practice. The authorities in Singapore attributed this decline to a combination of reasons: the danger of being discovered, the considerable inconvenience and distress of hiding in the hold of a ship and the high costs involved in bribing crew members. Tanaka, on the other hand, believed that the cause was more the marked decline in the number of ships carrying coal from Japan to Singapore, as Japanese coal was now channelled to the domestic market to meet the energy necessities of a rapidly growing post-Russo-Japanese War economy. Accordingly, the second method was the most conventional and had the highest rate of success. Tanaka suggests that this was due to the laxity of harbour officials in screening passengers. The third practice was allegedly a recent development and was used mainly by women from the *Kishū* region (Wakayama prefecture). Tanaka concludes his report by stating that the information collected by the British colonial authorities identified Moji as the port from which the highest number of women began their journey to Singapore, followed by Kuchinotsu and Kobe. The number of women leaving from Nagasaki, on the other hand, had reportedly fallen.[40]

A Diagram of a Journey

Social Knowledge: Working Maps of an Informal Kind

The new routes of informal migration to destinations outside of Japan were made accessible by the formation of a new class of brokers, namely 'traffickers' or 'procurers' (*zegen*). Their function and expertise was to guide others to overseas locations in exchange for money. To do this successfully, the procurer had to be familiar with things, people and events in dispersed and often distant geographical locations. The procurer's social capital lay in her or his ability to draw upon information concerning where ships berthed, what times they left or arrived, as well as alliances with those who worked in the harbour or on the ships. The procurer's knowledge of the intended destination, how to reach it and what might happen on the way, gave her/him power over those he or she was leading. People seeking work overseas were dependent on the procurer for direction on two levels: guidance as to the correct route of travel, and instruction in terms of the appropriate forethought and action required to reach their intended destination.

The work of such agents, which involved canvassing people in one place and transporting them by sea over great distances to another destination, has been documented in the (sensationalist and unreliable) biography of Muraoka Iheji dealing with his role in shipping Japanese women across South-East Asia in the international networks of 'slave-trading'.[41] The feminist-inspired writings of Yamazaki also focus on the procurer and justifiably point out the significance of this agency whereby men and women were bound up in relations of power in which women were dominated, highlighting the effects of the subordinate position women were placed in. I do not contest these arguments, but do wish to modify them. What I argue is a more complicated story. The localized knowledge that circulated in rural communities in western Kyushu – in the form of rumour, hearsay, gossip and letters from relatives abroad – was formative in grounding the experience of living abroad in truth claims that made travel to locations overseas plausible and attractive. The oral nature of this localized knowledge means that it has no formal archive or discernible events to mark its existence – but this does not mean that it was inconsequential. To recover this knowledge, I turn to contemporaneous narratives of observers who deplored the procurement of the young women of these rural communities, but who also saw them as agents and not merely victims. These forms of oral transmission point to a forgotten dimension of social practices steeped in the world of the everyday, which allowed the possibility of finding work abroad.

Procurers, female as well as male, based overseas, generally avoided returning to Japan if they could find a third party to do their bidding. Only when they were unable to mobilize or lost their connections in Japan would the procurers return, usually to their place of origin, where they would wander from village to village. If that proved unfruitful, the procurers would relocate to the nearest large port or railway hub town, where they would loiter in the streets, soliciting and enticing any young women willing to take up their offer of a 'better' life overseas.[42] Noma Seiichi, Japanese consul in Hong Kong, reported to Tokyo how Moji had become a harbour where hardly any ship left without Japanese women concealed on board. According to the testimonies of the women Noma repatriated to Japan, procurers were constantly loitering in or around Moji railway station, waiting to ply their 'crafty tricks' upon any young female passengers alighting from inbound trains.[43]

Procurers were able to win over young women by speaking from experience when they made their claims about life overseas. The women did not undertake travel innocently; they entertained various assumptions – some of which were valid and some not – concerning what life was like abroad, that prompted them to leave Japan. The successful procurer spoke to those assumptions. A pamphlet written in 1895 by a Japanese Christian organization aimed at eradicating Japanese prostitution abroad hints at how, in rural areas where many of the women originated, the local women were highly informed about what – in terms of work, economic and cultural possibilities – might be available to them in specified destinations overseas. The pamphlet argued that women working as 'prostitutes' abroad would return to their native villages dressed in gorgeous clothes and gold pins in their hair in the style of 'gentlewomen'. Seeing this display of abundance, the young women of the village, seeking to emulate the riches of the returned women, were willingly lured overseas by the promise of wealth.[44] An instance of this strategy of procurement in practice was the return of Yokoyama Kikuno to her native village in Nagasaki prefecture, after an absence of six years working in Taiwan and Hong Kong. Yokoyama returned to her village well dressed and claiming to be the owner of a successful 'Japanese restaurant' (*nihon ryōriten*).[45] She canvassed several houses during her stay in the village and managed to convince a twenty-year-old woman to accompany her. It seems that she persuaded the woman by assuring her that she could make 'easy' money working in Hong Kong as a hotel maid, earning as much as ¥25 per month, and much more in a brothel. The monthly wage Yokoyama promised was an enormous amount for the rural poor when one considers that a male day labourer would earn less than half this amount in a month.[46] The only reason Yokoyama's movements remain recorded for posterity is that her endeavours ended in failure: the Nagasaki authorities brought charges against her for trafficking in young women.[47]

Due to expense and the danger of being caught, whenever possible brothel owners tried to establish stable connections with third parties to ensure a constant supply of women to replace those who had ended their term of contract, became ill or died. One ploy was to use former employees, such as Yokoyama Kikuno, returning to Japan on the completion of their contracts, to recruit other women.[48] Another ploy was for the owners to write directly to parents offering substantial financial rewards if the parents agreed to send their daughters to work in their brothels.[49] The most common ploy, however, was to recruit young women through the services of *kuchi-ireya* (employment agencies), which existed in all of the large ports of Japan. In return for a handling charge, certain agencies would mediate for young women in finding employment overseas in such positions as domestic servants, waitresses and child carers. Households and families living on the periphery of these ports, alerted by the gossip of the returnees and the numerous stories found in newspapers concerning the money to be made overseas, would send their daughters to these agencies to find work.[50] Benefiting from such publicity, the *kuchi-ireya* directed a great number of young women to overseas brothels. A report filed in 1912 by Imai Shinoburō, Japanese consul general in Hong Kong, states that, without the establishment of a stricter set of regulations between the Japanese and the local colonial government, brothel owners in Hong Kong would conspire with the *kuchi-ireya* to recruit women to work for them.[51] A variation of this practice had been registered in the daily newspaper *Fukuoka nichinichi* several years earlier, reporting on how a procurer obtained women through a *kuchi-ireya* and 'lulled them into a false sense of security', only to smuggle them overseas and sell them into brothels.[52]

Resourceful Nobodies

Women from Kyushu did not migrate overseas blindly but tactically, following the footsteps of those who preceded them, with the aim of making the best of a bad situation, finding work, making money and hopefully striking it rich. A case in point is Onio, a native of Nagasaki who was found hidden aboard the SS *Tetartos* when it docked in Hong Kong in March 1888. In her statement to the

Hong Kong authorities, Onio revealed that at strategic points along the route she took to Hong Kong, she gained new social knowledges through exchanges with other intermediaries that helped her to proceed. For instance, Onio had to win the help of the washerwoman who worked at the harbour and the ship's boy in order to get onboard ship without being noticed.[53]

The point to note here is that the forms of knowledge Onio accessed and utilized in her efforts to migrate overseas were steeped in the world of the everyday. Letters from relatives or conversations with people who had been abroad, were formative in grounding the experience of living overseas in truth-claims that made travel to such locations plausible and attractive. Moreover, the presence of coal ships in the harbour, and the many groups of people who worked at the harbour loading, cleaning or maintaining the ships, formed an ensemble of local, but, nonetheless, effective and practical allies with the knowledge and resources to enable the women to emigrate.

Subterranean Economies

The dynamics of the underground economy revolving around the brokering of Japanese women was revealed in detail by an investigation compiled by Inuoe Kizaburō, Japanese consul for Hong Kong, in the summer of 1900. The impetus for the investigation was allegations made by local Japanese businesspersons against the Nagasaki police force accusing them of abetting the trafficking of Japanese women to Hong Kong and the Straits Settlements.[54] In his findings, Inoue reported that seven out of ten 'unsightly women' (*shūgyōfu*) arriving in Hong Kong did not have the appropriate travel documents. Furthermore, six of these seven women came with the consent of their parents. Only one out of ten women was deceived into taking the journey by the seductive words of the procurer, without parental consent. As for the three women out of ten who did possess proper travel documents, they had been obtained by bribing prefecture officials. The price of a passport was reported to be about ¥15–20.[55]

In cases where the women had no travel documents, the procurer used stealth to board the women on outbound ships, or by bribing the harbour police with approximately ¥20 per person. Once on board a Japanese or foreign vessel, the procurer would give the ship's captain or ship's pilot around ¥10 per head to take them to either Hong Kong or Singapore. On arriving in Hong Kong, the women were sold to the brothel owners for about ¥200–300.[56]

It was customary for the procurer to reach an agreement with the parents in advance over the amount of money they were to collect for the sale of their daughter. The amount was determined according to the woman's estimated physical appeal. The general convention was that if a woman was sold for ¥200, for example, then around ¥30–50 was due to the woman's family. The procurer usually collected ¥70–100 from each sale, as commission for having guided the women during their journey out of Japan. The procurer also took out the following expenses from the sale of the women: ¥10 for lodging expenses, ¥3 for two sets of night clothing, ¥5 for two *yukata* (cotton summer *kimono*), ¥3 for a headdress, ¥3 for *geta* (raised wooden sandals) and *tabi* (ankle-high socks worn with thonged footwear), ¥6 for a blanket and small wardrobe or chest. A further ¥15 was deducted for travelling expenses.[57]

The journey, as broken down by Inoue's report, is of interest for reasons besides the details of the costs involved in the brokering of women from Japan to Hong Kong. It also maps out an informal economy, which profited the male actors who participated: the procurer, the low-ranking civil servants and harbour officials, the seamen who worked the ships and the Japanese merchants who sold the women their clothing and furniture on arrival. The financial benefits gained in tacit cooperation were substantial in view of the fact that in 1900 the average daily wage for a ship's carpenter was 53 *sen*, 34 *sen* for a printer and 37 *sen* for a day labourer.[58] Sometimes the allure of big money proved too much for the people given the responsibility of preventing the informal migration of Japanese women abroad. There are recorded instances of patrolmen giving up their work and turning their hand to smuggling women overseas.[59]

The arrangements for financing the journey were organized in such a way as to work against the woman. The cost of the voyage became the woman's liability.[60] Until the woman repaid this debt, her labour in service became the property of the brothel owner who purchased the debt the woman 'owed' to the procurer. Similar to other forms of property, the ownership of the debt, and the women's labour, was transferable. The reason for this seems to be connected with the credit of the procurer. Most brokers of women had to borrow heavily to finance their operations, often at high rates of interest.[61] To cover their initial outlay, the procurers or brothel owners offered women as collateral. An example is the dealings of Takada Tokijirō of Osaka. In August 1888, Takada brought five Japanese women from Hong Kong to Port Darwin, Australia, whereupon he promptly sold one woman to a Malay 'hairdresser' for £50 and two other women to a Chinese man for £40. As for the remaining two women, he 'kept' one for himself as a concubine and the other he put to work as a prostitute.[62] The practice of selling women was very prevalent because British, Chinese and Malay men in the Straits Settlements were eager to gain access to concubines in order to constitute a patriarchal domestic space privileging themselves. A missive by Miyagawa Kyūjirō, Japanese consul of Hong Kong, to the foreign minister pays testimony to this fact. In his letter, Miyagawa reports on the stories emanating from the Straits Settlements regarding Japanese women being sold to Chinese and Malays, who would 'lead them off to wild and savage lands where they suffer unimaginable hardship'.[63]

Know No Border: See No Boundary

The subterranean economies and social practices involved in the informal migration of Japanese women abroad hint at another aspect of the world inhabited by the rural poor. The women were members of a larger transient community that transgressed linguistic and national boundaries, shaped by the rhythms of abundance and scarcity found in agricultural production. In the social territory occupied by the rural poor, the labour of children was a resource to be sought during cycles of abundance and shed when the consumption of the household had to be reduced during times of scarcity. The logic of preserving the household and propagating its patriarchal lineage morally obliged the child to supply the labour to ensure the household's survival.[64] The child–parent/child–adult relationship was not a black–white relation of exploitation but more of reciprocity implied by mutual utilization and the initiation of children into the adult world through social circulation, as seen through the custom of placing children in other families as apprentices or domestic servants. This preindustrial form of labour and all the social controls that accompanied it was transmuted by Japan's entry into a money economy.

As previously mentioned, as early as the eighteenth century the rural poor of the Amakusa and Shimabara regions migrated to Nagasaki in search of work. This practice of migrating for work extended beyond the nation's borders once Japan was incorporated into a capitalist money economy. The strategy of migrating abroad to escape dire poverty was asserted in an interview by a woman from the Shimabara region who had migrated overseas to find work at the turn of the twentieth century. In an interview taped in 1961 by Miyazaki Kōhei, owner of the Shimabara Railroad Company and 'gentleman' historian, S-san gave the following description of her life working overseas.[65]

A native of Shimabara village, S-san's father was mentally ill, and had turned, in her terms, into a 'dithering idiot', devoting himself to worship. He sustained himself and his family by the little money his wife and children brought in, and from the increasingly resentful benevolence of his relatives. The social ambitions the father nourished for his family were limited. His only demand on his wife and children was work. To make ends meet S-san was sent to work as a domestic servant to a local merchant in her early teens. She continued working there until she was sixteen, the year her mother died. The wages she received were not enough to sustain her father, three younger siblings and herself, let alone pay for any repairs to the house they were living in, which was more like an open hovel than a house, hardly offering any protection from the elements. Overwhelmed by the daily destitution her family faced, S-san and her sister took up the offer of a stranger dressed in a black coat loitering in the village to work in a 'far off place' for an advance sum of money.

The following night, S-san and her sister were smuggled on board different ships anchored in Kuchinotsu. After spending a gruelling week hidden in the hold, S-san's ship berthed in Singapore, whereupon she was immediately auctioned off to a Japanese brothel on Malay Street,[66] the heart of the Japanese red-light district in Singapore. On her arrival at the brothel, she was placed in the care of an older woman, a native of a village just east of Shimabara, and with whom S-san was faintly acquainted. The woman was the eldest daughter of a well-to-do peasant family. She and her two younger sisters had left their village to work as sex labourers in Singapore. After working for two years in the brothel, S-san was bought out of her debt by a young Englishman working for a big rubber plantation company on the Malay Peninsula. She spent the next eight years as his concubine/domestic housekeeper.

Another interview was carried out in the summer of 1992. The subject was K-san, a resident of Ushibukai, Shimo-Amakusa.[67] I met with K-san at her home at the introduction of my informant. K-san was born around thirty years later than S-san but, as we can see from her life narrative, the older forms of labour organized around the reproduction of the household still persisted. K-san first left her home at the age of twelve or thirteen to work at the spinning mills in Osaka. After five years of service at the mills, she returned home. Within a few months, she obtained a job as a child carer (*komori*) in Nagasaki through an intermediary in the village. Two years later, around 1935–6, at the age of about twenty-one, she left for Shanghai, together with five other women. In Shanghai, she worked as a chambermaid at a hotel located in the Japanese settlement. In contrast to the experience of S-san, K-san had little or no contact with people of other nationalities because the Japanese community in Shanghai was both well established and insular.[68] When I asked if she was scared at leaving Japan for the first time, she replied, somewhat mystified, that she had no reason to be, for she knew the people she travelled with, and there were other acquaintances from her village already working in Shanghai at that time. To her, the trip to Shanghai was not a frightening journey to the 'unknown'. The communal networks of solidarity she had recourse to in her village in Amakusa extended as far as her new destination.

Amakusa, Migration and Sex Work

In his classic text *Wasurerareta Nihonjin* (*The Forgotten Japanese*), folklorist Miyamoto Tsuneichi tells of the practices of his own rural household in Yamaguchi prefecture and the transmittance of wealth along matrilineal lines. Miyamoto goes as far as to argue that western and eastern Japan transmit wealth and culture in very different ways. In eastern Japan, the father is the key figure in transmitting culture and wealth. In western Japan, familial (and communal) authority is commanded more by age than gender, thus offering women greater authority in the household and the conditions of possibility for the matrilineal transmission of wealth.[69]

It seems that in the case of Shimabara and Amakusa regions at least, in the constructions of social personage for people from these areas, becoming a migrant labourer was one of the prescribed forms of conduct for women. In both regions, the village leaders did not try to prevent the local women from leaving. Indeed, in some circumstances they encouraged women to find specific forms of work overseas.[70] In 1920 a field study of the Amakusa area funded by the Japanese Woman's Christian Temperance Union discovered that over 5,400 people had left the island searching for work abroad. A majority of them were women who engaged in sex work.[71] The study was also surprised to discover that, regardless of economic need, it was a requirement of marriage for the local women to work for a period of time away from the islands (*onago no shigoto*: literally, women's work in the local dialect). Women of the Amakusa region were required by cultural convention to produce half of their dowry. A woman without a dowry remained 'out of the running', and under the domestic control of her family or whoever might want to use her for domestic and agricultural labour. The patriarchally perceived social value and marriage potential of the women increased directly in relation to the amount of money they earned and remitted. Moreover, the social status of the family itself within the local community increased according to the wealth and status of the employer and the amount of remittance received: the more affluent the employer, the higher the prestige of the family in the village social hierarchy.[72]

Although there were many women from the Amakusa Islands who were not fully informed by their parents, or persons recruiting them for work abroad, that they were being indentured into overseas brothels, many others evidently understood the nature of the work required. There is evidence that, at times, the parents would mediate in these negotiations.[73] This practice was still prevalent in the early 1920s. A young schoolteacher sent to a village on the Amakusa Islands for practical experience wrote that:

> An evil custom of this village is that they do not see prostitution as shameful. In the surrounding villages too, prostitution is regarded as a vocation. Moreover, what is extraordinary is that people with a good living follow this practice. If anything, these people treat those who do not engage in prostitution with scorn and ridicule.[74]

According to this observer, whom we can assume to be knowledgeable, in the case of the women of the Amakusa and Shimabara regions, it seems sex work was perceived as just another form of labour, without the attachment of stigma.[75] Moreover, the same occupation, by virtue of its economic outcomes, provided the island women with a relative degree of independence on their return to their native villages, which differentiated them from those women who remained under the aegis of family and local men. To illustrate this point, I turn to Sasaki Shigetoshi, a former low-class samurai involved in a Japanese migrant labour enterprise on Thursday Island, Queensland. In his 1892 petition to Tokyo, Sasaki describes how he appealed to the better nature of the brothel owners and women to cease working the brothels and how his best intentions came to naught. It is worth quoting at length:

> At times, we turn to the [brothel] owners and remonstrate, exhorting them to cease their occupation and to change to another line of work. Not only do they turn deaf ears to our remonstrations, it often happens that they turn around and rebut those giving advice saying things such as:
>
> You boors do talk a lot of rubbish. From the time we left Japan, let alone now when we are standing on foreign soil, you have no grounds to point an accusing finger even if you had the authority of the Japanese government behind you. What's more, if the [Thursday] Island authorities continue to find no fault with our business, why restrain our activities? I see no particular reason why I should change what I do. Haven't you caught on yet? Now, money talks in the world. No matter how base the occupation, if I can live the rest of my life in my own home in comfort, why should I concern myself? What matter to me the fortunes of the nation? We don't ask much. Yet, you demand a lot. What you advise, we will not do.
>
> Then, there are those amongst us, who turn to the women and advise them to become upright and honest, and to return to their homes in Japan as quickly as possible. The majority of these women are extremely simple and know no honour. Hardly any of them listen to the advice given. They feign unconcern and reply:
>
> Thank you for your gracious concern. Your words are fit for the innocent girls living back home who know nothing about the world. However, for ignorant women such as us who have crossed the open seas and have come to a foreign land thousands of miles away, your sermons are useless – like chanting sutras to a scarecrow. In Japan, poor people like us have sweat on our brow night and day working like beasts of burden. Far from having the wherewithal to cook our daily meals, we barely have that to rinse our mouths. Now that we are living overseas and engaged in such a profession, as for things heavy we pick up nothing more than a knife or fork. What's more, we wear gorgeous clothes and have our fill of fine food. All our wishes are respected. We have all that we desire. What could add to our happiness? We do, alas, regret most profoundly not to have been born daughters to such gentlemen as you.[76]

The major point of interest for me about this 'dialogue' is the silent battle raging between two codes of conduct organized around competing values of work and 'economic' interest. What underlies Sasaki's lament on the frivolous nature of the men and women making a living from sex work on Thursday Island is a distinction between productive and unproductive labour. For Sasaki, the 'unsightly behaviour' of the women is intolerable as he links the fortunes of Japan with the wealth of the nation defined as the aggregate of all productive labour. Sasaki vehemently objects to the existence of the brothels as it indicates a hatred for hard toil and a delight in relaxation, which erodes social order and, as such, the polity of Japan, for without the latter the former could not exist. In Sasaki's thinking, economic order is not the simple matter of accumulating wealth, but consists of reproducing and reinforcing the constituent elements of the state. As Sasaki laments, it is not only the humiliation, but

> also in relation to overseas commercial, agricultural and other enterprises, in political comparison to the Chinese, we Japanese are exceedingly inferior now because of the display of the likes of these filthy women ... If we [Japanese] want to exaggerate [our superiority over the Chinese] by means of our Japanese nation being the England of the East, the first thing that should be initiated is the eradication of unsightly women of this sort.

In his objections, Sasaki formulates a direct equation where good economic order is the prerequisite of political power. The ordered and continuous labour of his fellow migrants fosters the strength of the state in ways that will enable Japan to become the 'England of the East', a highly industrialized naval power capable of maintaining its autonomy within a framework of interstate rivalry.[77] On the other hand, the prodigal pursuit of pleasure Sasaki envisages the women enjoying behind closed doors implies leisure and the dangers that come with it: outright hedonism and stagnation.

For the brothel owners and the women, the acquisition of money was an end in itself if it ensured the maintenance and continuity of the household. The labour of household members was organized around the need for the household to ensure its survival.[78] As related by various contemporary observers, and consistent with the logic of the household economy in the Amakusa-Shimabara regions, in the eyes of the women, sex work was another form of labour that, foremost, made possible their maintenance and survival and, furthermore, secured the continuation and material development of their patriarchal household. For them, work as a prostitute abroad was undifferentiated from work as an agricultural labourer in Japan: sex work was neither unproductive nor immoral but one available tactic for their maintenance, survival and material comfort. In this instance, sex work was preferred, portrayed as being physically easier and more amenable to daily existence as far as food and clothing were concerned.

In fact, I did not find compelling evidence that the stigma of a moral and religious nature that the women wanted to avoid was related to premarital or commercial sex, but rather, with the failure to secure the prosperity and longevity of the household, the ultimate disgrace to one's parents and ancestors. The obligation to ensure the continuity of the household points to intimate and integral relations between daily existence and forms of worship and customary belief.[79] The concept of time followed by the women was of a different kind than the temporal discipline of a twelve-hour workday followed by Sasaki and his fellow labourers who harvested pearls from the seas of Thursday Island. In the cosmology inhabited by the women, time and work were informed by duties the living had with the dead. The household was an inheritance transmitted by the ancestors to the present, and the continuation of the household by the present generation to the next was an expression of worship and respect.[80] Bound by links to things unseen, the household occupied a world that was immutable and permanent. Work that secured the permanence of the household in the temporal order of the living was also an activity that continued the collective work of generating life in the future and, as such, an act of respect and fulfilment of obligation to parents and ancestors.

Following Sasaki, it is reasonable to assume that in the social arrangements and cultural dispositions of the Amakusa and Shimabara regions, there appears to have been no 'spiritual' milieu with a distinctive moralizing rationale concerning sex work. On the level of the individual, the lay Buddhist beliefs common in the region of Amakusa Islands did not see commercial sex as eternally polluting the soul. The experience of selling one's body for commercial gain was seen as morally redeemable if it was an act of filial piety, and spiritually redeemable through repeated prayer to Amida Buddha.[81] Women could move out of sex work and in and out of marriage without carrying the heavily stigmatized social status usually associated with the category of 'prostitute'. Illegitimate children conceived by the women while working overseas were, in general, readily accepted by the community and potential spouses.[82] On the collective level, the monies remitted by women engaged in sex work abroad were seen as an essential component for the physical maintenance of temples and shrines, the spiritual centres of their communities. In the 1920s, it was still exceedingly common to see, lining the walls of the shrines and temples of Amakusa Islands and Shimabara Peninsula, in large numbers, the names of the local women working overseas who had remitted donations specifically for the upkeep of their family temple or shrine.[83]

It would be overly simplistic to assert that the rural women who engaged in prostitution did not feel ambivalence about the sexual and moral conduct condemned by Sasaki Shigetoshi or the young schoolteacher who came to teach in the Amakusa region. Rather, the issue at hand is the rediscovery of a struggle between two competing sets of social beliefs about what it means to be a woman and a member of a community. On the local level, the women gained greater social capital and responsibility through the fulfilment of their duties in the maintenance and the survival and material development of their households and local communities. The conflict, though, lay at the general and collective level of the nation. In state-led programmes of nation-building, which emphasized values of chastity and female adolescent dependency as the general rules of progress to which all Japanese had to adhere if Japan was to meet the dictates of social advancement, there was no leeway for the women of Amakusa and Shimabara to continue working as migrant sex workers abroad.

End of Story?

This chapter has tried to bring to the fore the disqualified knowledge – in the face of popular knowledge – of the history of the *karayuki-san* as overseas migrant labourers. It has traced how localized cultural conventions and practices shaped the women's immediate communities and gave meaning to everyday life. It affirms that, at the level of the women's immediate communities, the women who took on sex work were not stigmatized as morally flawed individuals, or as a group found on the margins of local society. They were recognized as a legitimate component of village life, economically, culturally and socially.

The rediscovery of this disqualified knowledge raises a question concerning Japanese 'modernization' as social experience in the specific context of peasant women from western Kyushu. The history of the Japanese women migrating abroad to engage in sex work points to a whole series of local economic and cultural practices that informed the women of the expectations of their community and, at the same time, also endowed them with the capacity to integrate themselves fully into the social arrangements of their communities on their return. This body of local economic and cultural practices, however, was constantly in struggle with the more formal and general body of knowledge-cum-social interventions filtering into the region through the institutions and individuals representative of a 'better' or 'more effective' way of undertaking daily life: teachers, public servants and planners of economic development. The programmes of education and work introduced into the region under the rubric of 'modernization' looked at every opportunity to eradicate the local knowledge that made overseas migration plausible and the regional economic and cultural practices that located and gave status to women who engaged in sex work abroad in their communities. This provokes the question: by which historical process did female migrant labourers who sought work overseas for the maintenance and survival of their households and communities come to be designated as unsightly overseas prostitutes? How do we explain the refusal by people and institutions distanced from the Amakusa Islands and Shimabara Peninsula to understand the women in the terms they understood themselves? Why was the work of the women rejected as 'prostitution'?

2 CREATING THE ARCHIVE: THE POWER OF THE PEN

Prior to the Meiji restoration, sex work was a tactic available to poor rural women to keep destitution at bay. During the twilight years of Tokugawa rule, women recruited to work in the licensed 'pleasure quarters' more often than not came from the poorer strata of the peasant population.[1] A common practice for heads of peasant households fallen on hard times due to natural calamity, chance accident or sickness was to sell their daughters into prostitution. In return for a sum of money up front, the household head transferred his authority and patriarchal right to the creditor. The practice of selling daughters into prostitution also had political utility. In terms of governance, the licensed 'pleasure quarter' doubled as an orderly outlet for libidinal desire and as an institution for poor relief in Japanese cities and castle towns. The 'pleasure quarter' was a safety net to ease destitution among the rural poor and prevent urban vagrancy.

In pre-Meiji Japan, it was socially acceptable for destitute parents to send a daughter to a public house of prostitution. The communities around these families valued such an act of filial piety on the daughter's part as a repayment to her parents.[2] In contrast, destitute women who worked in the sex trade outside the licensed pleasure quarters were heavily stigmatized. Japanese authorities and moralists abhorred clandestine prostitution, which they regarded as a violation of the laws of society and nature. Officials categorized clandestine prostitutes as 'beasts with human faces' (*jyūkō naru mono*), a term signifying incorrigibility. Analogous to animals, these women lacked a sense of shame. Without the wherewithal to recognize right from wrong, such women were considered incapable of understanding the errors of their ways.[3] In and of itself, prostitution was not morally wrong.

In the years immediately following the Meiji restoration, the newly formed government's position towards prostitution was ambiguous. In November 1872, the Council of State (*Dajōkan*) issued the 'Ordinance for the Emancipation of Prostitutes' (*shōgi kaihōrei*), which made all contracts tying women to licensed brothels null and void.[4] In the early months of 1873, however, the Meiji government reinstated licensed prostitution under the 'room rental' (*kashizashiki*) system. Devised by the Tokyo Metropolitan Police, the 'room rental' system continued the Tokugawa practice of restricting licensed prostitution to designated areas of the city.[5] Itō Hirobumi, Japan's first prime minster, saw no moral complexities in licensed prostitution. In an interview with a foreign journalist, Itō explained that a Japanese woman who worked in licensed brothels did so from 'a lofty desire to help her parents or relations; and, when she forsakes the life, by good conduct she is readmitted to society'.[6]

In this transitional moment, the public too was split over whether licensed prostitution was a bane or virtue in view of the greater aim – that of Japan's achieving equality with the West. Debates over prostitution and the status of women crammed people into public gatherings, filled newspaper columns and dominated agendas in government chambers. The content of the debates was wide and varied. Japanese Christians saw a direct causal relationship between the lack of status of the wife in her family and the immorality of state-sanctioned licensed prostitution. Other public figures saw the custom of Japanese men taking concubines into their family as a sign of 'backwardness' which contributed to Japan's lack of standing as a modern nation.[7]

In the early years of Meiji, policymakers were also ambiguous in how to respond to impoverished peasant women migrating abroad for work. The administrators' ambiguity had nothing to do with ignorance. The Japanese government was aware of Japanese women travelling from Nagasaki to Shanghai to engage in sex work as early as 1872, for example. The Nagasaki prefectural authorities were issuing them with travel documents.[8] The lack of cohesion among Japanese administrators was because, as yet, Japanese women emigrating abroad in search of sex work was not seen as a political or economic issue.

The historical novelty that faced Japanese authorities in the early 1870s cannot be underrated. The Meiji rulers had the unenviable task of inventing a whole new form of government to accommodate an entire field of new realities when Japan became part of the global economy. A major challenge faced by the newly formed Meiji state was how to act on the economy and on public opinion. New ways of acting on the existing behaviours, opinions and mentalities of the Japanese people had to be created in order to change the ways the Japanese thought of themselves as economic and political subjects. Crucially, the Meiji rulers, unlike their Chinese counterparts, realized early on that state-building was ultimately constrained by the degree of engagement of Japanese merchants in global commerce.

The Meiji oligarchy was determined to improve Japan's long-term political stability by importing foreign technology and social practices. The rapid penetration of foreign imports in the 1860s and the resultant growing trade deficit brought on severe inflation that overwhelmed domestic handicrafts. Foreign imports were of higher quality, competitive in price and more often than not embodied technologies beyond Japanese capacities. To establish a manufacturing economy that would substitute domestic production for imports would require major institutional changes. However, gaining public support for a form of industrialization geared towards export trade was not an easy task. Confucian values, which saw merchants as parasites living off the labour of peasants – as well as the general hardships facing rural Japanese due to rapid inflation – made many wary of government mercantile policies.[9] Japanese modernization was a tricky business.

In 1875–6, the Meiji government suffered a further setback when it had to re-evaluate its import-substitution policy. A relentless cycle of inflation and increase in foreign imports ate away finances the government had earmarked for enterprises to industrialize Japan's manufacturing sector. As a result, the government embarked on a policy of export promotion instead. At the same time, the Meiji government restructured the role of the foreign ministry. On top of its diplomatic duties, the foreign ministry was to find new niche markets for Japanese exports and negotiate trade agreements for Japanese enterprises to sell directly to foreign markets. The restructuring turned Japanese consulates into conduits for the dissemination of commercial acumen to Japanese merchants.

On the surface, the implementation of consul reports to promote trade seems insignificant. However, without the consul reports, the emigration of Japanese women abroad to take up sex work would have remained invisible to Japanese administrators. Only when Meiji authorities began to correlate the movement of Japanese women abroad negatively with national security and economic development did authorities take measures to constrain the movement of these women. The world inhabited by the rural poor was transformed by Japan's incorporation into a global economy based on competition and inequality, and the Meiji state quickly linked national survival to protectionism and territorial expansion. The authorities took measures to protect domestic industries by directing domestically manufactured goods to potential overseas markets and providing Japanese entrepreneurs with privileged access to markets and raw materials. The Meiji government also sought to open new territories for settlement to increase production and to redistribute a growing population. In this context, overseas Japanese sex workers became problematized and subsumed into the broader governmental issue of how to develop Japanese economy and industry. Transforming Japanese peasants into good workers necessitated not only new skills in production but also the restructuring of interfamily relations. It became necessary to replace existing customs with practices that enhanced rather than impeded nation-building.

The systematic restructuring of bureaucratic knowledge was instrumental in transforming Meiji sensibilities regarding the sex life of the poor. Sex and bureaucracy are considered opposite forces, but bureaucrats redefined peasant women finding work abroad, who had previously been understood as filial daughters, making them into 'unsightly women abroad'. The conceptualization of rural female migrants as detrimental to Japanese nation-building had its impetus in the political showdown of 1873, when Ōkubo Toshimichi put economic development before military superiority as Japan's foremost political priority.[10]

Ōkubo's emphasis on economic development revolutionized bureaucratic practices. As Japanese merchants were inexperienced in matters of export trade, the Meiji government saw a need to create conditions in which local industries could export goods abroad without the mediation of foreign merchants. To this end, the Japanese foreign ministry was assigned the task of devising mechanisms to increase the international competitiveness of Japanese industry and commerce. Ōkubo directed the foreign ministry to isolate sets of indicators to ascertain the behaviour of economic actors, both at home and abroad. The foreign ministry came up with a solution: systematic consular reports. While there had been embassies, the foreign ministry opened the first consulate in Shanghai in 1870, and it gradually increased the number of consulates to 24 in 1884, 59 in 1900 and 92 in 1911. The primary role of these consulates was to 'protect and advance the wealth of Imperial Japan' by securing trade routes for the circulation of Japanese goods abroad.[11] Consuls began to submit reports on the economic, political and commercial developments within their jurisdiction in the early 1870s, and consular reports connected local economic interests with the global world market by identifying prices, demand and the market behaviour of buyers, consumers and importers.

Initially focused on economic activity, these consular reports were also instrumental in classifying the activities of poor peasant women abroad as a danger to nation-building. Meiji officials keen to increase the competitiveness of Japanese export goods, particularly within the foreign ministry (*Gaimushō*) and Ministry of Agriculture and Commerce (*Nōshōmushō*), eventually came to refute the idea that Japanese overseas prostitution was motivated by filial piety and was beneficial to the common good. Increasingly, consuls began from the early 1880s to narrativize poor peasant women involved in sex work as a direct threat to their efforts to create conditions favourable to Japanese trade and overseas labour. In consular reports, female peasant migrants were 'unsightly women', the embodiment of harmful customs that impeded the development of new productive practices, technologies and institutions necessary for full industrialization and optimal national security.[12] The redefinition of overseas Japanese sex workers as undesirable persons was not initially a moral prescription; it was, rather, part of a political and economic reconstruction linking a rigid new conceptualization of what counted as socially acceptable work.

In practice, consular reports were a form of bureaucratic knowledge that gauged the competitiveness of Japanese exports in the global economy. Consular reports took three forms. Monthly reports gave a general listing of the volume of Japanese trade covering items such as silk yarn, cottons, tea, coal, matches and textiles. Yearly reports were trade surveys of the major ports and commercial cities within the consulate's area of jurisdiction. Special reports detailed items that the consul felt worthy of notice for the Japanese manufacturers.[13] Under this ocular regime, impoverished peasant women migrating became visible and a target for government action.

Drawn into the Light

The year 1885 was the watershed year in which Japanese women engaging in sex work began to register increasingly in consular reports as a political and economic danger. In that year, the Japanese government began sending cheap Japanese labour abroad as one response to the finance minister Matsukata Masayoshi's policy to tackle inflation and mounting government deficits. The historical configurations that aligned migration with programmes for changing the economic and social life of Japan were the deflationary fiscal policies introduced by Matsukata in 1881, and the disastrous harvest in 1885. Matsukata's policy of stabilizing the economy by issuing less paper money led to rural distress as silk, rice and cotton prices fell sharply. Tenancy rates rose from 29 per cent in 1872 to 40 per cent in 1887.[14] An estimated 367,000 landholding farmers lost their property during this period, unable to pay land tax.[15] The rural recession also seriously impeded the Meiji government's ability to raise finances, as the land tax was the biggest source of government revenue.[16]

Matsukata's fiscal programme reoriented the government's industrial policy. The central government began working with local landed gentry to establish modern industries in their native regions. Driven by a mixture of nationalist sentiment and aspiration for local development, each region pursued their own policies for industrialization. In the case of Yamaguchi prefecture, the foreign minister and Yamaguchi native Inoue Kaoru joined forces with his protégé, the Yamaguchi governor Nakano Goichi, to recruit labourers to work in Hawaii under strict government supervision as a tactic to industrialize and introduce new technologies to the region.[17] Inoue was amenable to a government-managed migration policy (*kan'yaku imin*) because he linked government objectives such as regional economic growth and productivity with the displacement of Japanese labourers overseas.

From its conception, Inoue's policy of sending Japanese labour abroad was agro-centrist in nature. Inoue saw overseas labour migration as a policy of agricultural investment aimed at securing the well-being of landholding peasants. Emigrant remittances coupled with the skills brought back by returnee migrants were profit returning directly to the primary producers, the peasant landholding households, who in turn would invest the surplus back into the land. Inoue calculated that a government-sponsored and regulated programme of migration overseas would introduce new, and presumably more systematic, agricultural techniques and practices into his native prefecture. He predicted that new farming techniques brought back by the migrants would revolutionize agricultural practices in rural Japan within a period of ten years.[18] There was a national dimension to the policy too. The investment of monies and skill by landholders into agriculture production met the objectives of the Japanese government to increase economic competiveness both domestically and globally.

A crucial calculation was Inoue's expectations that, once overseas, Japanese labourers would remit considerable sums of money. This reckoning is evident in the administrative procedures designed to make the wages of the labourers calculable and, consequently, potentially manageable and usable as investment funds by the Japanese government. The conditions of the government-sponsored migrants gave the Japanese consulates in Honolulu access to approximately 25 per cent of the emigrant labourers' monthly wages. Every month, the sugar plantation owners sent around a quarter of the labourer's wage to the Bureau of Immigration, which transferred the money to the Japanese consulate. The consul then duly deposited the money in the Hawaiian Government Postal Savings Bank, which, in turn, sent the money to the Imperial Treasury in Tokyo. These administrative measures remitted and redirected a portion of the labourers' monies to rural household economies in Japan.

The government's promotion of Japanese labour emigration to Hawaiian sugar plantations brought a new awareness concerning how the conduct of rural women abroad was pertinent to the reproduction of economic relations and the circulation of Japanese goods and labour. In February 1886, Andō Tarō arrived from Shanghai to take his new post as Japanese consulate general. Andō's chief duty was to oversee the security and welfare of the first shipment of Japanese government-contracted labourers to the islands. The spectre of Japanese prostitution had haunted Andō endlessly during his tenure as consul in Shanghai.[19] It continued to hound him halfway across the Pacific. Soon after his arrival in Hawaii, Andō reported that gambling and prostitution were undermining the discipline of Japanese labourers (which included women) on the plantations, leading to a general malaise of laziness and depravity among the migrant population.[20] In March 1886, Andō's fears over the political liability of prostitution among the Japanese migrants contracted to work in Hawaii were confirmed. In a missive to Tokyo, Andō reported that the King of Hawaii, David Kalakaua, had threatened to renege on the labour convention signed by both countries in January 1886 unless he implemented immediate measures to prevent prostitution by Japanese women. The source of the king's agitation, explained Andō, was the rumours reaching Hawaii concerning the large number of Japanese women engaged in prostitution in Korea and China. The king feared that Japanese women in Hawaii would follow suit.[21] Andō also detected a further danger posed by prostitution to Japanese labour migration, noting that in Article 9 of the Convention between the Empire of Japan and the Kingdom of Hawaiian Islands, the Hawaiian government was liable for the cost of any Japanese subject repatriated before the term of their contract. The actions of 'evilly disposed' Japanese women engaging in prostitution, warned Andō, would make Japanese labour recruitment too expensive, as the costs of repatriation would be passed on to Hawaiian plantation owners, which would lead them to search for a cheaper source of labour.[22] In another report to Tokyo, sent in June 1887, Andō lamented that many of the wives who accompanied their husbands to Hawaii were selling sex to other Japanese labourers who travelled to the plantations by themselves, with the full knowledge and consent of their spouses.[23] Struggling to make sense of what could be the source of such behaviour, Andō put forward the proposition that the men and women coming to Hawaii were bringing with them the 'evil customs' of their villages, 'where men and women would gather in the temples and shrines, and in the dark of night, sleep together'.[24]

The perception of the incorrigibility of the rural poor as dangerous to Japanese economic interests was reproduced a year later, halfway across the Pacific, by Alexander Marks,[25] merchant-trader and honorary Japanese consul for Australia. In December 1887, Marks echoed Andō's anxiety concerning the political and economic danger the presence of Japanese women engaged in sex work posed. Marks warned the vice foreign minister, Aoki Shūzō, that every individual Japanese woman of 'disreputable character' entering Australia was an enormous threat to the development of trade between the two countries, and to the continuing recruitment of Japanese male labourers to work the sugar plantations in northern Queensland. The background to Marks's anxiety was the organized labour movement in Australia, which identified Chinese, Japanese and Indian workers as wilfully undermining the white working man's quest to earn a living wage because they chose to work for a pittance. Marks warned Tokyo that he feared 'considerable trouble would be the result' should 'unscrupulous men' introduce into Australia Japanese women of 'bad character'.[26]

Marks was filled with the same dread in 1891, when he received word from Samuel Griffith, the premier of Queensland, that two more 'women of the unfortunate class' had arrived at Thursday Island. Griffith's missive came in the wake of the restrictions placed on Chinese labourers by the Victorian colonial government. Marks immediately wired a reply asking for the immediate deportation of both women, before the public and press could call for restrictions against Japanese coming to Australia. Marks also wired Tokyo to express the danger of 'the present temper of the various Legislation of the Australian colonies' leading to 'a poll tax be[ing] levied on Japanese subjects should low women continue to arrive in Australia'. Marks's greatest apprehension, however, was that 'the Australian Governments (who act conjointly in these matters)' would enforce anti-Japanese exclusion legislation in all the Australian colonies. Marks urged the Japanese government to prevent rural poor women lacking such universal feminine properties as self-control, chastity and social decorum from leaving Japan to avoid giving 'the working classes who will not have cheap labour competing against them' grounds to advocate restrictions on Japanese labour migration.[27] The Japanese peasant women who made a livelihood as sex workers in Australia had a specific meaning for Marks. Their presence fanned his fear of the disenfranchised and reinforced the myths of the civilizing function of white settlements he shared with other Australian colonials.

Japanese consuls in California and British Columbia too began visualizing a causal relationship between the out-migration of poor rural women and anti-Asian legislation aimed at Japanese labourers. In March 1891, Chinda Sutemi, the San Francisco consul, informed Tokyo that Japanese prostitution was the issue most 'prone to incur the enmity of Americans', and become the 'basic pretext' for anti-Japanese agitation.[28] The necessity to stamp out all impropriety in the behaviour of Japanese women entering the US intensified in April 1891, when US authorities prevented a large number of Japanese labourers travelling on a succession of ships from landing. The immigration department deemed that the Japanese passengers had contravened recent legislation, which prohibited paupers, persons suffering from contagious diseases, prostitutes or contract labourers from entering the US.[29] Most of the male labourers on the ships eventually entered thanks to Chinda's intervention; nine women travelling on the vessels were deported, however. Chinda chose not to advocate for the women out of political expediency, thus rendering Japanese peasant women among the various categories of persons that the US government deemed to be less virtuous in political, moral and medical terms. The Japanese consul's affirmation of the threat of impropriety by Japanese women, combined with the certainty of restrictions being placed on Japanese merchants and migrant labourers by US officials, turned the escape from rural poverty by peasant women into a problem of government.

The increase in the number of Japanese women engaging in sex work overseas intensified the political contradiction faced by the Japanese government; namely how to promote and facilitate and, at the same time, control and limit the movement of Japanese subjects abroad. Successive consuls who took up their posts in the ports and cities along the major trade routes in Asia and the North American west coast were dismayed to discover that Japanese women working as prostitutes preceded them, and, more often than not, were the major Japanese presence in their jurisdiction. By 1890, consuls in every port east of Bombay had reported Japanese women working as prostitutes in their territorial jurisdiction.[30] Japanese consuls were not the only ones anxious about the increasing numbers of Japanese women engaged in 'unsightly behaviour abroad'. Between 1888 and 1890, the foreign ministry received over fifteen petitions via consuls from Japanese associations in Australia, Canada, Hong Kong, Singapore and the US calling for action against the large numbers of Japanese women undermining Japanese trade, commerce and labour migration.[31] The most frequent complaints came from Japanese merchants in Singapore and Hong Kong, who remonstrated that most of the women alighting in the two ports were 'barefoot' and 'dishevelled', had nothing to their name 'except the tattered clothes on their back', and were 'led from the harbour to a nearby Japanese inn', shadowed 'by large numbers of Chinese ridiculing them'.[32]

The naming of poor rural women as 'unsightly women abroad' signified an institutionalized contempt for any form of life not amenable to the project of socialization promoted by Japanese bureaucrats who spoke in the name of collective good and the state. A good example of this contempt in action is the reports by Saitō Miki, Japanese consul for Singapore from 1890 to 1895. Influenced by his meeting with Taguchi Ukichi,[33] an advocate of free trade and Japanese expansion in the Pacific, during his visit to Singapore in 1891, Saitō appealed to the foreign ministry for permission to tour the Malay Peninsula to assess the suitability of the region for the promotion of Japanese commerce and settlement. He duly received permission and funds for a series of fact-finding tours into the southern Malay Peninsula between October 1893 and February 1894. The Foreign Ministry Information Bureau (*tsūhōkyoku*) published the findings of Saito's expeditions in August 1894, with multiple copies distributed to the public.

In general, Saitō was unconcerned with Japanese women arriving in the Straits Settlements. As long as they did not disrupt the 'moral climate' of the region and did not hurt the standing of Japanese subjects, Saitō was not averse to them taking up work as prostitutes.[34] What he found objectionable, however, were the numerous requests from the Chinese protectorate asking him to enquire into the intentions of Japanese women visiting his office seeking registration to work in the settlement's licensed brothels.[35] Saitō objected to the time he had to spend investigating and filing reports on women seeking to work as licensed prostitutes because it prevented him from carrying out more important duties, such as extending the established rights of Japanese merchants in the Straits Settlements and promoting Japanese commerce. Saitō aired his frustrations to the Chinese protectorate over 'the great number of enquiries' that he carried out which 'could be done equally as well' by the Chinese protectorate themselves.[36] In another communiqué, Saitō clarified that the protection of this 'type of women' did not fall under his jurisdiction. The women 'had escaped from Japan', explained Saitō, and had 'no right to ask for any protection at the [*sic*] Japanese consul in any foreign country' without 'special instruction from [his] Government'.[37]

Saitō's indifference to poor Japanese peasant women was due to the women's lack of status as legal outbound migrants. The travel documents issued by the Japanese government substantiated the nationality of the bearer and their purpose for going abroad: student, merchant or labourer. In times of trouble, the bearer could call for protection to ensure their safety. However, if a person left Japan without a letter of travel, or failed to request one from the resident consul on arrival, then they forfeited all rights to call on the protection of the Japanese consul.[38] According to Saitō and government policy, as the women had 'escaped' from Japan without the necessary travel documents they were not entitled to any government aid or protection.[39]

Saitō's statement reveals a prevailing characteristic in the paperwork of Japanese consuls: namely, a plane of differentiation that marked rural poor women as social outsiders by the means in which they travelled abroad and the livelihood they made. The category of 'unsightly' (*shūgyō*) preferred by the majority of the consuls (if not all) to describe the peasant women migrating abroad was conceptually oblivious to the vulnerability of the rural poor and to the fragmentary and unstable forms of paid work that led them to seek work abroad. In general, the consuls despised the women's dress, speech and the daily tasks they engaged in as uncultivated and unworthy. Slipping into the consuls' condemnation was a gendered diagnosis of how the character of the Japanese poor was preventing new forms of womanhood from emerging to meet the current dictates of nation-building. In identifying rural peasant women as 'unsightly', consuls were effectively precluding any legitimate means of survival for the poor other than waged labour.

Emigration, National Security, Global Competition and Territorial Ambitions

In 1891, the foreign ministry attempted to restrict the travel of women abroad by institutionalizing measures to demarcate improper (*fuseigyō*) and proper (*seigyō*) occupations for emigration. On 3 March 1891, the House of Peers was hastily assembled to attend an extraordinary session to debate a matter of such delicate nature and vital importance that the doors were closed to the public. The extraordinary session had been called by the foreign ministry to discuss the draft of an important new bill – the Law for the Protection of Japanese Women in Foreign Countries. The purpose of the proposed legislation was to prevent Japanese women from conducting themselves shamelessly abroad.[40] The bill had two objectives: to target Japanese subjects unscrupulously avoiding honest labour by trafficking Japanese women overseas; and to scupper the belief, popular among the lower strata of Japanese society, that travel abroad led to easy riches. The foreign ministry claimed that this false belief incited greed among the rural poor, impelling them to seek work abroad recklessly, without due thought to the dangers involved.[41]

The Law for the Protection of Japanese Women in Foreign Countries read as follows:

> Article 1: Persons in foreign countries, who entice Japanese females for the purpose of prostitution or who procure them, or who hire rooms for the use of prostitution,

or who wittingly suffer prostitution to be carried out in their own houses, are liable to imprisonment with hard labour for more than one month and not more than six months, and a fine from ¥2 to ¥20.

Article 2: Women who proceed, or are about to proceed, abroad for the purpose of prostitution, shall be liable to imprisonment with hard labour from eleven days to two months, together with a fine ranging from ¥2 to ¥20.

Article 3: Persons who willingly assist women to proceed abroad for the purpose of prostitution, shall be liable to imprisonment with hard labour from two months to one year, and a fine from ¥5 to ¥50.

Article 4: Persons enticing women and sending them abroad, or about to send them abroad, are liable to imprisonment with hard labour for six months to three years, and a fine from ¥10 to ¥100.

Article 5: Persons under the provisions of this law are to be placed under police supervision from one month to one year.[42]

The foreign ministry was eager to implement the bill as quickly as possible in order to avoid further international attention and condemnation provoked by the misery and death of seven Japanese women and one man who had stowed away in the coal-hauler *Fushiki-maru*. The *Fushiki-maru* had left Nagasaki for Hong Kong loaded with coal from the Mitsubishi-owned mines on 21 March 1890. It reached Hong Kong four days later. On 26 March, the second day after having set anchor in Hong Kong, the engineers of the *Fushiki-maru* noticed a repugnant odour coming from somewhere on ship. Despite a thorough cleaning of the ship's mess, the strength of the ill smell increased. After a long search, the crew traced the stench to the cofferdam, a small compartment separating the engine room from the hold. The crew quickly removed the coal from the main hold to get at the sliding door tank. When the crew managed to open the door, they found twelve Japanese stowaways, eight dead and four barely alive, crammed in a compartment three feet high and two feet wide. The living lay naked across the dead in an effort to escape the intense heat coming from the adjacent ship's engine.[43] The morbid fascination of the international press detailing the circumstances of the women's deaths, or near deaths, and the bad light it shed on Japanese 'stateliness' prompted the foreign ministry to draw up a law to prevent a repeat of the events that befell the *Fukishi-maru*.[44]

The Law for the Protection of Japanese Women in Foreign Countries aimed to reinforce the Japanese foreign ministry's policy to restrict travel outside designated treaty ports in China and Korea to merchants, students and Japanese male labourers contracted to work the plantations and mines found on the west coast of North America, northern Australia and the European colonies in South-East Asia.[45] The foreign ministry penned the legislation not to protect female emigrants but to clamp down on the increasing number of women from western Japan working in lowly occupations abroad (*fuseigyō*).[46]

Cambridge-educated Ozaki Miyoshi, a career bureaucrat, presented the Law for the Protection of Japanese Women in Foreign Countries to the House of Peers for ratification.[47] Ozaki opened his address by imploring the House to recognize the national urgency in passing the law. Japanese consulates outside of Korea and China were powerless to take any action to curtail the presence of unsightly (*mikurushi*) women, who had become the object of amusement for people of other countries. The blame, claimed Ozaki, lay at the feet of those evil individuals (*warui yatsu*) who enticed ignorant (*muchi mōmai*) women blinded by the stories of easy wealth to a life of shame abroad. The reality, warned Ozaki, was that the number of Japanese women engaging in prostitution abroad had reached crisis levels. The 1890 census surveys on the number of Japanese abroad, completed by Japanese consulates, revealed 1,120 Japanese women working as prostitutes across an area spanning from Vladivostok to Vancouver.[48]

Because of the widespread presence of Japanese prostitutes abroad, continued Ozaki, foreign governments looked upon Japan in contempt. Foreigners 'cast a scornful eye upon the unsightly state of stowaway Japanese women especially when they first alight in foreign ports walking around aimlessly, barefoot and almost naked, without one *sen* to their name, nor one decent *kimono* to wear'. Unfortunately, 'foreigners inevitably judge the women as typifying the Japanese [race]'. Japanese inns at foreign ports added to the disgrace, as the innkeepers eagerly lodged the women, glad of the opportunity to make money off them, and 'care naught how the women arrive, nor that they are completely naked or blackened from head to toe in coal dust from hiding in the ship's coal bunker'.[49] To make matters worse, Japanese consuls in South-East Asia, Australia and North America were powerless to curtail the presence of these 'unsightly' women who led a life of shame in front of their very eyes.[50]

To highlight the daunting task facing Japanese harbour police, Ozaki gave an inventory of the endless ways in which women determined to travel abroad evaded detection. They boarded ships in stealth by 'disguising themselves as coal haulers and joining their ranks to load outbound ships with coal'; by 'secretly hiding in the cargo hold'; by boarding via the anchor hold; by 'hiding in the ship's funnel'; by 'secreting themselves in the ship's sails and life boats'; by 'using small boats to intercept and board outbound ships in the open sea'; or by 'concealing themselves in wicker baskets which are loaded into the cargo hold'.[51]

Ozaki informed the House of Peers that the Law for the Protection of Japanese Women in Foreign Countries was a temporary measure aimed at curtailing the ignorant and the incorrigible from seeking work abroad. The spirit of the law was to punish Japanese subjects directly or indirectly involved in the trafficking of Japanese women abroad, as this offence was not covered by the existing Criminal Code. Ozaki took pains to explain that the law was temporary. Over time it would become superfluous: recent progress in education would ultimately lead to improvements in the general moral deportment (*hinkō*) of the Japanese people. Ozaki was confident the people presently engaged in unsightly occupations (*shūgyō wo itonamu mono*) would begin to exert self-control (*mizukara yokusei*) and voluntarily cease their improper ways, leading to a natural decline in the number of Japanese women working abroad as prostitutes.[52] Due to the complicated legal implications of the proposal, discussion of the bill was deferred for two days. In the meantime, the House appointed Prince Konoe Atsumaro to head a nine-man working committee to review the bill.[53]

When the House of Peers next convened, on 5 March, Konoe presented a revised version of the legislation for open discussion. Konoe informed the House of changes to the bill proposed by the committee. The major change was where in the processes of peasant women emigrating abroad regulation should occur. The revision committee's position was that the most effective way to suppress Japanese prostitutes abroad was not by trying to control their movement once abroad – the emphasis of the initial draft bill proposed by the foreign ministry – but by preventing them from leaving Japan in the first place.

The revised legislation put forward by Konoe consisted of twelve articles aimed to 'prevent licentious behaviour abroad' by severely restricting the movement of Japanese women. The major changes to the legislation were the introduction of strict procedures for women to follow before they could travel to foreign countries and the assignment of greater power to port authorities. The revisions would make it compulsory for all women to obtain documentation from the village mayor or ward official stating their permanent domicile, status, age and purpose of travel abroad. Even women accompanying a husband or father would be refused permission to travel without the proper papers from their village head or ward. The women were to present the documentation to the port authorities three days prior to the date of departure in order to obtain permission to travel. The revised bill also gave port authorities the power to refuse passage to any woman they judged was leaving Japan for immoral purposes and to board any outbound ship if they suspected there were women on board travelling overseas for 'the purpose of making an immoral living'. Ozaki, speaking as a representative of the cabinet, had no objections to the amendments, as he believed they protected the welfare of Japanese women while also reducing the number of Japanese prostitutes abroad.[54]

The revised bill, however, came under attack when the floor was opened for discussion. Baron Kyōoka Takamoto, a member of the now defunct legislative review body, *Genrōin*, raised concerns regarding the wording of the bill.[55] He pointed out that in the original draft favoured by the foreign ministry the proposed law was specifically aimed at punishing persons going abroad 'for the purpose of prostitution' (*bai-in no mokuteki*). However, in the revised draft, the targets of regulation were persons going abroad 'for the purpose of making an immoral living' (*seijitsu naru seikatsu no mokuteki wo yūsezaru*). Kyōoka's objections had to do with the scope of the proposed law: namely, what specific actions did the legislation refer to, and how were legal measures to work when the letter of the proposed law targeted all forms of 'licentious behaviour' and not just prostitution?[56] Murata Tatomutsu, a career bureaucrat with experience working for the Cabinet, home and justice ministries, was also critical of the revised bill because it made the punishment for prostitution abroad more severe than the current punishment for unlicensed prostitution taking place within the shores of Japan. Murata referred to Article 425 of Police Offences, where punishment for unlicensed or clandestine prostitution was three to ten days' imprisonment and a fine exceeding no more than ¥2.[57] However, in the revised bill, the offence of clandestine prostitution carried out overseas brought a punishment of between one to six months' imprisonment with hard labour. To have two levels of punishment for the same act and conduct based purely upon the location worked against modern legal precedent for consistency in punishment.[58] In the end, the sum of all the objections proved too much and the House of Peers voted for the bill to be withdrawn for further consideration; the Cabinet officially abandoned the bill on 7 April 1891.[59]

The failure of the Law for the Protection of Japanese Women in Foreign Countries to pass as legislation reveals the struggle Meiji lawmakers had in realigning Japanese labour and migration abroad to a larger international context informed by notions of civilization and progress. The objections aired in the House of Peers echoed an earlier struggle over the wording of the bill that had occurred in January 1891. The foreign ministry, wanting to avoid any legislation that hindered normal women (*ippan fujo*) from travelling abroad, objected to the draft law prepared by Inoue Kowashi, head of the Cabinet Legislative Bureau (*Hōseikyoku chōkan*), who wanted to establish a strict set of administrative procedures to control the movement of women abroad.[60] In January 1891, Foreign Minister Aoki sent a letter to Prime Minister Yamagata expressing his concerns that Inoue was a greater impediment to the progress of Japan than was the presence of Japanese prostitutes overseas, as his plan to curtail the movement of Japanese women abroad eroded a necessary condition for the development of the human intellect and civilization. Aoki argued that the freedom to travel abroad was a critical yardstick for governmental action. He contended that the strength of the European powers, and the source of their 'advanced material development and knowledge', was due to the freedom of movement granted to all their subjects. To ram home his point, Aoki pointed out that Inoue's proposal was 'contrary to the principles of the (Meiji) Constitution', which nurtures and 'respects the rights and autonomy of (Japanese) subjects'.[61] Aoki's criticism was particularly barbed, as Inoue was one of the key architects of the Meiji Constitution.

The draft of the Law for the Protection of Japanese Women prepared by Inoue was a draconian piece of regulation that can be summed up by the motto: if a woman moves, regulate her. Inoue drafted the law on the presumption that, without supervision, the country girl learns little abroad other than vice. Consequently, his version of the law treats country girls who move abroad in search of work as 'voluntary' criminals who know no shame. The unsupervised movement of 'backward', 'ignorant' peasant women in the streets of foreign cities is thus equated with the offence of illicit prostitution. Inuoe's aim was to impart order onto the movement of poor country girls by subjecting them to a tight regulatory regime so that they can be socialized to the world of virtue and honest labour. In the figure of the overseas prostitute as 'voluntary criminal', we have the material and mental transformation of rural poor women into a delinquent form of Japanese womanhood that must be surrounded by apparatus of correction and control.

As we have seen, the foreign ministry resisted the measures proposed by the Cabinet Legislative Bureau on the conviction that a critical yardstick of good government was the ability of the state to secure the freedom of individuals. Aoki had followed the example of Inoue Kaoru, a principal figure in establishing a system of government-contracted labour migration to Hawaii, by identifying a causal relationship between social and economic progress, national strength and individuals endowed with the freedom of movement.

The gauntlet for fusing Japanese emigration with nation-building was picked up by Enomoto Takeaki, who replaced Aoki Shūzō as foreign minister in May 1891. In his capacity as foreign minister, Enomoto embarked on an ambitious project to expand Japanese sovereignty by territorial acquisition through peaceful migration settlement. Born in Tokyo to a shogunate retainer, Enomoto studied gunnery and navigation in Nagasaki under Dutch instructors from 1853. In 1858, he moved back to Edo to teach at the shogunate's naval school, created to bolster Japan's naval defences against the gunboat diplomacy of the Western powers. In September 1862, Enomoto left Japan for the Netherlands to oversee the construction of warships requisitioned by the shogunate. From 1862 until 1866, he resided in the Netherlands, handling the building of the warships while taking courses in Western law, military science and mechanics.

Enomoto's outbound journey to the Netherlands was on board a Dutch merchant vessel and involved a port of call to Batavia, the commercial and political centre of the Dutch East Indies. The port of call humbled Enomoto. Batavia awed him with its wealth of infrastructure, the prevalence of Western architecture and the volume of trade in quinine, pepper, tea, sugar, coffee and oil. During his stay in Batavia, Enomoto felt he had stumbled on the source of Western power and on a formula for Japan to escape Western subjugation. Enomoto grasped that overseas possessions enabled the Kingdom of the Netherlands to be in a state of permanent and collective enrichment through the creation of monopolist markets that controlled the supply of agricultural commodities and the distribution of manufactured goods. Enomoto's political realization was that the essential instrument and fundamental weapon in competition with other countries was monopolies in agricultural commodities.[62] As a result, Enomoto's career was characterized by advocacy of the opening of Hokkaido for cultivation, and keeping a constant vigil for opportunities to purchase overseas territory for large-scale agricultural settlements. Enomoto perceived territorial expansion as the most prudent form of economic development, as it would allow Japan the freedom to pursue an independent course of action on the international stage.

Enomoto first began advocating Japanese expansion into the Pacific in 1877. Inspired by the diplomatic acquisition of the Bonin Islands by Japan in 1876, Enomoto proposed that the Meiji government purchase the Mariana and Caroline Islands from the Kingdom of Spain. His plan included establishing an administrative centre in Guam as an offshoot of the main administrative centre on the Izu Islands. His proposal for settling the islands was inventive; suggesting that convict labour and dissatisfied samurai involved in rebellions against the government be used to grow tobacco, coffee and Cinochona trees to make quinine for the world market.[63] Settling disenchanted samurai on the islands was politically expedient: it defused the threat of armed rebellion, returned the samurai to the land and gave them a means to do productive labour, thus allowing for their rehabilitation back into the Japanese body politic. During the same year, Enomoto also put forward schemes for the Japanese government to purchase Papua New Guinea and the Solomon Islands along with all uninhabited islands in the western Pacific in order for Japan to secure a maritime-based economic sphere of influence extending from India to Australia.[64]

There are several noteworthy characteristics about Enomoto's proposal. His vision was agrocentrist, based on the plantation economies of Britain, the Netherlands and the US: the acquisition of unused or unoccupied land, the cultivation of large-scale agricultural settlements and production, and profit from agricultural return were the essential objectives.[65] Enomoto saw large plantation agriculture supplying distant overseas markets as the solution to Japan's economic and military weakness. Such a programme ensured maximum economic development and expanded the resources available within the sovereign territory of the Japanese state. In other words, for Enomoto, overseas land acquisition and large-scale plantation settlements translated into Japanese national security and autonomy on the international stage. Moreover, Enomoto, first and foremost a former samurai and loyalist commander who fought on the side of the Tokugawa shogunate, linked the purchase of land in the Pacific with the social and economic reintegration of the disenfranchised samurai class bereft of status and livelihood after the abolition of all fiefs and domains by the Meiji government in the early 1870s. Via Japanese agricultural settlements abroad, Enomoto envisaged the disenfranchised samurai providing direction and leadership to the Japanese overseas communities.[66] The fusion of samurai rehabilitation (*shizoku jusan*) with economic development came with Enomoto's unstated belief that former samurai were better suited to assume the responsibilities for increasing agricultural production and economic development than peasants. Unfortunately, his proposals coincided with a time when internal political developments took precedent. 1877 was a year of great domestic unrest. For most of that year, the Meiji government was preoccupied suppressing the Satsuma rebellion and a wave of nationwide peasant protests over rising rice prices. The government had neither the finances nor human resources to put Enomoto's colonial projects into action.

Enomoto received an opportunity to revive his policy for Japanese territorial expansion and agrocentrist economic development when he replaced Aoki Shūzō as foreign minister in May 1891. Aoki resigned to prevent further political damage between Japan and Russia after the failed assassination attempt by Tsuda Sanzō on Nicholas Alexandrovich of Russia (later Tsar Nicholas II) during a day visit to Lake Biwa in Shiga prefecture.[67] With the post of foreign minister, Enomoto also inherited the unwanted problem of how to deal with the flood of reports arriving from consulates and prefectural governors concerning poor rural women leaving Japan, more often than not to find sex work abroad.[68] The increased visibility of Japanese women engaged in prostitution overseas became problematic to the Japanese government in terms of race politics. The foreign ministry in particular was keen to ensure that Japanese subjects did not suffer the ignominy of being included in the Chinese Exclusion Act passed in 1882, which barred Chinese labourers from entering the US for twenty years because of the 'danger' they brought 'to the good order of U.S. society'. The foreign ministry feared the increase in the numbers of 'overseas Japanese prostitutes' would lead white settler societies such as Canada, the US and Australia judging the 'Japanese race' (*nippon jinshu*) as 'feeble and unskilled like the Mongolian races', opening the path for exclusionary measures to be implemented against Japanese subjects.[69]

From the start of his term as foreign minister, Enomoto forged a two-pronged foreign policy: to promote economic development via overseas Japanese agricultural settlements and to stop Japanese rural women from going abroad. On 5 August 1891, Enomoto established an emigration department (*iminka*) within the foreign ministry.[70] The administrative impulse behind Enomoto's decision was to demarcate acceptable and unacceptable forms of work for Japanese to pursue abroad. The department of emigration was established with two functions. One was to promote long-term Japanese settlements overseas, rather than the dispatch of contracted migrant labourers who returned to Japan upon the expiration of their labour contracts. The other task was to draw up administrative controls to stop 'the increasing number of Japanese women going abroad to work as prostitutes, whose presence undermines the credibility of the Japanese, and who evoke the slander of foreigners'.[71] Enomoto made one of his most trusted subordinates, Andō Tarō, head of the emigration department. Andō's loyalty was beyond question. He had fought alongside Enomoto as a Tokugawa loyalist in the last battle of the Japanese civil war in Hokkaido. Andō followed Enomoto into government service in 1872–3, accompanying Iwakura Tomomi to the US as an interpreter. Moreover, Andō had valuable field experience working with Japanese plantation labourers in Hawaii. The combination of dependability and first-hand experience in the practical everyday administrative and political problems faced in regulating Japanese migrants abroad made Andō the best man for the post in Enomoto's eyes.[72]

One of the primary tasks of the emigration department was to mediate with private investors to raise funds for overseas Japanese agricultural settlements. Here, Enomoto and the emigration department faced a lack of public consensus over the national usefulness of overseas agricultural settlements. These sentiments found expression in the newspaper editorials ridiculing the foreign ministry's plan for overseas settlements as lacking any economic and political practicality.[73] Editorial ill will was a political danger signal in mid-Meiji Japan. The press, more or less, acted as a mouthpiece for the different political parties made up by the propertied class, merchants and small-scale industrialists targeted by the foreign ministry to invest in overseas colonialization schemes.[74]

Enomoto's response was to take the initiative and call a public gathering to win support for his policy. His speech had two aims: to alleviate the fears and prejudices harboured against overseas emigration ventures; and to educate the Japanese public on the national and personal advantages in investing in projects to establish Japanese agricultural settlements abroad. A variety of newspapers printed all or portions of Enomoto's talk almost verbatim during the first week of August. This is fortunate for us, as Enomoto's speech reveals clearly his position on the importance of overseas agricultural settlements as a source of wealth, productivity and security for the Japanese nation.

The gist of Enomoto's address was that Japanese agricultural settlements abroad had the capacity to change the most pressing internal and external circumstances facing the Japanese government. Externally, Japanese agricultural colonies would 'improve the quality of Japanese (*kokumin*) residing abroad', and internally, 'better the livelihood of those residing in Japan'.[75] Japanese government-sponsored contracted labour migration to Hawaii (*teiyaku imin*, or sojourner migrant labourer) has been a 'favourable opening' for Japan, argued Enomoto. Since the opening of labour emigration to Hawaii, Japanese labourers had remitted around $1,300,000 to Japan, with an average of around $100,000 of the remitted monies finding its way to Yamaguchi, Hiroshima and Kumamoto (the prefectures of origin for large numbers of labour emigrants). However, the volume of 'sojourn emigration' to Hawaii was limited by the labour agreements between Hawaii and Japan. Thus, many people end up 'travelling to British Columbia, California and Washington'. Unfortunately, 'most of these emigrants fail to find steady work'. 'Uncertain in plans and without purpose', continued Enomoto, 'many fall into bad habits, becoming gamblers' or drifting menial workers 'wandering' from job to job 'in groups of threes-and-fives'. 'Sojourn emigrants', alongside 'Japanese women in unsightly occupations abroad' (*zaigai shūgyōfu*) warned Enomoto, were responsible for encouraging 'contempt among foreigners' and were a political danger. The US government had 'issued regulations to restrict the passage of Japanese emigrants', because of 'the call by the lower strata of the white race' (*katō hakujinshu*) for the expulsion for unskilled Asiatic workers.[76] Enomoto went on to lament the fact that the Japanese now shared the same status and circumstances as the Chinese, which had potentially dangerous implications. Enomoto projected how increases in the Japanese population would make 'employment scarce' in the not so distant future, and the Japanese poor labouring class would lack access to work abroad as the doors of countries would be shut to them.

It is 'imperative that the government take measures to prevent this', rallied Enomoto, by promoting overseas colonies (*shokumin*) or 'settler emigration' (*teijyū imin*). Enomoto took great pains to explain that 'settler emigration' did not denote appropriating another country and subordinating its territory as a branch of the aggressor country, but meant establishing Japanese settlements in 'underdeveloped regions with the objective of opening up the land and increasing its productivity'. Enomoto went on to explain the benefits of 'settler emigration'. Unlike the short-term migration of menial labourers, where the work was limited to unskilled tasks, 'settler emigrants leased or purchased overseas land and invested Japanese capital and labour to cultivate it'. He had no doubt that if able people ran the settlements, they would give emigrant settlers from the lower strata of Japanese society focus and 'fixed objectives'. Moreover, if the settlements made work available for women, with the 'right encouragement and guidance', the number of unsightly Japanese women would be, 'if not eradicated, drastically reduced'. To ensure that the listening public understood the urgent need to invest in 'settler emigration', Enomoto stressed that although the exclusion of Chinese from the US was widely attributed to 'differences in manners, religion and politics', the 'the primary reason was that they did not become landowners'.[77]

Enomoto's public address reveals the different levels of tacit assumptions in his policy to promote agricultural settlements abroad. The call to 'improve the quality of Japanese residing abroad', provides place of employment and investment for former samurai. In Enomoto's mind, former samurai were born for leadership positions. It was natural that they would oversee new enterprises abroad.[78] Moreover, Enomoto clearly believed that agricultural production was the original source of wealth, and that property ownership was the primary means by which people became fully socialized; the owning of land was the means by which to harmonize ethics, politics and economics. Economically, settler emigration linked agricultural investment and production and peasant well-being with commercial investment and Japan's ability to compete in the world market. Politically, large-scale agricultural settlements gave Japanese emigrants a greater independence and respect. Property ownership also defused the antagonism between the Japanese labouring poor abroad and the Caucasian labouring classes who saw Asiatic labour as undermining their ability to earn a satisfactory living. Ethically, large-scale Japanese agricultural settlements abroad offered the rural poor, both men and women, the means to make a befitting livelihood while, at the same time, bestowing upon them a real purpose in life.

In September 1891, Enomoto directed the research bureau (*torishirabekyoku*) within the foreign ministry to prepare a bill to prevent Japanese women from travelling abroad for the second session of the Imperial Diet. However, Enomoto soon scrapped his plans to draft a bill at the advice of Kurino Shinichirō, the head of the political affairs bureau (*seimukyoku*). Kurino informed Enomoto that to contend that Japanese women engaging in prostitution abroad were harmful to the interests of the state was an unavoidable emotional argument. If the situation was looked at objectively, however, 'there has never been any successful repression of prostitution, regardless of time and place' (*yo no kokon wo ronsezu kuni no tōzai towazu*). Prostitution surfaces throughout history because of the necessities of human society (*jinruishakai no hitsuyō ni dete*). Kurino pointed to the fact that all civilized countries openly regulated or tacitly accepted prostitution. Consequently, Japanese women in the 'unsightly profession' in countries where prostitution was state regulated could not be accused of injuring the standing of the Japanese nation. Moreover, if a bill passed prohibiting overseas prostitution because 'it was an injury to the standing of the nation' (*kokka no taimen wo kinson suru mono*), then the current licensed prostitution system in place in Japan would also have to be made illegal, or open Japanese lawmakers to the criticism of being 'hypocrites' (*jika-dōchaku*).[79] In one last effort, Enomoto approached Justice Minister Tanaka Fujimaro to see if 'persons who entice unemployed women abroad with false tales of wealth' could be added to the Criminal Code.[80] Tanaka too dashed Enomoto's hopes because of the impossibility of proving intent. There was no legal mechanism available to measure objectively if a woman harboured the motivation to become a prostitute once overseas.[81]

Enomoto faced a dilemma. The foreign ministry was eager to increase trade and secure the freedom of movement of Japanese labour abroad. Yet, the ministry also wanted to stop the movement of a floating and transient rural poor emigrating abroad and becoming vagabonds, paupers and prostitutes in foreign countries. The barbs of this dilemma were captured in a confidential dispatch sent by Enomoto to consuls in Korea, China, Hong Kong, Singapore and San Francisco on 23 March 1892. In his message, Enomoto confessed that the current feeling in the ministry was to stop the emigration of peasant women abroad.

However, as it was legally impossible for the Japanese government to prevent poor women from going overseas, the primary focus of the present administration was to promote Japanese interests abroad. As such, Enomoto instructed the consuls to 'tolerate' the presence of Japanese women engaged in 'base occupations' if the women were not violating any local laws or disrupting public order.[82]

Almost one year later, the foreign and home ministries issued a joint directive (*kunrei*) to all metropolitan and prefectural governors concerning the 'suppression of passage abroad of women under temptation'. The gist of the directive was that prefectural chiefs of police were to endeavour to hinder the operations of 'wicked persons who go around the country enticing young women overseas with tempting promises, and by threat have them take up immoral occupations, or deliver them to the hands of other people in return of profit'.[83] The police were also to warn rural poor women about the dangers involved in travelling abroad without following proper procedures.[84] In the end, Enomoto was happy to control the 'trafficking' of women abroad by administrative measures because he made facilitating Japanese migration and settlement a policy priority for the foreign ministry. During his tenure from May 1891 until the fall of the Matsukata government in August 1892, Enomoto instructed consuls in San Francisco and Singapore to investigate settlement in Mexico and the Malay Peninsula. He also successfully concluded labour agreements for Japanese labourers to work plantations in New Caledonia, Fiji, the New Hebrides, the Australian colony of Queensland and the Philippines.[85]

Enomoto's tenure as foreign minister was short. It lasted little over a year. However, his bureaucratic legacy was great. His reorganization of the foreign ministry to advocate and promote overseas agricultural settlements and trade institutionalized a bureaucratic culture that classified the rural poor, especially peasant women, as belonging to an incorrigible separate species of Japanese that were incapable of integrating themselves into the world of work. In March 1897, a year after the Japanese government initiated a policy of large-scale overseas labour migration as a solution to persistent rural underemployment and industrial underdevelopment, the deputy foreign minister, Komura Jutarō, informed consuls to ensure that the foreign ministry had full knowledge of Japanese 'prostitution' in their area of jurisdiction. The directive from Komura read:

> It has become necessary to acknowledge the fact that the number of unsightly Japanese women [*shūgyōfu*] living overseas and the circumstances of their lives have become intolerable. It is with good reason that I ask you to inform [this office] on the total number of unsightly women. Hence, I request you to report bi-annually, every June and December, on the number of unsightly women present in your locality, their movement to-and-fro, and their living conditions. The number can be included in a separate column marked 'miscellaneous' [*sonota shoyō*] in the mid-year list showing the number [of Japanese] entering and leaving, or in the end of year inventory on

> the total number of Japanese residents. In instances where it is necessary to make a specific report beyond the two above mentioned surveys, endeavour wherever practical, to investigate the real state of affairs, and place a report, although there will be instances where it will be hard to ensure accuracy.[86]

Komura's directive was significant for a number of reasons. The call for details on the women's lives reflected the belief that their opacity was the key to their unruliness, and the piercing of the opacity was the condition for combating their incorrigibility. The request for information was an attempt by the foreign ministry to acquire some purchase over the movements of the poor peasant women and the details of their everyday existence. The murkiness of the women's lives lay in the fact that their numbers, location, mode of dwelling and so forth were all unknowns. Even in cases where the circumstances of individual women's lives were known, the social milieu they inhabited appeared as a domain of social life resistant to the sobriety and discipline of work, and a breeding ground for unsightly and supposedly unsociable behaviour. The call for detailed numbers and information concerning the lives of the 'unsightly women' was also an expansion of the axis of political intervention. The subject of knowledge in consular reports was no longer just the market, but also those individual poor incapable of integrating themselves into the world – the prostitute and the destitute.

The second aspect of Komura's directive was that the information gathered and presented as tables and statistics to the foreign ministry would ensure the fidelity of Japanese consuls to the directives sent from Tokyo. The call for consuls to quantify the number of 'unsightly women' within their various jurisdictions standardized the understanding and experience of the consuls towards 'Japanese prostitutes'. The directives drew together a whole series of acts (vagrancy) and circumstances (destitution) that were not in themselves an act of injury against the Japanese state (the women were no more than 'unsightly'), but were now taken as proof of a character and an attitude that was morally defective and dangerous. By gathering information on 'Japanese prostitutes', the consuls were both producing knowledge about the women and, at the same time, subjecting themselves to an understanding of the women as an illegality that had to be controlled.

Lastly, the tables and surveys made obligatory by Komura's directive posited the 'reality' of the women's lives in a technical manner, as the 'know how' that promised to make the regulation of Japanese prostitutes abroad an actuality. The information on the women accumulated and disseminated in the consular reports created a new form of seeing and speaking about rural Japanese women migrating abroad as an illegality: a painful boil that needed to be lanced from the body of the Japanese nation. The foreign ministry's need to know stemmed from a structural contradiction inherent in the efforts of Meiji Japan to incorporate itself into a global economy. From the 1870s, the Japanese government used consulates to promote trade and build up domestic industries. In the mid-1880s, the Japanese government started offering peasants' labour to the global market. The government actively sponsored labour emigration to the plantations of Hawaii and Australia. Simultaneously, the Japanese government attempted to implement laws to prevent Japanese women going abroad and 'making do' as itinerant vagrants and prostitutes. This double move had two contradictory ends. One was the quest for 'freedom' crystallized around government efforts to promote the circulation of Japanese goods in the global economy and to secure the 'free' movement of Japanese labourers in the face of race restrictions placed on coloured labourers in North America, colonial Australia and the Dutch East Indies to name a few locations. The other governmental aim was 'restrictions', which coalesced around administrative endeavours to demarcate acceptable and unacceptable forms of work that the Japanese could pursue abroad.

The anti-itinerant prejudice engrained in the consul's bureaucratic duties was also found in the population surveys that became another function for consuls to perform on their post from 1886. The consul was to report on the number of Japanese residing in his area of jurisdiction, using the population surveys to obtain an accurate number of Japanese living in the area and to best identify what kind of information would be useful to disseminate to the local Japanese community to help promote Japanese trade. The foreign ministry sent the population surveys to officials in the home and agriculture and commerce ministries, and reproduced them for mass circulation among prefectural authorities. The population surveys classified overseas Japanese in minute divisions according to their work. This was instructive and transformative. The categorizing of overseas Japanese according to their role in the workforce made it easy for consuls to apply categories of what counts as work and what does not. Poor rural women who had no socially recognizable labour skills and who were not engaged in trade were lumped in the miscellaneous column. In 1917, three new classifications were added to the population surveys: two columns to represent Japan's colonial subjects (Koreans and Taiwanese) and a subcategory of family members to represent wives and children.[87] The statistical charts and graphs compiled by the consular census from 1917 onward divided the world into three distinct realms of existence. One realm was the diverse occupational groups of the socially useful, self-sufficient households and their dependants. Another was the realm of colonial subjects socialized into this world by the benevolence of the emperor. The last realm was for the incorrigible 'others' (*sonota shoyō*) – the indiscriminate mass of people deemed to be without social place (no stable familial relations) and utility.

The consular reports and population survey were scrutinized not just by bureaucrats, but also by people separated from the direct exercise of power, who themselves produced substantial amounts of quantitative data concerning the conditions and number of Japanese women engaged in acts of prostitution abroad.[88] The 'public opinion' forged out of the details supplied by the foreign ministry about Japanese prostitutes abroad became part of a wider social and ethical imperative: namely, how are we Japanese going to become modern?

The experience of the women as a symptom of some deeper disorder of Japanese society could not have surfaced without the coupling of economic principles with the belief that Japan's survival lay in an abrupt rupture with prevailing customs. The union of economics with social adaptation was introduced and circulated through the disciplines of philosophy and economics by the exponents of the Meiji Enlightenment, and by the religious belief of newly converted Japanese Christians, who saw in their faith both a voice of a higher calling and a superior form of reason, a moral science *par excellence*.[89] Both groups introduced into Japan a form of moral science devoted to the discovery of the natural laws governing the development of Japanese society, which would guide the Japanese as social beings to the means by which they could satisfy both physical and moral needs.

The union of 'free market' economic principles with the theory of civilization constructed a plane of reference that allowed external comparisons between Japan and other nation-states. The aim of these comparisons was to reach judgement on the current situation in terms of how far Japan had, or had not, evolved as a modern nation, where an abstract notion of the West functioned as a universal referent. Just as importantly, this index of the West as the apex of civilization allowed a newly emerging middle class, divorced from authority (journalists, civil servants and educators), to make internal distinctions between themselves and the rural poor. Although numerically small, this stratum of society affirmed itself as the spokesperson of the future, the embodiment of an advanced form of reason that would improve the manners and morals of the Japanese as a collective. The men and women situated in this social stratum saw themselves as ordained with the responsibility to lead the rest of Japanese society to its future. The responsibility, more often than not, was articulated in cultural terms, with much emphasis placed on character formation and moral cultivation. In order to compensate for Japanese backwardness, men and women from Japan's educated upper social strata elected themselves to speak for all Japanese, and turned to reason and Christianity to find the requisite tools for the Japanese race to avoid being consigned to a redundant past.

3 SEXUALITY AND CLASS: PROSTITUTION AND THE JAPANESE WOMAN'S CHRISTIAN TEMPERANCE UNION

The Japanese Woman's Christian Temperance Union (*Nihon Kirisutokyō Fujin Kyōfūkai*; JWCTU) was one of the first civic organizations to draw public attention to the flow of Japanese women going abroad to work as prostitutes. The JWCTU was a formidable organization in terms of mobilizing public opinion. In the late 1880s and early 1890s, its Tokyo branch organized public lectures in churches and civic halls to enlighten the public about the problem of Japanese prostitutes domestically and abroad. The editors of the Tokyo JWCTU monthly periodical, the *Tokyo Fujin Kyōfūkai zasshi*, also regularly printed articles describing the lamentable condition of Japanese prostitutes living abroad and the scandalous circumstances of their covert passage out of Japan. The lectures and printed articles were integral parts of an orchestrated campaign by the Tokyo branch of the JWCTU to gain public support for their crusade to persuade the government to ratify regulatory measures preventing young Japanese women from going abroad without proper supervision. In 1890, the JWCTU Tokyo branch submitted a petition with over 800 signatures to the foreign ministry imploring it to pass a law protecting all Japanese women abroad. How much influence the petition had on government affairs is hard to ascertain, but it seems more than coincidental that in March 1891 the foreign ministry successfully shepherded the passage of the Law for the Protection of Japanese Women in Foreign Countries through the Cabinet and submitted it to House of Peers for approval.

The formation of the JWCTU was a product of the first global wave in the feminization of politics that occurred in the last half of the nineteenth century. Women activists across the Atlantic and Pacific Oceans successfully extended their influence outside the domain of their homes by participating in orchestrated moral campaigns and philanthropic work advocating a healthy family life. These interventions strengthened women's rights by reinforcing and reconstructing the role of the mother as a primary agent in the socialization and moralization of her family.[1] The Woman's Christian Temperance Union (WCTU), one among many women's organizations engaged in moral and philanthropic work in nineteenth-century America, has been a subject of contention. Historians see the WCTU either as a reactionary organization whose main function was to protect and maintain the existing socio-political order, or as a progressive social movement that led to thousands of women assuming leadership roles and adopting feminist principles. Founded in the US in 1874, the WCTU expanded internationally to cover more than fifty nations by the 1920s. The organization began in Japan in 1886 with the visit of Mary Clement Leavitt. She was entrusted by Frances E. Willard, the founder of the WCTU, with the task of uplifting their oppressed Japanese sisters to Christian values.[2]

Recent studies have examined the politics behind the work of the JWCTU. Sheldon Garon, Elizabeth Dorn and Fujime Yuki argue that the group's moral campaigns against prostitution shed light on the failure of civil society in Japan to mature.[3] For Garon and Dorn, these campaigns reflect the way the Japanese state successfully breached the private domain of the family and sexual life. Garon in particular argues that the JWCTU's middle-class social reformers enthusiastically endorsed policies formulated at regulating 'illicit sexuality', which, for all intents and purposes, turned the organization into an organ of state regimentation rather than the defender and promoter of civil liberties and personal freedom. Fujime's conclusion is similar, but she formulates her argument differently, positing that the JWCTU's advocacy of a family centred on monogamous union reveals the intersection of capitalist economic structure and a repressive ideology of domesticity. The call for prohibitions on all other forms of sexuality is ideological, argues Fujime, because it imposes on lower-class families the values necessary to reproduce the compliant bodies needed to work the machines of the capitalists or to fight wars of aggression for the Japanese empire.[4]

Rumi Yasutake and Manako Ogawa challenge this view of the JWCTU as executor of state-sponsored social control, arguing that its campaigns propelled by American Protestant beliefs encouraged churchwomen to engage in aggressive social activism both at home and abroad.[5] Both Yasutake and Ogawa argue that the activities of the JWCTU, conceptualized from a transnational perspective, reveal a complexity unregistered in existing scholarship. On the macro level, the importation of Anglo-American ideals of domesticity based on the principles of monogamy, companionate marriage and domestic equality between men and women, imported to Japan by American missionaries, is an example of cultural imperialism. However, on the micro level, these new values provided Japanese churchwomen with the language and organization to advocate and demand their own distinct political and economic agenda. In short, Yasutake and Ogawa take the position that the JWCTU was an embryonic feminist institution formed around the concerns and interests of Japanese women. Both scholars maintain that the JWCTU was the first Japanese organization to draw critical attention to the social harm produced by the 'double standard' in sexual relations of Japanese men and women, which condoned male promiscuity, yet alienated women from their own sexuality by treating them as 'borrowed wombs', whose primary function was to reproduce the husband's lineage.

While useful and informative, these studies share methodological limitations. The first is the propensity to explain the JWCTU as the product of the alignment of capitalist development and individual rights. The implicit historical presumption to a greater or lesser degree is that Western historical experience is the central point of reference for the rest of the world, and that 'social progress' has its origins in the West and spreads to the East as peoples draw up constitutions that guarantee the equal rights of individuals to self-determination.[6] The second limitation is the emphasis on the downward diffusion of patterns of domesticity and womanhood from the former samurai strata to the rest of Japanese society via the processes of modernization. To argue that modern Japanese womanhood was achieved by a singular route, constructed on the basis of a general doctrine such as 'good wife and wise mother' (*ryōsai kenbo*), which was diffused across classes by example and the force of ideology, does not take into account the multiplicity of experience born out of class, age and place.

A key contention of this chapter is that the activities of the JWCTU involved a reorganization of familial space, which opened the possibility for new lines of interaction between the family and political power. This process began when the JWCTU, in the name of preserving the family household (*ie*), attacked the practice of men taking concubines. The organization emphasized the family as the primary social structure, the need for a cultivated and sound mother to socialize the child, and especially monogamous marriage as the ideal domestic relation between husband and wife, as it constituted the dynamism and strength of the nation generally and the vitality and good running of the household specifically.

The JWCTU also brought the subject of concubinage and prostitution into a wider debate concerning the Japanese need to overcome the 'evil practices of long-time ago' that harm family life, weaken the nation and hinder social progress. From this point of view, preconjugal chastity and monogamy as marital values became detached from familial values and assumed autonomy as moral ideals, and a lapse from either was seen as a moral failing with the potential to cause much harm to the Japanese people as a collective.

A significant characteristic of the new moral environment advocated by Japanese Christians was a sense of shame. The JWCTU used shame to promote the notion that it was better to die than to live without chastity. As Nikolas Rose has pointed out, shame in this context entails a self-directed investment in manner and appearance linked to a demand to discipline and regulate daily conduct in the name of the public manifestation of moral character.[7] That is to say, shame is primarily a social feeling; something that one feels in front of others, either when judgement is passed, or when the judgement is internalized and the individual becomes conscious of the sting of her disgrace.[8]

A remarkable feature of the activities of the JWCTU was that they involved an investment in fostering the life of a favoured group. The distinctive feminist content of the group's activism centred on a critique of the double standard of sexual morality for men and women; and a primary goal was to convince men of the same social strata as the churchwomen to commit to chastity and marital fidelity. The socially privileged women of the JWCTU thus attempted to inscribe on the bodies of their husbands and children a specific class identity, constructing premarital chastity and monogamy in marriage as markers of a boundary between respectable and non-respectable classes.

This chapter departs from existing scholarship to examine the way the JWCTU, in the name of promoting liberty and rights of women in their relations with men, constructed hierarchies to ascribe value to themselves through moral condemnation. First, the JWCTU used extramarital sex as a political issue to strengthen the position of the legal wife in the household as opposed to the concubine and prostitute. Second, its efforts to prohibit Japanese women from going abroad to make a living as prostitutes, while understood as an attempt to end a system of slavery that violated the inherent rights of Japanese womanhood, actually cloaked a desire to regulate the behaviour of the poor. The corrective moral work of the JWCTU to eradicate all forms of extramarital sex in Japan gave its members access to public life but at the expense of lower-class women whose sexuality did not conform to their sensibilities. Third, the JWCTU based its moral reform agenda on the importance of premarital chastity, strict monogamy and the obligation to work for the good of the nation. Its construction of prostitution as evil represents an important strand in the history of the relationship between prostitution and family as a socio-political issue in modern Japan.[9]

Chastity, Monogamy and Class Identity

The significance of becoming Christian differed for Japanese women and men. Irwin Scheiner and Karatani Kōjin have pointed out that in the decades after the government abolished hereditary status (1871), men from former samurai families responded more intensely to Protestant educators than to any other group because they were searching for a new basis for their sense of entitlement and self-respect. Scheiner posits that one of the major reasons for this was that American educators such as L. L. Janes introduced American Protestant tenets not as a higher calling, but as a superior form of reason – a *modus operandi* for the 'spiritual renovation' of the Japanese people so that they could complete the work of transforming Japan into a modern nation.[10]

The idea of the educator as social engineer grafted easily onto the existing ethos of Japanese rule.[11] In terms of the social imagination that existed in Japan prior to the Meiji Restoration (1868), humans were obliged to develop and respect the 'natural' divisions handed down to them as part of their unique endowment from Heaven. Each status group – samurai, peasant, artisan, merchant – stood as a measurement of social division.[12] The rulers, who possessed mental powers, were counted on to recognize the natural order of things, and had the responsibility of organizing society in its image. The ruled were enjoined to follow the commands of the rulers and to labour manually to overcome scarcity.[13] Samurai men readily embraced Protestant Christian tenets because they fortified both their sense of supremacy in relation to the mass of commoners and their social function as moral legislators with the inherent duty to direct those below them.

While most Japanese male converts saw Protestant Christianity as an indispensable moral instrument for meeting the demands of modernization, the churchwomen of the JWCTU perceived Protestant Christian faith as a powerful liberating instrument that would enable them to escape arranged, loveless marriages and abusive husbands. Although numerically small,[14] the women of the JWCTU situated themselves at the vanguard of Japanese civilization. The first chapter of the group, formed in Tokyo in 1886, went by the name *Fujin Kyōfūkai*, literally 'Woman's Moral Reform Union'. The literal translation highlights the fact that the core philanthropic activities of the JWCTU were not aimed at temperance (*kinshu*), like their American sister organization, but at correcting harmful customs (*fūzoku*) in Japanese life.[15] The group employed the word 'custom' with critical effect in order to target interfamilial relations, particularly the practice of men of rank and wealth investing in concubines and in sexual encounters outside of marriage. The JWCTU attacked the husband's right to take a concubine by grafting a Confucian model of social order, which depicted the family as the microcosm of civic virtues and skills necessary for good government, with Protestant expressions of domesticity that emphasized the view that wives were active partners in marriage rather than yielding subordinates.

Why did the members of the JWCTU identify patriarchal authority, which validated male sexual licence and the husband's prerogative to bring other women into the home, as the most pressing issue in need of reform?[16] An answer to this question has two strands. The first concerns the faith of the group's members. The churchwomen of the JWCTU inherited the prejudice held by American Protestant missionaries that Buddhist and Confucian doctrine degraded Japanese women by teaching them that they were insignificant. Protestant missionaries taught their converts that Buddhism denied women salvation until they were reborn as men, and that Confucian belief educated women to be inferior to men, and exaggerated the principle of filial piety to the extent that a young woman believed it was her duty to enter a brothel in order to assist her impoverished household.[17] The other strand is historical. In 1871 the Meiji leaders abolished all feudal caste statuses, thereby removing the prohibition on a man from a samurai background taking a woman from a lower social strata as his legal wife. As a result, high-status families no longer petitioned the national government for permission to marry. At the same time, the government began to recognize men and women in stable, ongoing sexual relationships as legally married even if they were not listed in the family register (*koseki*), thus further blurring the legal conventions that differentiated the wife from the concubine.[18] For the leaders of the JWCTU, such as Sasaki Toyoju, who came from a high-status family background where institutionalized concubinage was an accepted practice, the protection of the status of the main wife (*honsai*) in a samurai household was of pressing personal importance.[19] To make an unpleasant situation worse, the foreign missionary teachers could not differentiate the churchwoman-cum-legal wife from the concubine when they attended the same classes. The missionary teacher more often than not lumped together the legal wife with the concubine as 'heathen women' in need of salvation.[20]

The JWCTU linked its attack on patriarchal authority to the question of inheritance. The legal recognition of the concubine's child as a full member of the father's household became the key issue of contention for the legal wife in former samurai households. According to Mary Louise Nagata, in the first three decades of Meiji rule, the determination of the right to inherit between children of the legal wife and those of the concubine became highly tenuous. The Outline of a New Criminal Code (*Shinritsu kōryō*), issued by the Meiji government in 1870, endowed a second degree of kinship on both wife and concubine and gave equal inheritance rights to the children of concubines. In practical terms, this meant that the concubine gained the same legal status as the wife. Moreover, in 1878 one of the recommendations drafted by Japanese lawmakers for the 1882 Civil Code was that inheritance should change from succession of the family name to the bequest of the family assets. The recommendation set the legal precedent for the son of a concubine, upon having gained the recognition of his father and become legitimate, to inherit all of his father's assets and gave him the authority to evict his legitimate half sisters and his father's widow from the family home.[21]

The JWCTU affirmed the practice of monogamy and chastity as a mark of the legal wife's indispensable domestic role as moral educator. As such, chastity and monogamy became indicators of a superior, cultivated personality endowed with a sense of shame and of right and wrong, and the mark of a distinct class identity that distinguished the high-status legal wife from the concubine and prostitute.[22] In turn, the concubine and the prostitute embodied an inferior species of social being lacking the ability to exert control over sexual impulses and shameless regarding the conditions of their degradation. In short, the practice of chastity and monogamy became an index of superior cultivation and character and an indicator of the distinct individuality of high-status women *vis-à-vis* the uncultivated and non-respectable other.

Embedded within the notion of virtue espoused by the JWCTU was a programme to inscribe demands and regulations on the carnal activities of the body (eating, sleeping, defecating and copulating) in the name of preparing virtuous people for married life, preserving heredity, enhancing national dignity and strengthening the foundations of imperial rule. The wedding of chastity and monogamy with a higher authority is evident in the recruitment pamphlet written in August 1887 by Yajima Kajiko, leader of the Tokyo branch of the JWCTU. In the leaflet, Yajima epitomizes the imperial family as the model of domesticity and a natural moral order. The empress complements and sustains the natural wisdom (*eisei*) of the emperor through her high womanly virtues (*shikudoku*), thus ensuring that the Japanese people, men and women inclusively, enjoy the gifts of freedom and equality benevolently bestowed on them by imperial edict. Moreover, Yajima equates the principal position of the JWCTU – to reform antiquated customs that 'venerate men while belittling women, and take women into men's service as the latter pleased' – with carrying out the will of the emperor and the empress. Yajima argues that the continued subordination of women obstructs the imperial quest to achieve parity with the West as it harms the family, fetters the progress of women and weakens the foundations of the nation.[23]

Indeed, from its inception the JWCTU linked public objectives, such as the good order and vitality of the nation, with the private desire of its membership to affirm the role and authority of the wife in the domestic sphere. The extent to which the members of the group saw themselves as self-appointed moral legislators can be seen in the founding statement of the influential Tokyo branch in 1886, which pledges that '[t]he purpose of this society is to reform corrupt social practices, cultivate morality, prohibit drinking and smoking, and develop the dignity of [Japanese] women'.[24] The act of pledging was a moment of recognition by the members of the Tokyo JWCTU in which they affirmed themselves as a superior species of Japanese, morally calculable because of their capacity to promise monogamy, chastity and abstinence from tobacco, liquor and other uncivil behaviour. The capacity to promise – the force of will that places reason above the imperatives of immediate gratification – gave the JWCTU members the moral high ground to appoint unto themselves the authority and responsibility to undertake the generic training of others. In April 1887, the members reached consensus that their responsibilities as mothers and wives, coupled with their broader Christian calling to ensure the essential bonds of the family, coalesced around eliminating all forms of socially condoned extramarital sex.[25] Consequently, from 1887 until the enactment of the Anti-Prostitution Law in 1958, the JWCTU membership tirelessly petitioned the government to encode the natural laws of civilization – premarital chastity and strict monogamy – on the social body.[26]

Until the turn of the twentieth century, the JWCTU focused on circulating petitions and holding open public meetings with the aim of gaining broad public support for this struggle to make monogamy and chastity compulsory for all. Petitions were an established practice within Japanese history by which the ruled submitted to the ruler demands for social justice.[27] In the first twenty years of Meiji, voices that struggled for political recognition or opposed government policy and legislation, which Japanese historians refer to as the Freedom and Popular Rights Movement (*jiyū minken undo*), used petitions to make themselves visible as speaking subjects and to make their recrimination noticeable as a worthy object of dialogue.[28] Via the petition, the JWCTU were hoping to reconcile the family and the sphere of law by anchoring the principle of equality between men and women to the authority of the state in order to eradicate prostitution and other evils such as concubinage and socially tolerated contempt for women (*danson johi*: literally, venerate men, despise women) from everyday life.

These tactical ends did not involve any egalitarian vision. Nor were they based on a commitment to liberate women from existing gender roles or to emancipate them from obligatory sexual reproduction or maternal and domestic functions. Instead, the petitions and public meetings were a double-pronged strategy by the members of the JWCTU to force men from the same social strata as themselves to commit to premarital chastity and marital fidelity. In fact, the call for universal monogamy by the group was part of an overall strategy to secure property and inheritance rights for married women in high-status families, which ultimately worked to reinforce the link between property ownership and patriarchal and patrilineal social organizations.

The link between property ownership and patriarchy was possible because of the ambiguity of the word 'household' (*ie*). JWCTU campaigners used the word *ie* to connote both a social grouping and an object of property. The inclusion of property in the criteria of the concept of consanguinity can be found, for example, in a petition submitted to the government by Yuasa Hatsuko on 27 June 1889. The petition, signed by over 800 people, calls for raising the legal status of the lawfully wedded wife and her children over that of concubines kept by the husband and any offspring of such unions. It argues that *geisha* and prostitutes who enter the household as concubines would 'steal the property of the household' and displace and eradicate the legitimate family in order to make their offspring the household head.[29] The petition further articulates a concept of property defined by the consanguinity of its owners. The father possesses the property and the mother the blood. Together, they form the twin criteria for both kinship and inheritance. The switch between the two meanings of the word *ie* from social group to real estate brought about the conjunction of the mother's blood and the father's property. The mother provides the successor who will inherit through the blood of kinship, and the father provides what is to be inherited. The blood of the mother provides the subject of property and the blood of the father provides the object of property.

The conjunction of blood and property conveyed in the principles of marriage brought together two issues of great importance to the members of the JWCTU. The first issue was the necessity of monogamy so that the Japanese people could accurately specify their relations to each other based on the purity of blood. The second was the concept of national progress based on a notion of protecting the future – embodied in the present by the family founded on the harmony of 'two equals' in marriage and the natural right of property – from the threat of degeneration personified by the prostitute.

The JWCTU membership feared the 'public [licensed] prostitute' (*kōbai-in naru mono*) and the dangers she brought to their lives through the contact she had with their spouses. Members of the JWCTU argued that the prostitute threatened the quality of the Japanese race, because husbands engaged in extramarital affairs exhausted the inheritance of the next generation, in two corresponding ways. First, a husband who violated the conjugal laws of marriage sabotaged his active commitment to the social promotion of the family through the economic and cultural betterment of its members. Second, prostitution diverted the energy of the father away from the family to self-indulgent desires that consumed both the wealth and the impetus needed to secure and sustain the happiness and well-being of all present and future household members. Contact with prostitution brought naught but misery and unhappiness because, like all parasites of nature, the prostitute was a contagion sapping the vitality necessary for life and, by logical extension, the accumulated vitality of the Japanese race on which the strength of the nation rested (*teikoku no genki wo suiboseshimuru genso*). The character and integrity of a nation lay in self-disciplined subjects (*kokumin*) who engaged in industry (*kinbengoto*) and avoided indulging in idleness and lust.[30]

Personal Conduct and National Integrity

Every year from 1890 until 1927 the JWCTU unwaveringly petitioned the government to stop the flow of Japanese women going abroad to work as prostitutes. This campaign ended when the Japanese government decided to adhere to the League of Nations' convention regarding the trafficking of women and children. The petitions were one tactic used by the JWCTU to try to persuade the Japanese authorities that their beliefs exemplified the necessary moral and ethical orientation for Japan to become a powerful, wealthy and modern nation-state. The organization first articulated the link between 'moral character' and Japanese global prominence in the mid-1880s, when it identified poor rural women engaged in prostitution abroad as an insult to Japanese womanhood. The root of the churchwomen's ire was the fact that Westerners could not distinguish between respectable Japanese women (*seigyōfu*), such as themselves, and the disorderly and shameless women who not only made a living by charging for sex, but also had fallen into degradation and become the 'playthings of foreigners'.[31] The improper conduct of a 'base class' (*senmin*) of Japanese women abroad – whom the government and the JWCTU alike called *shūgyōfu* (unsightly women) – injured the Japanese as a collective social body because it gave the impression to the international community that Japan was a nation of prostitutes.[32]

In the mid-1880s, the migration of poor rural women abroad was blamed for restrictions being placed on the movement of Japanese merchants and labourers travelling to Australia, Canada and the US. Japanese consuls in Australia and north-west America were anxious to avoid the ignominy of anti-Asian laws – legislated in both continents to stem the flow of Chinese coolie labourers – being amended to include Japanese labourers.[33] For instance, in the first months of 1891, US harbour authorities prevented a succession of ships carrying large numbers of Japanese labourers from landing. The passengers were deemed unfit to disembark based on recent legislation that prohibited paupers, persons suffering from contagious diseases, prostitutes or contract labourers from entering the US.[34] The Japanese consuls feared that the increase in the numbers, and consequent spread, of Japanese women working as prostitutes in foreign ports would convince lawmakers in Australia and the west coast of North America that the Japanese race was on a par with the feeble and unskilled Mongolian races and, as such, an appropriate target for exclusionist measures.[35]

The JWCTU also worked to end licensed prostitution at home, arguing that it had effectively eradicated any feeling of shame, 'the quality that gives dignity to superior countries', thus creating an environment that was detrimental to the moral development of the young, the cause of destruction for tens of thousands of families and ruinous to the economy.[36] The condition of shame became a common referent among the members of the JWCTU to affirm and further distinguish the superiority of their specific form of life founded on the practice of monogamy and premarital chastity. The group saw the attribute of shame as a hard-fought and fragile faculty of human nature constantly under threat as immorality produced physical and mental changes that undermined character development. In December 1889, Asai Saku, the president of the Tokyo branch of the JWCTU, delivered a petition to the Japanese government, appealing for the abolition of licensed prostitution.[37] The petition argues that the government's policy of regulating prostitution by linking a licensed prostitute with compulsory medical examinations had failed to curb the spread of venereal disease and poisoned the morals of the country (*kokufū wo doku suru koto*).

In March 1890 Asai Saku sent a further petition to the Imperial Diet concerning the need for government action to stop the predominance of Japanese prostitutes in China, South-East Asia, the Australian colonies and the west coast of North America. The petition beseeches the 'gentlemen of both Houses' to right a wrong by taking legislative action to prevent the flow of Japanese women going abroad and subsisting as prostitutes. The unbearable (*iunishinobizaru*) disgrace of Japanese women eking out a living as prostitutes had spread across Asia and the expanse of the Pacific. Backward (*mōmai*) and ignorant (*muchi*) women had become entangled by their greed in the crafty schemes (*kassaku*) of procurers. Many, however, repented their actions and longed to return home but were unable to because of the circumstances in which they found themselves. The petition warns the Japanese government that the existence of Japanese prostitutes abroad is a national shame because the 'indescribably awful' circumstances endured by the women are worse than slavery and without parallel. As a solution, the JWCTU formally requests that the government implement comprehensive laws to prohibit the trafficking of Japanese women abroad. Until regulations restricting the movement of young women were in place, asserts the JWCTU petition, crafty persons (*kankatsu yakara*) would continue year after year to slip through the mesh of the law, deceiving and abducting ignorant women abroad to a life worse than slavery. The petition concludes by emphasizing the urgency of government action to avoid further harm to the Japanese nation and race:

> [I]f Imperial Japan aims to be a supreme power in the East, a wealthy and militarily strong country, and furthermore, to spread its righteousness to the four corners of the world, [the presence of many young Japanese girls living in conditions worse than slavery] will stain the Japanese flag for a long time.[38]

What is fascinating about this petition is the call for creating some kind of punitive legislation by which 'shameless' women who peddled their bodies overseas could experience and appreciate their shame. The petition identifies the free movement of rural Japanese women as a grave threat to the strength of the nation because of the potentially negative effects that their 'unsightly' existence has for honest and virtuous (*seigyō*) Japanese.

In the language of the petitions we catch the women of the JWCTU constituting for themselves a class identity that they saw as the future of the Japanese race. The petitions acted as a surface on which the members of the group could reflect their enlightenment as well as their rank and place in Japanese society. The familial relations promoted by the JWCTU were constituted as vital for the good running of the household specifically, and as an essential link to the dynamism and strength of the nation in general. The enlightened homemaker and the chaste husband withdrawn from the temptations of the pleasure quarter were the ideal parents because the children of such a union were best able to shoulder the responsibilities and burdens of transforming Japan into a strong, modern nation-state. Unarticulated but implicit in the petitions of the JWCTU was that other forms of Japanese female sexuality had to be negated if Japan were to evolve socially into a qualitatively different society from the past and take its place among the ranks of advanced countries.

Although the JWCTU deflected the problem of Japanese prostitution abroad to the field of personal conduct and morality, they also aligned political objectives with the transformation of personal conduct. This is evident in a pamphlet produced jointly by two organizations loosely affiliated with the Tokyo branch of the JWCTU – the Kyoto branch of the Women's Reform Society (*Fujin Kyōseikai*) and the Young Men's Moral Reform Association (*Seinen Kyōfūdantai*). The pamphlet, entitled 'Warning Bell: A Warning to Our Compatriots at a Time of National Prosperity' (*Keiteki – kōkoku no jiki ni saishi tsutsushinde waga dōhō ni keikokusu*), was written in April 1895, in the wake of Japan's military success against China in the first Sino-Japanese War (1894–5). It addresses the social disorder emanating from excessive consumption – an unwanted effect of victory – and the harm this brings to the dignity of the Japanese race, and sees the ever-growing number of Japanese prostitutes abroad as a symptom of the increasing commercialization of prostitution, which has the potential to undermine the advances gained by Japanese victory over China.[39]

The *Keiteki* presents Japanese prostitutes abroad as a source of moral degradation to Japanese expatriate communities and to their native villages. It maintains that the dependence of men on the earning power of women undermines the natural harmony of Japanese families abroad. Women working as prostitutes end up looking down on their male compatriots because of their greater capacity to earn money. To compound matters further, the women spread moral degradation to their native villages. They return to their homes in the manner of 'gentlewomen', adorned in gorgeous clothes and gold hair pins bought from earnings made as 'concubines to foreigners'. The other women of the village look on this gratuitous display of wealth with envy. Driven by the desire to emulate the wealth of the returned women, young village women are easily lured on board outgoing ships by promises of wealth, only to have their dreams turn into a nightmare of depravity and addiction to drink.[40]

Keiteki also attacks the character of the ignorant, backward, peasant woman caught in a web of vice at home. These 'unsightly women' live a hand-to-mouth existence, getting by on irregular, low-paid, squalid work. They are poor rural women who lead transient lives and who are thus free from the obligations and duties of household and regular work. Their main offence is their inability to integrate themselves into society, their preference for idleness over family and the routine of work, and their disorderliness. The *Keiteki* painstakingly chronicles the irregular conduct of women of 'bad' character as proof of the dangerous disposition and attitude of the incorrigible – a species of poor unqualified for moral training because they lack the capacity to be guided to their own improvement by conviction or persuasion.

In the oft-reiterated history of the fight by Japanese women against an unyielding and essentially unchanging patriarchal domination, the JWCTU lost the struggle to abolish all forms of sexual liaisons outside of marriage. However, such historical narratives miss a significant point. The group's campaigns focused on placing sexual restraints on men; the evil customs of concubinage and prostitution could be defeated when men committed themselves to chastity and marital fidelity. If viewed in this context, the activities of the JWCTU had positive effects. The group was successful in transforming and reconfiguring the power relations between high-status men and women inside the family. The JWCTU also managed to increase the domestic power of the wife contra the concubine and gain public recognition for the value of premarital chastity and monogamy in marriage. Legally, the Civil Code of 1898 removed the concubine's legal status and disqualified children born to concubines from inheriting property ahead of children begat in matrimony. Moreover, in the 1890s the Japanese state reinforced the idea of the educated and cultivated mother by mandating the establishment of higher schools of learning for women in each prefecture.[41] Indeed, the efficacy of the mother to the cause of the state was based on women's level of education, for the diffusion of information was through the written word.

From the mid-1880s until the mid-1890s the tactics of the JWCTU were based on a strategy of exclusion aimed at disqualifying all stable ongoing sexual relationships outside the conjugal bed. By the 1910s, however, having affirmed the legal wife's position in the family, the group shifted to reform work based on a strategy of inclusion aimed at binding all families to a shared culture of premarital chastity and conjugal fidelity via moral training and reform work. To this end, the JWCTU turned to resocializing fallen women, bringing them back into society by coupling advice and moralization with correction and reform. Moreover, the 1910s was a specific time in history in which those doing charitable works in Japan entered into governmental relationship with the objects of their philanthropy, and turned themselves into important social actors in the process. We cannot assess the importance of the JWCTU if we ignore its alliance with social philanthropy.

Philanthropy and Social Control

This research is sceptical of the argument that the JWCTU was co-opted by the Japanese state.[42] Rather, the position of this chapter is that the moral campaigns of Japanese Protestant Christian organizations to abolish licensed prostitution and the philanthropic work aimed at saving 'fallen women' set up the conditions for state intervention in areas of social life that were previously seen as outside the domain of government.

After the Russo-Japanese War, the philanthropic social work of Japanese Christians – which targeted character reform through education – began to coalesce with government objectives. Urban centres grew at an astonishing rate as men and women from farming families left the countryside to find work in the city, giving rise to growing urban anxieties.[43] The moral dangers of the city came in many forms: gambling, delinquency, prostitution, squalor, slums, destitution and homelessness. The biggest fears, however, were social: the fear of the spread of degradation due to the squalor of the slums that arose almost overnight around Osaka and Tokyo, the fear of the slum as a breeding ground for an underclass prone to open revolt, and anxiety concerning the inevitable increase in crimes against property and order.[44]

During this time, organizations such as the JWCTU attributed the cause of prostitution to a lack of moral education and attempted to right the wrongs by targeting the family and sexuality of the poor for correction. The result was the growth of a field of social administration in which Protestant Christian reformers emerged as specialized personnel who held expert knowledge about the collective moral regularities of the nation. It was in this realm of social and educational administration that networks of convergence and alliance formed between Japanese Protestant reformers and state bureaucracy. Japanese authorities at the municipal and national level turned to Japanese Protestant reformers to help them find some solution to the threat the poor posed to the moral order of the city.[45]

Here, it is important to note a subtle but significant difference in interpretation between this research and Garon's work over the conditions of collaboration between Japanese Protestant reformers and state bureaucracy. Garon frames the association between reformers and civil servants as an alliance based on shared class attributes such as income, status, education, living conditions and personal life experiences. That is to say, the collaboration of civil servants and Christians rested, 'above all, on the common desire to improve the morality and behaviour of the ordinary people below them'.[46] This research does not share Garon's sociological model of power, which situates the middle-class family as a semi-autonomous institution of social cohesion and normality, and introduces an ideal type of family across classes by example and by force of moral suasion. Rather, it follows the lead of Jacques Donzelot, who sees the modern family as a mechanism of interventions, which works by the disparity between individual and family interests, between one family member and another, and between middle-class and lower-class families.[47] As we have seen, for the first thirty years of its existence the JWCTU for the most part aimed at strengthening the position of the mother and diluting the father's authority. In the 1910s, however, its anti-prostitution crusades changed from protecting the status of the wife, by trying to convince men of their social strata to commit to chastity and marital fidelity, to the goal of creating a universal moral standard for all Japanese. It would achieve this end via education programmes in each prefecture informing the public how licensed prostitution enslaved women, undermined the family and impeded the evolution of Japan into a democratic nation-state.[48]

The impetus for the change in tactic can be traced to April 1911, when the JWCTU started a campaign to prevent the rebuilding of the Yoshiwara quarter, a major Tokyo red-light district, which had been destroyed in a fire. Believing the fire was the work of God, Yajima Kajiko, the president of the JWCTU, paid a visit to the Home Minister, the Mayor of Tokyo and the Tokyo chief of police to give her evaluation of how best to respond to the destruction. The JWCTU also allied with the Japanese Salvation Army and other Christian organizations to run a series of public lectures, coordinate petition drives and lobby the press to join them in their crusade against the rebuilding of the Yoshiwara. In July, the JWCTU formally joined hands with other Christian reformers, establishing the Purity Society (*Kakuseikai*), a Japan-wide organization committed to the abolition of licensed prostitution.[49] A key component of their efforts to abolish prostitution was the moral re-education of the prostitute back into the fold of respectable society.[50]

From the mid-1910s, members of the JWCTU worked closely with churches, mission schools and the Japanese branch of the YMCA to expand the reach of the abolition movement by giving talks at churches, factories, schools and stores on the merits of chastity for (unmarried) men and women.[51] All members were asked to mobilize in the fight to eradicate prostitution by pledging five *sen* to fund the necessary rescue and moral work.[52] As a result, the activities of the JWCTU, along with those of other Protestant organizations and philanthropic bodies, mutated from a focus on personal immorality to the need for social work to overcome the social and economic conditions that forced women to resort to prostitution. In this shift in focus from the individual to the aggregate, Protestant organizations and the Japanese government were attuned in terms of tactics and goals aimed at alleviating the external circumstances that led to deviant behaviour.

Knowledge, coercion and assistance converged in the alliance between Japanese Protestant philanthropic groups and the government. The initiative for educational campaigns aimed at correcting and reforming popular mores to induce the right kinds of habit came from the philanthropic bodies. Christian philanthropists also acted as self-designated social cartographers, whose main duty was to identify and investigate subjects who threatened the moral order of society and who needed to be redirected to the path of virtue. In order to achieve this aim, Protestant philanthropists needed information about the subjects targeted for intervention. Consequently, much of their work during this period consisted of investigating the target groups for moral education via a cross between assistance and coercion. Through its philanthropic work, the JWCTU, along with other Japanese Protestant reform groups, turned the sexuality of the poor into an object of assessment in the name of social problems and national interest. Gradually, the social work of Japanese Protestants became one element of government social policy.

It is important to note that Protestant Christian bodies such as the JWCTU, and not the state, first identified the causal relationship between underemployment, poverty and prostitution. A case study *par excellence* of how such social investigations constituted both the object of assistance and the target of correction is the way the JWCTU along with other Christian reformers identified the Amakusa Islands and Shimabara Peninsula in western Kyushu as the source of Japanese women working overseas as prostitutes.[53]

The JWCTU organized a fact-finding tour of northern Manchuria and Siberia in early 1919 to examine the conditions of over 6,000 Japanese women living in the region.[54] A large number of these women had followed Japanese troops sent by the Terauchi Cabinet in August 1918 to help the White Russian forces assembled in Siberia fight the Bolsheviks. The leader of the fact-finding expedition, which left Japan in late February 1919, was Hayashi Utako, the president of the Osaka branch of the JWCTU. Miyagawa Shizue, editor of the JWCTU's monthly magazine-cum-newsletter *Fujin shinpō*, which regularly featured articles on women's rights, temperance and prostitution, accompanied Hayashi. Her role was to report on the facts unearthed on their 27-day tour of Vladivostok, Khabarovsk, Harbin, Seoul, Taegu and Pusan. It should be noted that Hayashi and Miyagawa had little contact with Japanese women engaged in prostitution. They spent most of their time meeting and speaking with Japanese consuls, military commanders, superintendent commissariats to hospitals, Japanese Christians and Japanese business groups in the region.[55]

The JWCTU organized the expedition in response to a letter from an American member of the WCTU informing the 'mothers of Japan' that Japanese prostitutes were enticing American soldiers in Siberia to a life of sin.[56] The JWCTU delegation found that 5,000 Japanese women were residing in 'unsightly' living conditions eking out a livelihood as prostitutes in the remote regions of Manchuria and Siberia. The mission found this unacceptable. Not only did the women defile their souls and ruin their bodies by selling sex, but they also covered in mud the dignity of Japanese womanhood. The overwhelming numbers of Japanese prostitutes subjected honest, good countrywomen to unjustifiable discrimination and prejudice from the local foreign communities and to criticism from transnational sister organizations. Moreover, the almost 'slavelike' existence of the Japanese women working in brothels sabotaged Japan's standing *vis-à-vis* other 'advanced' nations.[57]

The JWCTU delegation also discovered that the majority of women in Manchuria and Siberia originated from Kyushu, especially the Amakusa Islands and Shimabara regions. Moreover, they found that most of the women were beyond help; their health was broken and too much psychological damage had been done for them to take on the vocation of a 'married woman' (*fujin toshite no tenshoku*). The delegation noted that it was a waste of resources to aid women already fallen into prostitution in Siberia. They were either too damaged or beyond help because they were ignorant daughters of peasants who lacked any sense of shame.[58] Armed with this discovery, the JWCTU leadership planned to obtain the cooperation of the Japanese authorities to take measures to prevent further disgrace to the reputation of Japan by informing the public of the conditions of Japanese women abroad. On their return to Japan, 3 March 1919, Hayashi and Miyagawa immediately sent a written statement of their findings to the foreign, home and education ministries. Two days later, both women addressed an audience of over 1,000 people in the Kanda district of Tokyo on the 'prostitution problem in Siberia'.[59] Moreover, the JWCTU announced at its 27th annual convention that the moral education of Amakusa and Shimabara women was to be the organization's next major project. The JWCTU committee charged with implementing a programme of reform in the Amakusa and Shimabara regions quickly realized that first-hand information on the social circumstances that led large numbers of women from these two locations to migrate overseas to work 'immorally' as prostitutes was imperative for success. The committee formally nominated and accepted three outside experts to help in collecting this data.[60] The experts were Kitazawa Shinjirō, a Waseda professor, the Reverend Kubushiro Naokatsu – husband of Kubushiro Ochimi, perhaps the JWCTU's most aggressive campaigner for the abolition of licensed prostitution and Yamajima Kajiko's niece – and Nunokawa Magoichi, a professor of sociology at Meiji Gakuin University, a founding member of the Sociological Society (*shakaigakkai*), and a consultant and researcher for various Japanese ministries.[61]

Out of the three, Nunokawa's contribution was most significant. He shared with the JWCTU a heightened sensitivity to the harm caused by Japanese prostitutes abroad to Japan's standing amongst other nations due to the nature of his commissioned work for the Japanese government. Nunokawa had first-hand knowledge of the living conditions of Japanese women residing in northern China and Siberia. He had spent the last 18 months travelling across Siberia doing field research commissioned by the Japanese home ministry on the living conditions and numbers of Japanese women working as prostitutes in the area.[62] Nunokawa also shared the JWCTU's sense of civic responsibility and activism. He had written about the wretched existence of the women and the damage they incurred to Japan's international standing in the women's magazine *Fujin Kōron* in February 1918, under the heading 'The Soiled Honour of Japanese

Women' (*Nihon fujin no tsura yogoshi*).[63] Akin to the JWCTU, Nunokawa was personally committed to finding some way of implementing reforms. In February 1919, he had financially assisted in the return of three Japanese women from Siberia who had sought shelter in one of the Japanese Christian rescue homes.[64] The JWCTU did not hesitate to commission Nunokawa to carry out an inquest into the reasons why a prolific number of young women from western Kyushu worked abroad as Japanese prostitutes. Thus, during the summer of 1919, Nunokawa travelled to the Amakusa Islands, where he completed a survey on the local practice of women migrating abroad as sex workers.[65] His survey and analysis was published by the JWCTU in 1920 as 'The Problem of Overseas Prostitutes: Amakusa Survey'.[66]

Nunokawa studied the social and moral milieux of the Amakusa Islands with the aim of discovering what factors led local women to a life of 'disrepute' abroad. The study reveals a systematic concern with the relationship between 'cultural backwardness' and the creation of a subspecies of Japanese womanhood that did not recognize the social evil of prostitution. Nunokawa identified four primary reasons why young women from Amakusa felt no shame working overseas as prostitutes: overpopulation and lack of industry; cultural underdevelopment and the inability of the women to learn and follow directions; the lack of inherent ideals relating to chastity and virginity; and the worship of 'mammon' (i.e. material wealth).

Nunokawa condemned the life led by Amakusa women on the grounds of their lack of character, epitomized by the incompatibility of the world they inhabited with the norms and cultural conventions of modern Japan. He was particularly scathing about local marriage customs and gender relations, which encouraged women to leave the islands to engage in sex work. Nunokawa saw the women as having no social value and the tasks they performed abroad as driven by avarice and harmful to the collective interest of the Japanese people embodied in the state.[67] He attributed the irreconcilability of the local Amakusa women to the modern ideal of Japanese womanhood as an agent of moral and social cultivation to their lack of integration into the world of industry, which engraved social utility onto the body of women through the regulations, control and training found in legitimate work (*seigyō*) in such places as textile mills.[68]

Nunokawa's ability to map out the social ills of the Amakusa Islands was possible because of a perceived connection between moral and character development and accountable and responsible Japanese subjects. The propensity of women from Amakusa to engage in sex work abroad was reduced to the specific environmental factors that affected the character of the islands' inhabitants. The politics in Nunokawa's report reveal the contours of moral judgements from the perspective of an invested class position, which only recognizes others of like quality. In the eyes of Nunokawa, Amakusa women's lives needed correction as they bore the mark of an inferior form of humanity on two accounts. First, they lacked value. They bore no sign of the cultivation that distinguished the high-status women of the JWCTU above all others, namely, the developed inward forces and dispositions of personality and character that gave them the capacity to demarcate good from evil and judge life accordingly. A woman of such character and personality would die rather than expose herself to the shame of selling her body. Second, the women of Amakusa lacked social utility as they did not belong to the world of work, and as such did not possess any of the social competencies beneficial to the objectives of the nation-state.

The JWCTU decided that the solution to eradicating the problem of Kyushu women going abroad to sell sex was via education. In winter 1919, the Kyushu chapters of the JWCTU announced a prize essay contest for young men. The essays were to deal with the health and psychological damage caused by licensed prostitution at the individual and national level, the harm to Japanese womanhood and national prestige by Japanese prostitution abroad, and the evils of drink. The local JWCTU chapters felt that the essay contest was the most appropriate means to forewarn the young men and women of the region of the dangers of prostitution and to cultivate public opinion for the eventual eradication of prostitution from the island.[69] The national committee also became involved. In January 1920, Moriya Asuma and Kubushiro Ochimi undertook an educational tour of Kyushu to inform the public about the evils of prostitution, giving public presentations to government bureaux, schools and civic associations, and speaking informally to social gatherings organized by wives of high-ranking officials.[70]

Although comprehensive reform of family life in western Kyushu failed to materialize, a mutually expedient alliance grew between high-ranking civil servants and leading Protestant reformers in the 1920s. The ambitions of the city authorities and Home Ministry to implement comprehensive reforms were severely curtailed by budgetary constraints and so they began to work with and subsidize Christian philanthropic efforts to initiate educational campaigns in an attempt to combat poverty and social unrest in Tokyo and Osaka.[71] The JWCTU and the Japanese Salvation Army were happy to cooperate with the home ministry to (re)socialize the Japanese poor, as they firmly believed that destitution and deprivation might be prevented by the intervention of educated, virtuous, social actors such as themselves, who possessed the rational capacity to steer the wayward towards a right way of life and to protect them from inappropriate impulses.

It was in this realm of social and educational administration that the home ministry bureaucracy relied extensively on the expertise of Christian reformers to identify the subjects that needed to be worked on and the apparatuses of control and restraint that would improve their thoughts and behaviour. For example, the Japanese government subsidized the rescue shelters run by the JWCTU in Tokyo for women who were destitute or who wanted to leave prostitution. The

Japanese government also recognized the churchwomen's moral authority and responsibility for determining the disciplinary order necessary to reintegrate the women to a society where sex outside marriage had no place.[72] In return, the JWCTU women gained access to an appropriate sphere of employment and a degree of independence outside the family.

Conclusion

A key concern of this chapter has been to assess the importance of the feminism of the JWCTU in the context of its alliance with social philanthropy. The organization recognized sexual relations as being of primary social importance and a key socializing force. Moreover, the women's encounter with a religion new to Japan, American Protestantism, allowed them radically to problematize and critique the existing status of sexual unions in Japan around the question: what is the precise relationship between natural aptitudes and social functions when our new beliefs overturn the least disputed model of marriage – the sexual division of ability and tasks? The attempts of the JWCTU to transform the Japanese family through universal norms of monogamy and chastity wed individual conduct with improving the qualities of the Japanese people to achieve parity with the West. Marriage in the sense of self-mastery and ethical responsibility served as a point of reference to a particular individuality-cum-personality, while marriage in the sense of monogamous procreation served as a point of reference to a collective way of conducting oneself to strengthen the nation in general.

Bearers of the 'worthiest instincts', Japanese Protestant Christian organizations believed that moral and social policies would improve the moral character of the Japanese people. As much as the reforms were driven by philanthropic zeal, their real function was to regulate the behaviour of the poor and to ensure the reproduction of descendants by emphasizing the purity of blood and the necessity to prepare people for monogamous married life. In the conjugality envisaged by Japanese Christians, we see a new social and moral code slowly being imposed, with the help of the state, which had different repercussions for the upper middle class and the poor. The increase in the domestic power of upper-middle-class women gave them an expansive role in the field of educational and charitable work focusing on the lives of women from the lower strata of Japanese society. All forms of female sexuality exhibited by the lower classes that did not conform to the sensibilities of the Christian philanthropists were targeted for reform as being injurious to the collective good of society. Members of the JWCTU willingly called on government intervention to help them in their reform work because ultimately they saw the state as the organizing agent of society.

A key characteristic to the new humanism advocated by the JWCTU was a sense of shame. The group saw shame as a hard-fought albeit fragile faculty cultivated by the forces of civilization. This shame took two forms. All those who espoused shame were bathed in a righteous glow, and never felt the prick of shame's barb. It was always 'others' – outside the realm of righteous illumination – that felt the full sting of this shame and had to endure it. The humanist shame touted by the Japanese Christians as the future of an enlightened Japan measured others by its values, which held that it was better to die than to live ignobly as a prostitute. This harmonized well with the Japanese state's espousal of the universal worthiness of being a Japanese subject, as both spoke the language of illumination, righteousness and the need to cleanse the world of all evils that polluted Japanese civilization and empire. Japanese Protestant Christians and the state made good bedfellows as both burdened others with shame and invested it in God and empire.

That they worked so well together perhaps should not surprise us. The JWCTU and the Japanese state shared the deepest concern over how to achieve cohesion between the principles of political action, the transformation of Japan into a modern nation-state, and personal conduct. Both also agreed that there was a need to coach Japanese subjects for the task ahead, not only in terms of gaining the capacity to carry out the various functions expected, but to do so habitually. For example, the moral persuasion campaigns run by the government in the 1930s, calling on the Japanese to save, be frugal and lead austere lives, sought to control and regulate the conduct of the many by casting a web of public codes and embarrassments calculated to shame people into readjusting their behaviour. As such, the JWCTU and the Japanese state shared a common preoccupation with the connection between the government of oneself – the importance of ethical responsibility to a higher authority and self-mastery – and the government and regulation of the many.

There is another history that is revealed in this chapter: the vital role that sexuality has played in the constitution of the Japanese upper middle class as a distinct and separate socio-cultural entity. The upper-middle-class women of the JWCTU tried chastity, monogamy and virtue on for size and liked the fit. The moral superiority of the upper middle class lay in the strength, vigour and life of its offspring. The healthy sexuality of their offspring became a political affirmation of their authority. Without the wholehearted belief in the superiority of its physical sex-body in contrast to the supposedly degenerate poor, the upper middle class would never have been able to maintain their exclusivity from the masses that was once the characteristic of the samurai strata. To paraphrase Foucault, with this investment of its own sex which it had itself invented, the Japanese upper middle class 'underscored the high political price of its body, sensations, and pleasures, its well-being and survival'.[73] Its authority was dependent on the cultivation of this type of class-body.

4 SEX AS PROGRESS: FUKUZAWA YUKICHI ON TRADE AND OVERSEAS PROSTITUTION

> If we Japanese will begin to pursue learning with spirit and energy, so as to achieve personal independence and thereby enrich and strengthen the nation, why shall we fear the Powers of the West? Let us associate with men of truth, and be rid of those that are not. We shall achieve independence only after we achieve personal independence.
>
> Fukuzawa Yukichi, *An Encouragement of Learning*[1]

Public interest in overseas prostitution was clinical in nature. The overseas prostitute was an indicator of a deeper disorder within Japanese society. However, diagnosing the women proved elusive. The JWCTU's self-prescribed role as the educator of progress was an attempt to change the interfamilial behaviour of the Japanese public by manipulating public opinion. They were not alone, however. Other contemporaneous reformers, such as Fukuzawa Yukichi, used the same strategy. The churchwomen and Fukuzawa both advocated monogamy in marriage as an end to the practice of upper samurai families and aristocracy placing concubines in their homes. However, they were at opposite ends of the spectrum when it came to their position on Japanese prostitution abroad. Whereas the churchwomen made the moral blight of overseas prostitution into a primary crusade, Fukuzawa saw 'the freedom of prostitutes to work abroad [as] ... a necessity' in the context of state affairs.[2]

Fukuzawa Yukichi's is the face on the Japanese ¥10,000 banknote. He is *the* face of Meiji Japan and its modern transformations. The iconic canonization of Fukuzawa tells us that he was a translator, author, founder of Keio University – one of the most prestigious private universities in Japan – journalist, entrepreneur and political theorist. His ideas about government, modern family, education and business changed Japan from a marginal feudal realm into a powerful industrialized world power. Fukuzawa is the renaissance man of Japanese history. He realized the modern ahead of anyone else, and it was only the lack of resources and technological support that held back his immense genius. His remarks on overseas prostitution matter because of his iconic status.

The iconography of Fukuzawa's life has two threads. One is Keio University, which has made an industry out of Fukuzawa scholarship. The other, and for this research the more important, is the significance of Fukuzawa to post-war Japanese intellectuals. Exemplary of this is his intellectual legacy to Maruyama Masao; one of the most influential public intellectuals in post-war Japan. In his studies of Fukuzawa undertaken in the early 1940s, Maruyama found a means by which to critique the present. This revelation defined Maruyama's intellectual persona. Hiraishi Nao'aki, a specialist on Maruyama's thought, quotes him from a 1966 public lecture stating that Fukuzawa allowed him to think 'the very limit of what is possible, and then use this as leverage ... to criticize Japan's modernity'.[3] Maruyama recognized that Fukuzawa and he were engaged in the same ethical struggle; namely, how to correlate the psychological transformation of the Japanese people with the cultivation of independent action.

Maruyama understood that the challenges facing post-war Japan were analogous with the trials faced by Meiji Japan: how do we create the conditions that restore Japan to independence and freedom? In the wake of the Meiji Restoration, Fukuzawa identified Chinese learning as leaving Japan vulnerable to Western imperialism. He was especially critical of Confucian thought, which Fukuzawa saw as irrelevant because its impracticality and fixation with the past offered no models of action for contemporary questions. Fukuzawa's struggles to change the intellectual culture of Meiji Japan were salient for Maruyama and facilitated Maruyama's most important insight: the militaristic manifest destiny of the Japanese empire was not just the world view held by the rulers, but also permeated to the inner world of the ruled, who accepted this perspective as their own.

The key to Fukuzawa's critique of the present lay in his radical comparative method. Cued by contemporary trends in Western thought, he saw civilization as following the physics of progress. Human evolution involved unlocking the laws of progress via the continuous accumulation of knowledge.[4] The different social organization and means of subsistence that differentiated the peoples of the world sprung from deeply rooted cultural customs grounded by habit and education. Unlike other contemporaneous Japanese advocates of Western learning of his time, Fukuzawa saw history (civilization) as open ended. Commitment to progress did not mean imitation, but overtaking 'the present level of attainment of the West'.[5] Europe was not the end point of this civilization, but the geographical location of communities that had advanced further in accumulating and adapting knowledge to the laws of progress. The historical specificity of habit and education as the primary difference between people and nations made civilization itself a contingent historical artefact. Progress was directly proportional to the mental advancement of the different communities bound together by race, territory and custom.

Fukuzawa's dictum, the independence of an individual is the prerequisite for the independence of a nation, also inspired Maruyama. Fukuzawa's position was that the best defence against the predatory nature of the West was to 'fill the country with the spirit of freedom and independence, and let everyone regardless of difference in rank, wealth and knowledge, do one's duty for the nation by accepting their countries interest as their own interest'.[6] This motto helped Maruyama find intellectual direction; the post-war Japanese too had to transcend their 'habit energy' of siding and flirting with the powerful, and cultivate independence and self-respect. Maruyama spent the rest of his career offering a critique of rationality and its effects of domination. Parallel to Fukuzawa, Maruyama also dedicated himself to promoting ethical transformation, on an individual and communal level.[7]

The significance of Fukuzawa as an indigenous model of liberal democratic principles and internal transformation does not come without controversy. Japanese political and feminist historians have called into question his liberal credentials. Historians of Japanese intellectual thought are often critical of narratives that ascribe principles of universal freedom and independence to Fukuzawa.[8] One of the most vocal is Banno Junji, who points out that Fukuzawa's view of independence was curtailed by his nationalist aspirations, most famously in 1885, when he advocated for the government to increase Japanese influence on the Korean Peninsula, by diplomatic and military means, for the sake of national security.[9] Feminist historians too question Fukuzawa's position as a champion of individualism and equality between men and women. Testimony to their suspicion is Fukuzawa's piece written for the *Jiji shimpō*, 18 January 1896, promoting the migration of Japanese prostitutes abroad on the grounds that it encouraged Japanese overseas settlements.[10]

This chapter embraces the ambiguity and ambivalence in Fukuzawa's thought by asking: what is the interrelation between his articulations of the need for the Japanese citizenry (*shimin*) to acquire a spirit of independence, nation-building and overseas prostitution? It is important to note that Fukuzawa's use of the notion of *shimin* is double-sided. It stands for the ideal of the autonomous individual given in naturalist terms as the innate and developed inward forces and disposition of personality or character. Yet, at the same time the notion of *shimin* is evaluative. It also stands in for the value and affirmation of certain distinct and superior moral qualities, such as the enjoyment of free behaviour and individual self-determination, which are viewed as the apex of the natural universal progression of human experience. However, before our investigation can proceed, one has to ask: what is the nature of Fukuzawa's article for the *Jiji shimpō*?

My position is that Fukuzawa's article on overseas prostitution, like his other writing, was a response to a historical moment, intended to goad and warn the reader with regard to the actuality around him. Why him? Because Fukuzawa's intended audience was men; specifically, second, third and fourth sons of landowners and former samurai families who could not inherent property and status and had to make their own path to success and prestige.[11] His journalistic writing aimed to disturb the terrain of the debate in which it was inserted, and to reveal the possibility of openings for men of 'talent'. Throughout his writing Fukuzawa focuses on a novel distinction between the historical and the current based on a diagnosis of how elements of the past were preventing new forms of Japanese life from emerging to meet the dictates of mental and material progress. His power to persuade was based on his carefully cultivated reputation as the mouthpiece for the coming civilization of change: the man of truth telling the reality of global competitive modernity and the consequent obligation of all Japanese to adapt and explore avenues of innovation. Fukuzawa's article was a strategic attempt to set a political agenda concerning the tricky business of correlating the 'spiritual development of the common mind of the people' with the new global reality of the market.[12]

Social Adaptation, Morality and Progress

Fukuzawa spent most of his adult life agonizing over how the Japanese could maintain their own identity in the face of the virus of Western civilization that was sweeping into Asia and altering all before it.[13] He saw the solution in 'self-aid'; maintaining the finest of Japanese custom whilst absorbing the best the West had to offer. In short, Japanese survival rested on the capacity of the Japanese people to adapt to the germs, steel and guns of Western imperialism.[14] For Fukuzawa, a pressing political concern was the configuration of the family; more specifically, the upper strata family of the former samurai and large landowners who were to provide the leaders and innovators for the future Japan. In particular, he saw family-centred Confucian beliefs and practices as directly impinging on the physical bodies of women and on the space of personal existence pertinent to the reproduction of the current political order. Analogous to the mantra of late twentieth-century feminism, Fukuzawa saw the personal as political.

For Fukuzawa, the survival of the Japanese race *vis-à-vis* a stronger and more industrially advanced West centred on reversing the declining vitality of the Japanese, and overturning the slow degeneration in their mental and moral qualities. He identified the lack of association open to Japanese women of the samurai status as the key issue that had to be addressed. He noted pointedly that Japanese women were denied all freedoms and social responsibilities; making it 'impossible to expect them to improve their health or develop as human beings'.[15] Consequently, Japanese 'women, having grown weak in both body and mind', are 'worthless in the support of the family and country'. Mothers without freedom and the opportunity to take on social obligations and duties bring forth unhealthy infants, and 'the hereditary physique of the Japanese' is weakened. Urgent action was paramount, or in the near future the Japanese would have the 'worst physique in the world', and they would have no-one to blame but themselves because of 'the ill-treatment we have given women through the past history. Anyone who cares for his or her family and country and the future generations must stop and give serious thought to this matter'.[16]

Changing gender relations inside and outside the family was 'a long-term project of a hundred years for the good of the whole nation', according to Fukuzawa. And the solution to improve 'the physique of the present Japanese men and women and thereby produce more perfect children' was monogamy in marriage. He linked restrictions on the movement and emotional development of samurai wives to antiquated Confucian learning, which '[d]uring the peaceful two and a half centuries of the Tokugawa period' had made 'the members of the middle and upper classes ... weak and effeminate'.[17] Paralleling the criticism of the JWCTU, Fukuzawa saw the 'forced logic' of a mother's womb as being 'borrowed' for the temporary abode of future generations as the core of the damage done to the minds and bodies of Japanese women of the samurai strata. Confucian logic supported a double standard of morality. Husbands could easily divorce their wives at 'their convenience' if they did not satisfy his personal needs and ambitions as the head of the household. Moreover, men were 'free to take as many concubines as desired' while infidelity by women was prohibited. As a result, argued Fukuzawa, over the years Japanese men have managed to monopolize 'freedom in indulging promiscuous behaviour' to the extent that 'licentiousness' has 'almost turned into their nature'. Men, he surmised, have successfully 'thought up all sorts of devices to bond women' and devised precepts found in interpretations of Confucian doctrines such as *The Greater Learning of Women* to create a safe and free world for their shamelessness by suppressing all women's objections to their promiscuity.[18]

The present gender relations undermined the future of Japan, because of the 'restrictions on women's pleasurable life', cautioned Fukuzawa. Women in middle- to upper-class families lacked the wherewithal to 'express their warmth and sentiments' as they were 'kept from associating with people' and 'prohibited from going outdoors'. Given no responsibility inside or outside the home, samurai women 'were confined throughout their lives' to 'courting their men's whim'. Consequently, their minds and bodies, starved of pleasure and social meaning, became feeble. Middle- and upper-class women who knew naught but a life of confinement and frailty, 'accumulate their melancholy within themselves', causing 'morbid sensitivities and brittleness of the body, which is handed down to the next generation and on to posterity'. 'When the mother's body' is not robust, 'the child's body cannot be strong or healthy'. According to Fukuzawa, this accounted for the 'small size and weak constitution' of contemporary Japanese, especially in comparison to Westerners.[19]

Fukuzawa did not believe Western women to be superior to Japanese women. He noted that women's behaviour in the West was at times beyond the realm of social decorum; 'they make light of men; their minds are sharp, but their thoughts may be tarnished and their personal behaviour unchaste; they neglect their own homes and flutter about society like butterflies'. However, he could not hide his admiration of the Western practice of monogamous marriage, women's right to divorce and legally own property and their dynamic social involvement outside the household, which 'exhilarate and develop both the mind and the body' of Western women and resulted 'in the birth of strong offspring'. However, whilst Fukuzawa advocated equality between husbands and wives (*fūfu dōken*), he dissociated himself from notions of equal rights for men and women (*danjo dōken*). Although he advocated for women to take a more active role in the upbringing of Japan's future generations, 'the basic purpose' of his argument was 'not to side with women to contest their rights', but for 'the improvement of the Japanese race'. To improve the physique of the next generation, 'the first necessity is to make our [Japanese] women more active mentally and physically'.[20] Despite advocating for greater personal freedoms for upper-class women, Fukuzawa subscribed to the belief that biological differences between men and women gave specific duties and obligations to each gender in civil society. Men were best suited to public life and action. Women on the other hand were psychologically adept at running a household and nurturing the next generation of talent for service to the empire.[21]

Fukuzawa made his most succinct statements on prostitution and morality in late November 1885. Unlike the JWCTU, his primary concern was not the festering boil of licensed prostitution on the body of Japanese womanhood, but on the relationship between ethics and good government. He linked a set of personal character achievements as the prerequisite for democratic government, with the relationship between husband and wife as a primary criterion whether an individual was fit to govern others. Changes in the current relationship between Japanese men and women were an indicator of a shift from paternalistic benevolent government that left the Japanese unable to 'talk and act in the ways they wanted', and a new form of government that came 'with respect and the granting of the rights' to the people 'to take part in governing'. Fukuzawa explained:

> Suppose now that the man is the government of the household and the woman the people. What is their relationship? It is difficult to describe because it is worse than oppression or despotism. The man deals with all the family property in any way he pleases, never telling his wife what he is doing with it. That is like the government robbing the people of their rights over personal property. And the man's forbidding his wife to have any say in household matters is exactly like the government prohibiting any discussion among the people. Even worse is the man's licentious pleasures and his monopolizing good times while the woman is confined to the home with no freedom, resulting in her gloom and melancholy and leading to her physical deterioration. This is equivalent to the government monopolizing profits and forcing hardships on people. Even the man who is faithful and professes to love his wife only

> cares for her as if she were a cuddly dog or cat. His behaviour resembles that of the crafty politician making fools of people.[22]

Fukazawa's wrath focused on the leading Meiji political leaders who graced the parties and formal Western balls held at the *Rokumeikan* (Hall of the Baying Stag). Built on the commission of foreign minister Inoue Kaoru, the two-storey *Rokumeikan* created an elegant atmosphere for the delectation and felicitation of foreign luminaries to impress upon them that they were dealing with cultural equals. Inoue's hope was that the merry splendour of the *Rokumeikan* would incline foreign dignitaries to reassess their negative view of Japanese cultural achievements, and open negotiations for the abolition of extra-territorial privileges. Fukuzawa believed that the impression Japanese leaders aimed to give was marred by the scandalous behaviour of high-ranking officials attending the functions in the company of concubines and *geisha*. Japanese leaders cavorting without shame with such women in front of foreign luminaries lost the gravitas necessary to add 'weight and dignity to our country so that it may stand proudly in the eyes of all other nations of the world'.[23] Meiji leaders such as Itō Hirobumi (whose womanizing gave the fledgling Japanese press endless material for scandal-mongering, and who married a former *geisha*) were oblivious to the fact that associating with *geisha* – who were no more than glorified prostitutes – was 'obnoxious and immoral'. Accustomed to the open and boisterous culture of the Yoshiwara 'gay quarters', where the 'customers show no signs of embarrassment or the least hesitation', noted Fukuzawa, current Japanese leaders are ignorant of their *faux pas* – that is, that 'one must never bring up [prostitution] before a civilized foreigner!'[24]

It was imperative, admonished Fukuzawa, that the Meiji leaders acknowledge that the work of *geisha*/prostitutes 'is shameful', 'absolutely against human morality' and that it has no standing in civilized society. Who in the 'modern nineteenth century', he asked rhetorically, would 'entrust the lives of the people to a prostitute-coddling pleasure seeker?' He urged that for the sake of national standing and 'in order to lead the young generation in the right direction', the present leaders of Japan stamp out their nonchalant attitude towards prostitution, or at the very least moderate their behaviour by conducting their liaisons with *geisha* secretly, away from the eyes of foreigners and the public. To help facilitate a 'policy of secrecy', Fukuzawa put forward several suggestions to 'decrease illicit acts'. First, exclude all concubines 'from the society of ordinary women'. He advocated that women who were initially concubines and 'rose to the position of legal wife' after the Meiji Restoration should not be granted this status. Any person who was a concubine 'had ignored the dignity of human ethics and sold themselves for money'. They were, in actuality, a purchase and 'must not be accorded the respect due to a legitimate wife'. Second, *geisha* and prostitutes should be ostracized from 'human society and barred from association with honourable people' and treated with contempt. Once *geisha* lost their social allure because they would no longer be considered human beings, upper-class and educated women would cease to enter this profession voluntarily, and 'those remaining will be the uneducated, without poise, without shame, the lowest sort of female – some like hag or she-devil'. The 'unsightliness' of such women, fantasized Fukuzawa, would make 'wanton' upper-class men think twice about an illicit tryst, or if they found themselves attracted, they would 'do their best to keep it a secret and put up a dignified front, which would help preserve the outward appearance of society'.[25] At the very least, Fukuzawa was pragmatism personified.

However, Fukazawa was not a moralist. Unlike the churchwomen of the JWCTU, he did not believe in universal moral prescriptions and loathed 'the idea of meddling in someone else's private affairs with the cold and logical teachings of a righteous moralist'. He believed that moralists such as the JWCTU churchwomen who advocated the eradication of prostitution were building castles in the air. History had shown that it was impossible to keep 'the animal instinct under control by will power'. He believed, as prostitution was impossible to suppress, a wiser policy would 'be to permit and prevent worse results'. Therefore, whereas the JWCTU churchwomen saw licensed prostitution as a moral blight on Japan, Fukuzawa believed it was a permissible outlet for the male desire of the poor, who could not support wives, and single men, thus acting as a safety valve for respectable women by preventing widespread sexual violence. If the red-light districts were closed, he argued, 'within a few months, the accumulation of the animal urge will reach the breaking point and it will manifest itself with illicit activities among the children of good families, or violation of lonely widows'. Although prostitution was 'lowly, ugly' and, for the woman involved 'physically and spiritually degrading', society depended on it for the 'preservation of order'. For Fukuzawa, prostitutes were the 'martyrs' or, in modern parlance, 'collateral damage' sacrificed to male desire for the greater good of legitimate households and their womenfolk.[26] For the JWCTU, death was preferable to such martyrdom.

National Autonomy and Individual Independence

The world that Fukuzawa inherited was fraught with internal and external dangers. Internally, the social upheavals of disgruntled samurai plagued the first ten years of Meiji. Many samurai took umbrage at the Meiji government's insistence in treating its citizenry without distinction. Samurai agitation often took the form of armed rebellion, the most famous being the Satsuma rebellion (1877), where Saigō Takamori, one of the main military leaders of the Restoration army, attacked the edifice that he helped create. In 1874, a non-violent form of opposition emerged from the fissure among the Meiji oligarchy. Itagaki Taisuke initiated this new and more enduring form of opposition, which questioned the legitimacy of the Meiji rulers based on a critique of the usurpation and abuses of power. Itagaki's anti-government stance appealed to the rural landed gentry, who bore the fiscal burden of the oligarchy's policies to industrialize and militarize Japan, and to peasants, discontented with high prices and low wages. By 1880, the broad base of dissatisfaction had evolved into various political fraternities and associations calling for the establishment of representative institutions and limits to the oligarchy's authority under the banner of the Freedom and Popular Rights Movement (*jiyū minken undo*). Externally, the challenge was Western threats to Japanese sovereignty. The Meiji oligarchy saw investment in industry, arms and Western bureaucracy as the technical means to assure Japan's territorial borders and to eliminate foreign consular jurisdiction (extra-territoriality) and Western control over Japanese tariffs and foreign trade policies.[27] The Meiji policy of 'enriching the nation and strengthening the armed forces' aimed at replicating Western commerce and military might as the best form of defence.

The inability of the Meiji state to maintain sovereignty *vis-à-vis* other national powers was for Fukuzawa the greatest crisis facing Japan. Douglas Howland shows that by 1875 Fukuzawa was keenly aware of the threats posed by Western domination. Western governments made competition into a virtue; for profit in commerce and for victory in warfare. Survival in such an international setting meant success in both trade and war.[28] Fukuzawa also recognized that the global market was based on inequality rather than equality of exchange. Trade always favoured industrialized countries at the expense of less developed countries such as Japan. In his *Outline of a Theory of Civilization* (*Bunmeiron no gairyaku*), Fukuzawa explained that the world was divided into two types of nations – those that manufacture and those that farm. Economically, national wealth depended far more on techniques of production and less on agricultural surplus. Manufacturing nations such as Holland, which produced scarcely any agricultural products, were rich because they 'make use of their unlimited manpower', through trade and colonial enterprises that held monopolies in agricultural commodities via the creation of large-scale plantations. On the other hand, peoples that lacked the ambition and mental wherewithal to develop industry became the muscle and sinew of foreign traders.[29] Fukuzawa pinpointed Japan's diplomatic and military vulnerability to the outflow of capital and loss of employment due to the monopolistic advantages Western commerce enjoyed in global markets.[30]

However, Fukuzawa was critical of the government's policy to enrich the country and strengthen the military. An element of his scepticism was the anti-oligarchic critique that guardians of the state must be distanced from the seductions of wealth and not be able to make money from their functions.[31] Another element was a concern for opinion, namely what is going on in the minds of the governed. He believed it was folly to think that the purchase of technology and military hardware readied the Japanese people for the task ahead. The enforced isolation of the Japanese people and a feudal system that prized obedience and deference to authority had left the Japanese people bereft of the value of autonomy necessary to compete with foreign merchants.[32] The only merchants involved in foreign trade were *seshō* merchants personally connected to the government in the mould of *goyōshonin* – privileged merchants and traders who were regular purveyors to the shogunate and the daimyo domains during the Tokugawa period – who lacked any enterprising spirit.[33] Two hundred years of commercial isolation and a feudal legacy of dependency had left Japanese entrepreneurs lacking the necessary skills to succeed in international competition.[34] Good government, according to Fukuzawa, had to act on the consciousness of people, to modify their opinions and behaviour as economic subjects.

Fukuzawa was also critical of the Meiji oligarchy's policy of using government funds to subsidize private industries deemed important to 'national security'. By the late 1870s, the government was in dire financial straits. The general expenditure of modernization programmes was beyond the government's fiscal means, and many of the industry subsidies were unprofitable. According to Fukuzawa, the direct intervention of the government in financing industries went against the grain of 'the natural principle of competition'. Because of the oligarchy's despotic tendencies the Japanese people continued to be 'stupid, spirited and powerless', and the little progress made was 'out of all proportion to the energies and money spent'.[35] In his 1880 work *Minkan Keizairon* (*Essays on Private Business*), Fukuzawa reiterated the 'great mistake' of the Meiji oligarchy to ignore the principle of competition and intervene in the economy and 'compete with people in industry and trade'. Only competition leads to industry, trade and a self-adjustment in prices, all of which encourage further industry. Equality of individuals lies in competition, as 'all people are equally concerned with making a profit, and thus (naturally) inclined to compete'. On the other hand, a government that 'spends without due consideration of gain' is wasteful and interferes with the mutual competition among individuals, leading to the double loss of wealth.[36]

Fukuzawa's solution to the internal political friction between the Meiji oligarchy, interested in keeping control of political power, and the Japanese people, agitating to secure political participation and representation in government, was national sovereignty (*kokken*): the development of national power requiring all people to take as their guide the principle of independence.[37] Naoki Sakai finds Fukuzawa's linkage of state (*kokken*) and people (*minken*) a radically different way of framing social obligations without recourse to the 'webs of kingship relations' and familial ties.[38] Feudal domainal autonomy was based on Confucian virtues – Ruler and Ruled, Father and Son, Husband and Wife, and the Elder and the Younger – which delineated all social relations in terms of kingship relations.[39] The ethos of Confucian virtue transferred familial bonds to relations of government that privatized power as a political privilege rather than as a socializing force for the common good. The Confucian ethos of virtue and loyalty undermined Japanese sovereignty as it encouraged widespread unrest and competition between exclusive factions, dragging the people's attentions and energy away from their higher obligations as citizens (*shimin*). Fukuzawa attributed the fall of the Tokugawa regime to a failure to rule for the genuine public good, leaving it unable to sustain itself in external relations as it lacked universal support. However, as Sakai astutely points out, Fukuzawa was experimenting with new ways of institutionalizing relations of solidarity around horizontal relations of associations defined by shared membership and common experience that would allow the Japanese to form a national body (*kokutai*).

> *Kokutai* refers to the gathering together of a species of people who share suffering as well as pleasure, the creation of a distinction between fellow countrymen and foreigners, the fostering of more cordial and stronger bonds with one's countrymen than with foreigners. It is living under the same government, enjoying self-rule, and disliking the idea of being subject to foreign rule: it involves independence and responsibility for the welfare of one's own country. In the West it is called 'nationality'.[40]

The definition of nationality based on the permanence of government and a natural community made up of shared customs, race and destiny allowed Fukuzawa to make the corporate body of the state (*kokutai*) into the necessary precondition for overturning the unequal treaties and monopoly rights of the West, and for the granting of rights of movement and equal exchange to Japanese merchants. In other words, a powerful national sovereignty enhanced the ability of the individual Japanese to compete in the global market from a position of strength rather than weakness.

As many scholars point out, Fukuzawa's views on 'nationality' defended the unity and power of the central government by putting national security before individual autonomy.[41] Such critiques, however, overlook the way he inserts the concept of freedom of association. According to Fukuzawa, national unity and national industrial freedom were necessary if Japan was going to overcome the current international division of labour established by British principles of free trade. British power lay in their ability to buy raw materials from Japan such as silk, transforming it into silk cloth, and selling it back to Japan at considerable profit. To escape dependence on a global system of exchange built on an international division of labour detrimental to Japan, he argued, the Japanese economy needed the protection of a powerful state to allow individual Japanese to 'advance their usage of clothing, food, (and) housing', and 'exist freely and independently'.[42] As such, national unity and national industrial freedom were interrelated.

Fukuzawa insisted on equality liberated from the constraints of social rank as a necessity for the promotion of national productivity via the power of horizontal associations and the development of individuality.[43] *An Encouragement of*

Learning (*Gakumon no susume*), one of Fukuzawa's most widely read texts, gives the best examples of how the power of associations works. In section five, a transcript of a speech delivered at Keiō Gijiku in January 1874, he informed his male student audience that the great inventors of the industrial revolution – Watt and Stevenson – belonged 'neither to the government administrators nor the labouring masses'. They came from the middle position of society, which 'leads the world by power of intellect. Once some device or invention takes the form in someone's mind, a private association is founded to concretize it in practical form.' At that moment, the duty of government is to 'let the creativity of the people take its own course without interference, to understand and protect the direction of public sentiment'. He then proceeded to illuminate how the freedom to make associations and competition between private individuals allows the state to profit:

> Therefore the people should initiate the affairs of civilization as if it were their private property. They should compete and dispute with one another over forms. They should take pride in their achievements. The whole nation should respond to each commendable achievement made within the country ... In such a situation the matters of civilized progress will all become the instruments of strengthening the spirit of the nation. Everything will be conducive to fostering national independence.[44]

The private sphere was brought forth by Fukuzawa as the correlate of the state wishing precisely to provide the freedom for competition necessary for national autonomy. He lamented the fact that scholars, the 'Japanese middle class' able to 'advocate national independence and modern civilization', were more concerned about their private well-being than that of the nation, choosing the security of government service rather than enter the risk-filled world of commerce and industry. The only way to overcome that, he argued, was for educated people of talent to apply their knowledge and 'advance Japanese civilization' through the magic of association:

> Business, law, industry, agriculture, the writing and translation of books, publications of newspapers – almost every affair of civilization – must be made our own ... and act in concert with government, so that the proper balance of powers will increase the potential of the whole nation.[45]

Fukuzawa's commitment to the power of association was not limited to his lectures and writings. He used the considerable wealth made from his early writings to establish one of the first Japanese joint stock companies, Maruya Trading (1869), become a leading shareholder of the Yokohama Specie Bank (1879), started in partnership the *Yugensekinin Boekishokai* trading company (1880) specializing in silk trade, and was the principle founder of an independent newspaper, the *Jiji shimpō* (1882).[46]

Education and progress were interrelated for Fukuzawa. Education was the means by which the natural laws of economic and cultural development revealed themselves. However, as Earl Kinmonth has brilliantly noted, the freedom to participate in competition for wealth and honour was the only right advocated by *An Encouragement of Learning*. Fukuzawa's opening paragraph to his book states that all men are equal, 'and stand in the same rank'. Men with no distinction 'between honored and despised or high and low' 'contribute to all things on the basis of the working of a heart and body which join with the spirit of all things'. Mental ability was not equally available to all, as intellectual work was 'difficult work'. The 'principle of things' revealed that occupations were distributed according to aptitude.

> Looking over the people in the world it will seem that there are clever people; there are foolish people. There are impoverished people. There are menial people. What is the cause of this difference ...? [I]f a man does not study he is without wisdom. A man without wisdom is a fool ... The distinction between wise men and fools comes for whether they studied or did not.[47]

The distribution of talent functioned as a distribution of gifts of unequal value. Fukuzawa also drew on the correlation between education and talent to explain the division of labour to the political order. Social inequality was the natural evidence of social utility:

> The man who performs difficult work is called a man of important rank; the man who performs easy work is said to be a man of insignificant rank. All work that requires use of the heart and demands concern is difficult work. Work done with the power of the hands and feet is easy work. Therefore doctors, scholars, government officials, merchants who buy and sell on a large scale, and farmers who use many servants – men such as these are important in rank and are honoured.[48]

Importantly, Fukuzawa saw no virtue in the poor. The ignorance of the 'principle of things' – what he called the laws of nature – caused human suffering. There were 'no men more pitiable and despicable than the ignorant and illiterate. And the height of ignorance is to be shameless.' Ignorance was also the source of resentment and political danger to the unity and order of the Japanese nation. 'When people through their own ignorance have fallen into poverty and are hard pressed by hunger and cold, they recklessly hate the rich around them instead of blaming their own stupidity.' If the poor were filled with resentment they became 'shameless and law-defying' and 'mount rebellions and insurrection to press their demands'.[49] In '*Jiji shogen*', an essay written in 1881, Fukuzawa further elaborated on this theme by stating that the natural endowments of men come from the bloodline of parents and ancestors, the product of hundreds of years of education handed down in the family.[50]

Clearly, Fukuzawa had no love for the poor, whom he considered to be no more than the flotsam and jetsam of society; their lack of 'wisdom' indicated a lack of self-mastery and a danger to state order. The only virtue that the poor could exhibit was submission to the state. Issues of social equality and justice did not concern him. Yet, in January 1896, he wrote in favour of Japanese prostitutes migrating abroad. Fukuzawa's promotion of rural women finding work abroad seemingly contradicts his ethical principles and moral sensibilities on the laws of progress. Was he just being opportunist? Most likely. However, to assess the nature of his opportunism we need to ask: in his promotion of Japanese prostitution abroad, to what was Fukuzawa asking the women to submit?

Trade, Security and Nation

The year 1881 marked a change in economic development policy by the Meiji oligarchy. Inflation and increasing dependency on foreign loans provoked policy change. In 1880 the government was divided by Finance Minister Ōkuma Shigenobu's call for large-scale foreign borrowing to continue financing loans to Japanese enterprises important to trade (mass production of consumer goods) and national security (mines, arsenals, shipyards). Ōkuma was ousted by the Minister of the Right Iwakura Tomomi, and replaced by Matsukata Masayoshi. Matsukata quickly introduced a policy of fiscal restraint, reducing drastically the distribution of government funds for industry promotion, which had the intended effect of curbing inflation and stabilizing currency. The new economic policy also led to severe deflation, which resulted in an economic depression that lasted until 1885. During this cycle of depression, unemployment was prominent and many banks and companies became insolvent.

During the recession, Fukuzawa encouraged young men of talent to show 'independent spirit' and seek work abroad. Through public speeches and newspaper editorials he promoted migration as a solution to underemployment among ambitious young men. In his writings and speeches, he admonished the 'weak-spirited nature' of the Japanese who 'crowd in the land of their forefathers and complain bitterly' about the lack of work. Fukuzawa identified the US as the most suitable country for emigration, as the success of Chinese emigrants returning home with 'large amounts of saved gold' testified. He especially encouraged the educated to emigrate, as wealth and status waited for them abroad as entrepreneurs once they became accustomed to their new surroundings and had established themselves.[51]

Fukuzawa's vision of Japanese entrepreneurial migration to the US paralleled the ambitions of Enomoto Takeaki. Japanese emigrants would form associations in the major US trading ports and provide a link for Japanese commerce to their new place of residence. Fukuzawa's hope was that emigration would be the means for Japan to emulate Great Britain and transform itself into a major mercantile power. In another article entitled 'Venture to Leave Your Homeland', he waxed:

> The wealth garnered by individual English traders abroad has become part of England's national assets. The land the English claimed has turned into regional centres of trade, if not formal colonies. This is how Great Britain became what it is today. In a similar fashion ... [Japanese emigrants] engaging in various enterprises abroad is an indirect show of patriotism.[52]

A spirit of independence and enterprise was directly linked to the goals of nation-building. However, akin to his early views articulated in *An Encouragement of Learning*, emigration to the US was limited to educated men endowed with the talent, intellect and superior disposition to succeed in life abroad. As yet, Fukuzawa saw no utility in the actions of the gendered poor to the goals of national autonomy.

However, by the late 1880s the economic and social utility of large-scale overseas emigration became a topic of much public debate in government and opposition circles as it became inserted into issues of economic development and national security. In 1890, constitutional government came into effect after the country's first general elections. The newly established constitution gave the House of Representatives, controlled by political parties that emerged out of the freedom and people's rights movement, power to attack the Meiji administration and obstruct policy goals. The main discontent for the political parties was taxation and wasteful government spending. As a strategy to overcome calls by the political parties to reduce budget expenditure, the first Matsukata Cabinet submitted a budget leaning strongly towards military expansion. The government heavily funded the construction of a blue-water navy with a battle fleet in the interest of national security and protecting Japanese merchant routes.[53]

The initial profitability of Japanese shipping companies was due to labour emigration to Hawaii, which boosted revenue with fares and freight. For example, the Nippon Yūen Kaisha managed to establish a profitable trans-Pacific route in 1885 helped by heavy subsidies and a government-sanctioned monopoly in transporting labour emigrants to Hawaii.[54] Due to the relative success of Japanese labour migration to Hawaii, Japanese entrepreneurs, who advocated commodity export trade as the best policy for Japan to achieve commercial competiveness in the global market, started to form societies that advocated integrating emigration with the promotion of Japanese sea lanes as a way to increase foreign trade. Associations such as the *Tokyo Keizaigaku kyōkai* (Tokyo Economic Society, formed 1887), *Tōhō kyōkai* (East Asian Society, formed 1890), *Kaigai ijū dōshikai* (Friends of Overseas Emigration, formed 1892) and *Shokumin kyōkai* (Colonization Society, established 1893) started with the purpose of raising public support and capital for ventures involving overseas emigration and settlement. Some of these societies had well-established connections with the government. A founding member of the *Shokumin kyōkai* was Enomoto Takeaki. He was also a driving force behind the societies' attempt to raise venture capital for a Japanese agricultural colony in Chiapas, Mexico, in 1897.[55]

In 1891, the newspaper owned by Fukuzawa, the *Jiji shimpō*, began a series of editorials linking Japanese emigration, overseas expansion and national security. The editorials encouraged Japanese emigration abroad for its economic utility and as a means of preserving domestic order. Japanese merchants of good standing, 'who were likely to succeed in the struggle with competitors' and 'whose conduct would reflect the honour of Japan', were encouraged to try their talents abroad. Their success would bring profit and trade to their home country. The editorial advocated that the underemployed – especially educated youth without fixed occupation – be given financial aid to seek work overseas. This would have the advantage of saving the youth from joining the *sōshi* (politically dissatisfied) class and, like the labouring poor, give them the ability to find meaningful work.[56]

The year 1891 was also the first time the *Jiji shimpō* raised the issue of Japanese prostitution abroad. What is significant about the article is that it defers from moralizing and attempts to identify the right relationship between the spontaneous movement of Japanese prostitutes abroad and nation-building. The *Jiji shimpō* downplayed the cries that Japanese prostitutes and other lower-class persons in foreign countries were a national disgrace, and continued by pointing out that the people 'whose lives are most frequently brought to the notice' of Japanese were 'not fair representatives of the Japanese community in any one place'. It was an overreaction to 'judge the character of the people under consular jurisdiction' by only focusing on 'law-breakers'. 'Is it true', asked the *Jiji shimpō*, 'that Japan's national honour is tarnished by the bad characters that exist abroad?' The editorial answered in an emphatic 'no'. The *Jiji shimpō* analysed recent attempts to enforce legislation to restrict the movement of Japanese women abroad (the Law for the Protection of Japanese Women in Foreign Countries) as reactionary.

> The restrictions put upon foreign travel during the past few years have been based rather on what foreigners might say than on what they have said. Constituted as the world is, the crossing of women of bad character from one country to another, or the wanderings of habitual loafers is unavoidable. Japan is not the only country which has subjects who bring her no credit ... Good and evil is mixed in the world, and the best thing to do is to recognize the fact. Restriction on foreign travel is ... productive of more evil than results from the importation of bad characters into foreign lands.[57]

The message of the *Jiji shimpō* was clear. Restrictions on any kind of travel overseas were more of an impediment to emigration and expansion than the relatively small numbers of 'Japanese prostitutes' found abroad warranted. The *Japan Weekly Mail* endorsed the article with a small editorial statement: '[w]e think undue prominence has been given to the subject here, and that Japan has no fear of being reproached for an abuse which exists in all countries alike, and is likely to do so to the end of time'.[58]

The argument of the *Jiji shimpō*, endorsed by Fukuzawa himself by his prerogative of editorial authority, centred on the political discovery that too much intervention thwarted the very ends of government. The perception was that any state action leading to restrictions on the ability of Japanese subjects to migrate freely overseas frustrated progress. Any element of compulsion implemented by even the most well-meaning government contributed to the weakening of the very vitality that the action of intervention sought to promote.

Trade, Security, Nation and the Need for Prostitution

The decisive changes which created favourable conditions for investing in mass Japanese emigration came between the years 1894 and 1896. In 1894, Japan signed its first equal treaty: the Anglo-Japanese Treaty of Commerce and Navigation. Article 1 of the treaty granted the Japanese the unrestricted reciprocal right to travel, reside and buy property on a most-favoured-nation footing.[59] The treaty was buoyed by pro-mercantile legislation subsidizing merchant shipping and ship-building in 1896. Japanese companies also overcame their dependency on Western financing for industrialization. The finance ministry channelled the savings of the poorer classes to the Yokohama Specie Bank, which converted the funds to competitive credit for Japanese commerce and industry.[60]

The government linked labour migration abroad to a cluster of policies designed to buttress maritime trade in 1894, when the government handed the recruitment and transport of Japanese labour emigrants to the private sector, namely the *imingaisha* (migration companies). The government promulgated the Emigration Protection Ordinance (*Imin hogo kisoku*) in 1894, which, with minor adjustments, was ratified as the Emigration Protection Law (*Imin hogohō*) in 1896.[61] On the surface, the new legislation seemingly protected the rights, life and property of Japanese emigrants. However, the underlying administrative objective was to establish cumbersome screening procedures at the prefectual level to sift the solid and honest emigrant from the undesirable vagabond.[62]

In 1896, Fukuzawa penned a series of articles on the eve of the passing of the Emigration Protection Law. These articles, published over the month of January, presented a sustained argument as to why commerce, the expansion of shipping lanes and Japanese migration abroad were necessary for the future of Japan. His aim was to shape an emigration legislation that worked in harmony with the natural laws of the economy, population growth and gender relations rather than draconian measures emphasizing prohibition and prevention. What made Fukuzawa's articles about Japanese labour emigration and overseas prostitution unique was that he did not take a position on what must be prohibited or what was obligatory behaviour. Instead, he preferred to stand back and try to understand the movement of Japanese prostitutes abroad as a social index by which to identify the stage of development Japan was entering according to universal laws of progress.

In his first article, published 3 January, Fukuzawa introduced the idea that natural processes of population and economy give rise to the need of government to adjust the means of subsistence to accommodate and adapt to the growth in population. Calling upon statistics, which reveal the natural laws of life, labour and production, he revealed that the Japanese population had increased at a yearly rate of around of 400,000 people in each of the last ten years. Improvements in diet, industry and science had decreased mortality rates, leading to a rapid rise in Japanese population since the Meiji Restoration.[63] Calling upon Malthus's principles of population, Fukuzawa warned that for the sake of the longer-term stability of the economy, it was necessary for the government to take immediate pre-emptive measures to prevent distress and misery in the near future.[64] In his next article, printed the following day, Fukuzawa answered his own call for prudence and planning by identifying emigration as a solution to inescapable demographic pressure. He saw a general law of causality between national strength and population. In countries past and present, he argued, population increases and the development of national strength are interrelated. Logically, if Japan was to continue in its efforts to increase national wealth and strength for the overall prosperity of its people, then the Japanese should follow the example of the Anglo-Saxon race and migrate. Fukuzawa identified the newly acquired Japanese colony of Formosa, the neighbouring countries of China, Korea, Siam, the islands scattered in the Pacific and South America as locations promising success to Japanese subjects enterprising enough to migrate. He did not envisage migration through piecemeal territorial acquisitions, but through the opening of territories free of European colonial settlement. Developing Japanese communities in these areas would result in the promotion of commercial relations between those locations and Japan, as was the case with Great Britain and her colonies.[65] His next article, published on 7 January, dealt with the question of whether the Japanese were suited to the purpose of settlement abroad. Fukuzawa answered in the affirmative. The Japanese, parallel to the British, he argued, appreciated the comforts of their own home and therefore were comparatively indifferent as to where they lived as long as they had their families and their own firesides. His nominated proof was that Japanese migration to Hawaii had proved an unmitigated success.[66]

Fukuzawa's article on overseas prostitution appeared on 18 January. This article followed a piece published the previous day on the importance of Shinto and Buddhist missionaries in reconciling Japanese migrants to life in a strange country.[67] He began 'The Migration of [Japanese] Subjects and Prostitutes Working

Abroad' (*Jinmin no ijū to shōfu no dekasegi*) marvelling at all the commotion on the issue of overseas prostitution. He argued that just as alcohol and tobacco were ceaselessly condemned for reasons of health, prostitution, too, no matter how loudly denounced on ethical or moral grounds, would never disappear as long as human society (*ningen shakai*) existed. Fukuzawa sarcastically rejected the idea that the women's prevalence discredited Japan in the eyes of the world. He likewise mocked the thought that efforts to keep prostitutes at home could delude the world into believing that prostitution did not exist in Japan.

In the past Fukuzawa had made his views on marriage clear. From the late 1860s he advocated a nation founded on a universal family composed of one husband and one wife together with their children. He argued it was the dictate of nature that over generations the association of men and women in marriage expand to form nations; the cluster of families sharing similar language and customs. In 'The Equal Numbers of Men and Women', composed in March 1875, Fukuzawa further defined his views on the importance of monogamous marriage to the natural and universal laws of progress. In this article, he posited monogamous domestic relations as a natural universal law; a 'simple point' embedded not in religion or morals but in the truth of the 'mathematical computation of the *soroban* [abacus or counting tray]'. Men and women were equal in number and because the natural harmonious law of association between them was for one husband to marry one wife.[68] Following this logic, Fukuzawa, recognizing overseas emigration was at first a predominately male enterprise, believed that a gender imbalance favouring males in Japanese communities abroad would undermine permanent settlement as it was contrary to the natural laws of domesticity and civilization based on an equal number of men and women. The major point concerning the existence of Japanese prostitutes abroad, contended Fukuzawa, was that they served a necessary purpose, which was in harmony with the evolution of the Japanese state.

> There is only one reason that I deal with this question [overseas prostitution] in particular. It is because I recognize that, for the encouragement of overseas settlements by our people, it is necessary for prostitutes to go abroad. The best scenario would be to try and have migrants move overseas as much as possible with their wives, taking with them the pleasures of a happy family home; by having the reassurance of their family it would be the same as if they were in their native homeland. But, migrants are not just married men. Indeed, one has recourse to appeal that in the beginning, aspirants who want to migrate to the so-called unknown lands abroad, are mostly single men without dependants. Moreover, in the case of married men, they initially migrate alone with the purpose of calling for their wife from Japan after they are settled. Accordingly, the proportion of women to men in settlements abroad is meagre. As there are many people who recognize the necessity of domestic prostitution because of our country's increasing population, I cannot help feeling more and more keenly the need for prostitutes given the circumstances found in newly opened lands.[69]

To support his argument that promoting prostitution was a necessary and inevitable stage in the process of nation-building, Fukuzawa turned to historical evidence. During the twilight of the Tokugawa reign, British authorities in Hong Kong requested Japanese women to service British troops stationed in the colony, he reported. Russian authorities in Vladivostok also made numerous requests for Japanese prostitutes. He ended his article with a final word of advice: 'the encouragement of migration and the freedom of prostitutes to work abroad are, in the context of the conduct of state affairs, a necessity'.[70]

Fukuzawa's position was that the role of proper government in this instance was not to impede or restrict the migration of women abroad. There was no need to prohibit it because once the character of Japanese communities developed and evolved, the need for prostitutes would cease. The mechanisms to stop women going abroad were not in the form of prohibitions but in the form of a progressive self-cancellation of the phenomenon by the phenomenon itself. For Fukuzawa, the overseas prostitutes were one alongside many other developments aimed at stimulating overseas migration and settlement, such as wealthy merchants guaranteeing a fully subsidized passage for migrants, the improvement of overseas communications, the expansion of Japanese maritime resources, and government investment in overseas settlements for future profit and security.[71]

The motivation behind Fukuzawa's articles was to encourage his reading audience to seize the moment, support Japanese efforts to trade, and settle abroad. For the government to prevent the movement of women abroad by instructing Japanese subjects, as a father would his children, on how they should lead their lives, was parallel to despotism. The main task of the government was to encourage the desire of self-improvement by promoting useful enterprises and the maintenance of agencies supporting commerce. The key word for Fukuzawa was *patriotism*, not *paternalism*, for the ultimate ends of both government and the individual were the attainment of the most harmonious development of the individuals' powers that would also work for the greater good of the Japanese state. However, the way patriotism was exercised differed according to rank and status. The educated men of talent from 'middle-class' households were to exercise their patriotism by becoming innovators and leaders in commerce, industry and finance. The men who comprised the labouring poor were to show industry and courage by emigrating and establishing Japanese colonies abroad. The role of the female rural poor was to provide consolation to labouring males abroad by supplying them with sex and the comforts only a woman can give.

Fukuzawa's understanding of civilization as the unfolding of a society built on the pragmatics of rational knowledge meant that historical order was revealed rather than constituted. He was convinced that he had discovered the purpose in nature – the quest to refine the intellect and harmonize human action with the laws of progress. He was also a nationalist. He agreed with the Meiji oligarchy that the growth of the state to its full potential in strength and wealth was crucial to Japanese survival. However, he was critical of the despotic tendencies of the Meiji oligarchs, which, for him, undermined Japanese efforts to industrialize and achieve equality with the West. He believed that Japan's quest to overcome the West depended on the right relationship between state resources and the Japanese people; sovereign autonomy and individual independence were concomitant. From this insight, Fukuzawa inserted the cultivation of autonomy as a key ingredient for good government. According to him, the challenge facing the Meiji oligarchy was not at what point do the people say no, but the opposite, how can they say yes. First, associations formed by private individuals (what we would call civil society) were brought forth as the correlate of the state which synchronized natural social process with human action. Second, population emerged as a new problematic for government. The natural increases in population brought about by the development in economy meant that the government could no longer control through prohibitions but via management of 'natural freedoms'. Good government involved removing artificial impediments, mental and material, thus allowing progress do its work. Third, freedom would give rise to economic activity, the circulation of goods and the action of markets.

Fukuzawa believed that the natural forces of progress would cancel out any inherent dangers found in the circulation of people and goods. In the context of overseas prostitution, this process of self-cancellation would occur when Japanese settlements became well established, attracting a more refined type of Japanese emigrant, who would relocate abroad with his wife and family. At that historical moment, the settlers would realize that prostitution was harmful to their society and put a stop to it. Because demographic growth and migration were 'natural' physical processes with their own internal logic, policymakers needed to resist the urge to take draconian measures. Over-regulation would impede rather than enhance nation-building by forestalling the necessary conditions of association between men and women, the foundation of labour and production, vital to the long-term success of Japanese overseas settlements.

There is another level where Fukuzawa was innovative. He conceived Japanese survival in a hostile world of competition as a bio-economic problem. He connected the economic and social conditions of reproduction with the public and public opinion. His self-prescribed role as the educator of progress was an attempt to change the economic, familial and political behaviour of the Japanese public by manipulating public opinion. He was not alone, however. Other contemporaneous reformers used the same strategy, such as the JWCTU. Unlike Fukuzawa however, the JWCTU made the eradication of prostitution, domestic and abroad, a primary crusade.

Fukuzawa and the churchwomen both advocated monogamy in marriage, but were at opposite ends of the spectrum when it came to licensed prostitution. Whereas the churchwomen saw it as a moral blight on Japan, Fukuzawa believed licensed prostitution was a necessary outlet for male desire and acted as a safety valve for respectable women by preventing widespread sexual violence.[72] The divide between Fukuzawa and the JWCTU was due to a fissure over the political embodiment of the 'ideal' female citizen/imperial subject. Fukuzawa's premise was that associations – the social contracts that create relations between individuals – give rise to institutions. The thrust of his argument was that Confucian forms of association operated to the detriment of women because they were not incorporated into the civil order as individuals. However, he did not advocate equality between men and women, because their natural eternal biological differences demarcated civil society into distinct male and female spheres with their specific and separate duties and obligations.

The JWCTU, on the other hand, recognized sexual relations as the most important of social relations and a key socializing force. The churchwomen saw all prostitution as an institutionalized form of violence by men against women. Moreover, the women's encounter with a new religion to Japan, American Protestantism, allowed them radically to problematize and critique the existing status of sexual unions in Japan around the question of the sexual division of ability and task based on equality, monogamy and, for upper-class women at least, the entitlement to social, if not political, recognition.

5 DISCIPLINING GLOBALIZING: THE COLONIAL SINGAPORE EXAMPLE

Japanese peasant women migrated to Singapore to circumvent poverty. This flow of transient women, found on the fringes of the narrative of national development, wealth and industry, was the other side of Japanese modernity. To representatives of the Japanese state, the transient poor seeking work in Singapore were the incorrigibility of 'backward' Japanese customs embodied in the 'base' (*seimin*) peasant woman. To compound matters, the largest Japanese presence in Singapore until 1920 was women engaged in sex work. According to empirical research carried out by Shimizu Hajime, between 1907 and 1915 women made up over half of the Japanese population in the Straits Settlements and accounted for 79 per cent of the total number of Japanese residing in the area in 1908. The largest number of Japanese women working as licensed prostitutes was recorded in 1917, when the Japanese consul counted 1,912 women, around 62 per cent of the total Japanese population, working in the brothels of Singapore and Malaya.

This chapter focuses on Singapore to address the wider question of how gender hierarchies and political economy entwine and develop. The regulation of Japanese prostitution in Singapore reveals a plane of differentiation by which the Japanese government marked the vagabond, the pauper, the destitute and the prostitute as lacking dignity and unworthy of social and political recognition. Japanese authorities viewed the work that Japanese prostitutes performed as lacking quality ('unsightly'), performed by persons without worth: the women's labour counted for nothing because their occupation was not recognized as having social value. Sex work failed to comply with the unconditional requirement of all Japanese imperial subjects to realize their role as producers of state wealth, vitality and advantage.

The challenges faced by successive Japanese consuls in trying to shape and regulate the Japanese community in the Straits Settlements reveal the contradiction inherent in the processes of globalization; namely, the frantic negotiation between the need to promote and facilitate the flow of money and labour and, at the same time, to control and limit the movement of workers in order to exploit their labour to the hilt. It was a negotiation requiring bipolar dexterity. The 'freedom' of Japanese subjects in the global world market was dependent on the executive and administrative functions of the Japanese state. Via law – treaties, conventions and administrative procedures – the Japanese state obtained political recognition to allow Japanese merchants and labourers to trade and offer their labour to the world market without hindrance.[1] Yet, the state endeavoured to deny rural women the 'freedom' of trying to find work, earn money and, if fortunate, get rich. The story of the policing of Japanese prostitutes in Singapore reveals how the 'freedom' offered to the poor by the market and secured by the state was highly selective and limited.

The Limits of Authority

For the Japanese foreign ministry, the problem of Japanese peasant women engaging in sex work abroad revealed the fissure between the goals of nation-building and personal conduct. Japanese consuls in particular were keenly aware that for Japanese subjects as a collective to gain political prestige some way was needed to structure the behaviour of the women so that their actions enhanced, rather than undermined, the political and economic goals of the nation. The greatest frustration faced by Japanese consuls in British colonies was that they had no means to regulate and control the women's behaviour. The women's actions persistently escaped the established boundaries of Japanese authority.

One limitation on the Japanese consul's ability to control the Japanese community was the colonial character of Singapore and the contingent forces of globalization, which, as if by magic, transformed a rain-forested island into a hub for global trade. From the late nineteenth century Singapore flourished as an international entrepôt – no import and export duties – linking the West with Asia via the movement of finance, labour and commodity trade. Singapore's standing as a prized commercial port was a product of the revolution in transportation and communication, which coincided with a global demand for tin, cotton, rubber, sugar and coffee. Singapore's wealth was built around volume in trade. Shipping companies and trading companies established branches in Singapore to profit from the increasing flow of commodity trade in the region. The trading companies varied in size and function and, broadly speaking, formed two distinct commercial groups: European merchants and intra-Asian traders. European merchants monopolized the export of manufactured goods from the factories of Europe, but despite this monopoly European (predominantly British) trading firms were dependent on Indian, Arab and Chinese merchants to distribute their manufactured commodities via intra-Asian trade routes. Well established and acquainted with local languages and commercial practices, non-Western traders acted as middlemen between European merchants and the local markets in Indochina, Thailand, Burma and the Dutch East Indies. Asian merchants were responsible for distributing the greatest volume of Western manufactured goods throughout South-East Asia. They also bought and transported primary commodities from South-East Asian markets to Singapore for sale to Western merchants, who in turn exported the commodities to Europe.[2] Because Singapore functioned as an interface between Western and inter-Asian trade, by the turn of the twentieth century the port boasted one of the strongest trading performances in both imports and exports of any British colony.[3]

The success of Singapore as a major global entrepôt was not due solely to the vision of British colonists, entrepreneurs and traders who transformed economic potential into industry and profit, however. The other story to Singapore's globalization is labour exploited to the brink. The labour force attracted to the area was predominately single, male and poor. The development of the Straits Settlements relied heavily on Chinese and Indian indentured labourers. Male peasants from southern China – mostly from Fujian and Guangdong provinces – formed the largest migrant group, and they came to Singapore for a single aim: to find work. Chinese labourers worked the mines, plantations and docks that kept British banks in the black and gave English stockholders investment satisfaction in colonial enterprises. To put the amount of peasant labour offered to Singapore and the rest of the Straits Settlements into context, from 1870 until 1930, the colony's population increased between 24 and 43 per cent each decade.[4]

The sharp increase in the colony's population aided the development of Singapore as a major Asian entrepôt. The flow of migrant labour into the region gave rise to a demand for daily necessities – food, clothing and perhaps the pleasure of a drink. Rice and other daily commodities were imported in large volume from Thailand, Burma and Indochina to Singapore, where, in turn, they were redistributed to the Malay Peninsula and Dutch East Indies to feed the labourers working the mines and plantations there.[5]

The 'heroic' accounts of economic development in South-East Asia omit the resources of the poor in the processes of globalization, especially the cultural achievements created by them to make the best of a bad situation. Narratives that focus on the 'magic' of development confine the achievements of the poor to a shadowy and muted criminal existence, outside any social role in the established order of the city. Cultural institutions created by the poor, often for self-protection and promotion, were very powerful and, ultimately, just as exploitative: for example the dreaded triads and secret societies that coloured the history of Singapore. In an effort to suppress the resistance of Chinese 'coolie' workers to the regime of work imposed by the colonialists in Singapore and Penang in the late nineteenth century, the British created the office of Chinese protectorate. In 1877, the first of a chain of Chinese protectorates was established in Singapore with the aim of curtailing the abuse of incoming poor migrant labourers, to repress the secret societies and to bring 'the Chinese within the control of the [British] Administration'.[6]

The Chinese protectorate was also in charge of supervising the colony's brothels. Prostitution in Singapore was organized around the guidelines of the Contagious Disease Ordinance (CDO) of 1870. The main administrative aim of the CDO was to stop a venereal disease pandemic among British troops. British medical officers advocated some form of sanitary infrastructure for reasons of national interest, public health and economic prudence. It was a waste of public money to train soldiers only for them to lose their ability to fight to the ravages of a disease that could be prevented, instead of in the line of duty and service to empire. In addition, the lack of preventive measures to stop venereal infection among troops harboured a greater social negligence. Troops shattered by venereal disease returned home broken, unable to work, and became a burden that society could ill afford.[7] Thus, the CDO enforced the registration of all women working in public brothels, compulsory medical examinations, certificates for the healthy and hospitalization for the infected.[8]

Another administrative objective of the CDO was to prevent the traffic in women and children. Phillipa Levine's research reveals that the Straits authorities implanted the CDO in Singapore in a radically different way than police authorities in Britain. The greatest difference was the registration process. The onus of registration in Britain fell on the individual woman, known to the police and medical authorities as working in the sex industry. According to the police, the weakness of this system was that few women volunteered to name their 'fall from grace'. The police surmised that no women, however desperate, would welcome the public shame of being a prostitute (and thus cleverly avoided any debate about the draconian measures faced by the women, and why it would be in their own and their families' best interest to avoid detection). In the Straits Settlements, the colonial authorities assumed that Asian societies were naturally licentious, and that Asian women needed saving. The CDO in Singapore was implemented on the premise that prostitution involving Asian women was a form of chattel slavery, and that the colonial authorities were benevolently offering the vulnerable protection against coercion and bondage. Consequently brothels, and not the individual sex workers, were required to register with the Chinese protectorate.[9] The function of the registration system was to identify the keepers and incorporate them into the colonial administrative system to protect Asian women from cruelty and slavery.[10]

As the regulation of prostitution in the Straits Settlements fell to the office of the Chinese protectorate, Japanese consuls to Singapore did not enjoy police powers over Japanese women working in Singapore as licensed prostitutes. The extent of the consul's power was negotiation with the Chinese protectorate to implement some mechanism to control Japanese women engaged in sex work.

In general, the Chinese protectorate was quick to repress the exploitation of women by brothel keepers, especially if there was a suspicion that the women were being forced into prostitution against their will. However, Japanese consuls noticed that British authorities were reluctant to intercept and search vessels for women being smuggled into the settlement unless they were certain that women were hidden on board. They reasoned that the colonial authorities did not want to undermine the prosperity of the region by obstructing the volume of shipping entering and leaving port.[11] Moreover, the Japanese consul could not ask the Chinese protectorate to take action to 'save' women they suspected of being trafficked to Singapore for sale to local brothel owners. Unless individual women came forward and testified to the colonial authorities that they were taken overseas against their will, no action could be taken against the 'evil persons' (*yakara*) who lured them there.[12]

Another major limitation to the Japanese consul's authority was that they had no purchase within the Japanese community. The local community ignored him. Successive Japanese consuls pointed out that the mores of the Japanese community were topsy-turvy in Singapore and, as a consequence, their efforts to enlist the local Japanese community to rid themselves of women working as prostitutes met with few results. One of the first missives of Nakagawa Tsunejirō, the first Japanese consul to Singapore (1889), pointedly noted that the Chinese, Indian and Malay merchants 'made a point of despising and ridiculing the Japanese' residing in Singapore. This was unavoidable, explained Nakagawa, as 'apart from a few small merchants and itinerant peddlers, the majority of the Japanese (community) are prostitutes and seamen' who turned to 'pimping'. To rub salt into the wound, lamented Nakagawa, Japanese 'gentleman travellers and merchants' alighting in Singapore in transit visited the Japanese brothels in the red-light district, leading 'everyone to scorn' Japan as a country run by prostitutes.[13]

Seven years later, the consul Fujita Toshirō – a former subordinate to Inoue Kaoru and one of the architects of government-sponsored emigration to Hawaii – informed Tokyo of similar circumstances. He too was quick to note that among the 460 Japanese living in Singapore, only 20 were involved in occupations fitting the description of 'respectable'.[14] Fujita also was of the opinion that the lack of legitimate Japanese merchants in Singapore stemmed from the low moral quality of the Japanese community, which idolized men who had several women working for them as prostitutes. The reason for this, deduced Fujita, was because Singapore was the major centre for the trafficking of Japanese women. Several traffickers (*zegen*) worked from Singapore, organizing and coordinating the traffic of large numbers of Japanese women to Australia, the Pacific Islands, India and South Africa. These traffickers were venerated because they were models of success. They led a swanky life and had 'numerous underlings to do their bidding'. As a result, legitimate merchants, who saw and admired the lavish life of the traffickers, came to believe that their occupations were inconsequential in the scheme of making money. As a result, when small-scale Japanese merchants – such as drapers (*gofuku-sho*) or haberdashers (*bekko-zakkaten*) – brought in enough money to invest in a business, they would immediately depart for Japan to recruit women to work as prostitutes abroad. He also noted a lack of collaboration by the local Japanese communities to help them quell prostitution. Fujita put the reason down to self-interest. Japanese merchants, inn-keepers, restaurateurs and taverniers all relied on the traffic in Japanese women and on the patronage of Japanese prostitutes for their livelihood.[15]

A History of Ignoble Failures

Successive Japanese consuls throughout Asia called upon the government to implement measures to stop Japanese women migrating abroad to work as prostitutes. The foreign ministry, however, was unprepared for the increasing number of such women. The initial response was to mimic the solutions found in Korea and China. Policing Japanese women on the Asian mainland involved utilizing extra-territorial rights gained by Japan in their treaties with China and Korea.[16] In 1885 the foreign ministry revised the first clause of the 'Rules for the Regulation of Japanese Residence in Korea and China' (*Shinkan zairyū nihonjin torishimari kisoku*), giving Japanese consuls the authority to extradite Japanese subjects deemed as 'offensive to public morality'.[17] The revisions allowed Andō Taro, then consul to Shanghai, to extradite 200 Japanese women involved in the sex trade to Nagasaki in 1885.[18]

Despite his success, Andō did not see extradition as a useful long-term policy. In a missive to Tokyo, dated 15 August 1885, Andō bitterly noted that even as he wrote, many Japanese prostitutes in Shanghai were pretending to be domestic servants or, worse, had become the chattels of unscrupulous 'Occidentals'. Ando reported that 'eight–nine out of ten Westerners who report to the consul claiming to be employers of Japanese women are sordid individuals who have been bribed by the women or received sexual favours. In some cases they are the woman's pimp.'[19] To counter the cynical exploitation of loopholes in residency restrictions, Andō recommended adapting migrant labour contracts to safeguard Japanese women seeking legitimate employment in Shanghai. Andō's aim was to control the flow of itinerant Japanese women to China by making the receipt of a work contract conditional for the issue of travel papers. This plan was based on the Japanese migrant labour contracts (*dekasegi imin keiyaku*) negotiated by the foreign ministry as a prerequisite for Japanese labourers to work in Australia in 1883.[20]

For Andō, the beauty of the model was its flexibility. On one hand, the necessity of having a work agreement before travel would prevent women's migrating overseas aimlessly. And yet, women with a valid work contract would obtain travel papers and protection from the Japanese government, thus offering them a safety mechanism to evade destitution and the temptation to turn to prostitution to make a living. Andō also proposed making it mandatory for women travelling abroad to deposit the fare of a return passage at the closest Japanese consulate on arrival to their destination of employment.[21]

However, Andō's suggestions did not solve the problem of Japanese women seeking sex work in colonial Singapore and Hong Kong. The reasons were two-fold. First, the Japanese poor were skilled in avoiding detection – their principle tactic of survival was to live in the shadows.[22] They voluntarily went abroad without having the prerequisite travel documents. Second, the women, the traffickers and brothel owners used deception and flight, going to regions where Japanese consuls did not have the power to extradite them.[23] The poor understood that, unlike their counterparts on the Asian mainland, Japanese consuls in British colonies did not enjoy police powers. Moreover, to their advantage was that the main British colonies in South-East Asia, Hong Kong and Singapore, were 'free ports'. As we have noted, the colonial authorities were reluctant to establish any policing mechanisms that would hinder the flow of goods and labour into the area.

During 1885–6 the Japanese consul in Hong Kong exerted considerable energy to limit the number of Japanese women arriving at the British colony applying for a licence to work as a prostitute. In May 1885, Asada Tokunori, head of the Communications Bureau, sent detailed instructions to the Hong Kong consul on implementing 'guidelines for providing moral instruction to Japanese subjects abroad'. Asada instructed the consul to identify any injurious Japanese subject and educate them in the error of their ways.[24] Three months later, Foreign Minister Inoue supplemented Asada's directives, ordering Hong Kong consul Minami Sadatsuke to use his authority discreetly to extradite Japanese subjects who had offended public morals (*fūzoku kairan*) so as to 'avoid obstructing [the freedom of] upright [Japanese] subjects'.[25]

Minami never put Inoue's instruction into action, however. The major obstacle was the Hong Kong colonial government. The British authorities rejected the idea of granting what was tantamount to extra-territorial rights to Minami.[26] Disappointed but undeterred, Minami continued negotiating with the colonial authorities. After a series of meetings, Minami and the Hong Kong register-general came up with an informal agreement to restrict the number of Japanese women working as prostitutes.[27] Both parties agreed to limit the number of Japanese women registered in public brothels to 52.[28]

However, by 1887 it was agonizingly clear that the informal restrictions were not deterring the flow of Japanese peasant women seeking work abroad outside established legal and administrative procedures. Traffickers in Japanese women were using Hong Kong as a base of transit. The Japanese consul in Singapore reported an increase in the number of Japanese women alighting from ships arriving from Hong Kong. He also pointed out that there were already 200 Japanese women working in Singapore's licensed brothels.[29] Over time, Japanese consuls in Singapore and Hong Kong came to the conclusion that the increasing number of peasant women leaving Japan was due to an organized network in the trafficking of women abroad. 'Cunning' and 'unscrupulous' procurers were luring ignorant women to 'a life of slavery'.[30] The 'ignorance' of 'base' peasant women allowed unsavoury individuals to make 'an industry out of smuggling Japanese women overseas'.[31]

Consuls in Singapore and Hong Kong used their initiative and tried to find an administrative solution to curtail the entry of 'undesirables'. In October 1886, for example, Minami advocated introducing a passport system similar to the one introduced by the Spanish to regulate migration from Hong Kong to the Philippines. Regardless of the number of people travelling to the Philippines, reported Minami, each individual person had to apply to the Spanish consulate for a passport. The bearer of the passport handed the document to the ship's captain on departure. On arrival, the captain handed the passports directly to the harbour customs officials, who then checked every passenger off with the passports at hand. The regulations appealed to Minami because shipping companies would not issue a ticket unless they saw evidence that the customer possessed a valid passport.[32] Saitō Miki, who took up the post of Hong Kong consul after Minami, offered a different solution. He wanted stricter police action against traffickers. Saitō called for the foreign ministry to open communication between Japanese prefectural authorities and consuls to exchange and coordinate information about the movements of procurers.[33] Saitō's successor Miyagawa Kyūjirō too stressed the victimization of innocent, albeit ignorant rural women who needed protection from the 'evil schemes' of traffickers. For Miyagawa, traffickers were heartless creatures 'who enticed women to travel overseas in the most dangerous circumstances for the sake of a quick profit'. The most public and dramatic example was the *Fushiki maru* incident (March 1890), when seven Japanese women died a horrible death in a bungled attempt to travel to Hong Kong secreted in the cofferdam deep in the ship's hold (see Chapter 2 above). Miyagawa pointed out that in the present circumstances even if traffickers were discovered by British authorities on board inbound ships without proper travel papers, they were set free. As a result, the traffickers believed they had nothing to lose, and plenty to gain. The lack of punishment meant that Hong Kong had become a 'breeding ground for shameless people' who did not give a second thought to 'selling their country women to a life of indentured slavery'.[34] The situation was so dire that the colonial government, inundated with requests, had lost its resolve to restrict the number of licensed Japanese prostitutes.[35]

Unlike Minami, Miyagawa did not see passports as an effective method of control, however. He noted that traffickers used the same passport repeatedly. The reason was the composition of Japanese passports, which in the late nineteenth century did not carry a picture of the bearer; just their name, age, destination and general appearance (colour of hair, eyes and any distinguishing features such as scars). The bearer's height was given as a general description of size, such as 'tall' or 'small', and not as a specific figure.[36] The lack of a police function to Japanese passports was not an oversight by the Japanese government. The administrative purpose of the passports was to facilitate Japanese emigration rather than to choke an exodus from Japan. The Japanese foreign ministry primarily began issuing passports in the 1880s to ensure the entry of Japanese migrant labourers into Hawaii, Australia, the US and Canada.

When it came to taking measures to prevent Japanese peasant women going abroad, consul reports from Hong Kong and Singapore stressed the victimization of the women. The reports described women in puerile scenes that illuminated their ignorance and the danger and degradation they faced. The moral focus on the purportedly 'ignorant' women at the mercy of individual, evil men reactivated an essentially parental–puerile relationship between the ruler and the ruled, men and women, and the cultivated and the corrupt. This demarcation harked back to a pre-Meiji form of authority, where the rulers, who possessed mental powers, would lead and guide because they best understood the order of things, and the ruled, mired in ignorance, were enjoined to follow their commands. It was repetition with a difference, however. Rural women, turned into vagabonds and prostitutes by the forces of the global market, were being chastised for becoming 'voluntary criminals'. In the process, the content of the women's lives was reduced to deviance and violence.

Soliciting the State: Excursions in Everyday Interventions

As mentioned earlier, the belligerence of the resident Japanese community was a major obstacle to consul efforts to eradicate Japanese prostitution in colonial Singapore. The main reason for this resistance was because the women engaged in prostitution were the economic and social heart of the Japanese community, at least until the outbreak of the First World War. As noted previously, in November 1895 Consul Fujita Toshirō reported that only 20 Japanese people out of a total 460 residing in Singapore were involved in a 'respectable trade'. The rest of the population were making their livelihood, directly or indirectly, from Japanese women engaged in sex work, either by running brothels or by owning various stores which catered to the needs of women and their male clientele.[37] Small-scale Japanese merchants in Singapore were dependent on the women's presence to survive economically. The majority of the Japanese-owned enterprises – laundries, barbers, photographers, dentists, drapers, jewellers, inns, restaurants and drinking houses – were located in and around Hylam, Malabar, Malay and Bugis streets, the heart of the Japanese red-light district in Singapore.[38]

The customers who frequented the brothels worked by Japanese women were usually Indian and Chinese labourers. There is evidence to suggest that it was customary practice among Singapore-based Japanese brothels not to take Japanese males as clients. This seems to have been a tactic aimed at cutting the expenditure of constant recruitment. Most Japanese brothel owners feared that their fellow male compatriots would try to entice Japanese women to run away, either to marry and/or to work for them.[39] This informal restriction on Japanese clients by Japanese-run brothels was more or less in place until the outbreak of the First World War, when Japanese banks and trading and *zaibatsu* firms established themselves in Singapore. The change in policy had less to do with 'white collar' employees of such companies comprising a 'better' type of client, and more with the pragmatic realization that these men were less likely to run away with the 'merchandise'. The discipline of white-collar work, with its demand of diligent work at the same table, in a closed room, for eight to ten hours most days, intrinsically restricted and controlled the movement of the employees of the banks and *zaibatsu*. *Zaibatsu* employees were also extremely well paid, lived apart from, and enjoyed a standard of living beyond the imagination of the Japanese community built around Hylam and Malay streets.

Japanese sex workers also played a major role in the maintenance and daily running of the Japanese community in colonial Singapore from 1890 until 1915. Allow me to give several examples. One is the founding of the Japanese cemetery in 1891. The move to establish a place to bury the Japanese dead in Singapore was organized by the three most successful brothel owners-cum-traffickers in the settlement.[40] Initially, it was used as a resting place for Japanese women who had died destitute in Singapore, and its upkeep was shared by women working in the licensed brothels. However, as the Japanese population grew the maintenance of the cemetery was taken over by a mutual aid society (*kyōsai kai*), an independent association comprising all members of the Japanese community. The society was formed to provide aid for the Japanese ill and to ensure the dead were buried with dignity and the proper rites for their journey to the afterlife. The initial membership of the mutual aid society was over 800 people, with the majority comprising Japanese women working as prostitutes. Membership in the society's managing committee was very political as the responsibility brought distinct financial advantages. Members of the committee controlled access to the funds, and any opening was highly contested among the Japanese community.[41] Another example is the 1897 Diamond Jubilee Year of Queen Victoria's rule. The Japanese community in Singapore participated in the celebrations by financing a fireworks display to mark the auspicious occasion. Few people outside the community knew that the consul gathered the money for the display by carrying out a door-to-door appeal of all Japanese brothels.[42] Similarly, in 1915 Japanese women working in the registered brothels raised and donated money to the war-relief fund for displaced people due to the fighting in Europe.[43]

Japanese women engaged in sex work were also the main source of finance and credit for Japanese petty merchants in Singapore. Shimizu Hiroshi and Hirakawa Hitoshi have pointed out that the Japanese community had limited access to credit. Until the First World War, capital available to the Japanese community was limited to cooperative credit associations whose main membership was Japanese prostitutes, or high-interest loans from *chettyars* – Singaporean moneylenders. Japanese finance did not extend its reach to Singapore until the 1910s. The reasons for this state of affairs were various. Up until the outbreak of the First World War the import trade in industrial goods was the monopoly of European merchant houses in Singapore. Japanese commodities became available in the Straits Settlements in the late nineteenth century, however, this was not due to Japanese investment. Rather, overseas Chinese merchants in the Straits Settlements began to cultivate a market in ceramics, lacquer ware, dried cuttlefish and cotton piece goods. Using their extensive commercial connections throughout Asia, the Japanese branches of the Chinese merchant houses would commission goods and buy at below wholesale prices in cash, and sell them in the Straits Settlements at retail prices.[44] In fact, the first Japanese bank to establish a branch in Singapore to help finance local Japanese industry and trade was the Bank of Taiwan in 1912.[45]

In general, when Japanese individuals borrowed an advanced payment from Singaporean moneylenders, they did so under specific terms and conditions to ensure that the moneylender would minimize the possibility of losing his advance. It seems Chinese, Indian and Arab moneylenders were willing to loan money to Japanese individuals involved in trafficking, as the women stood in as a form of security. The consul's report on Nishiyama Yūzō in 1892 gives us a glimpse of such a transaction. Nishiyama had borrowed money at a very high interest rate from an Indian moneylender in order to open a boarding house in Hong Kong, which also doubled as a gambling den heavily frequented by Japanese pearl divers returning from Thursday Island, northern Queensland. Nishiyama's main source of income, however, was as a broker in human trafficking; the buying and selling of Japanese women to ports throughout South-East Asia. In September 1892, financial difficulties forced him to close his lodging house. He was unable to meet the demands of his Indian creditors due to a combination of a drop in the demand for Japanese women in Singapore, tighter restrictions on them obtaining licenses to work as prostitutes in Hong Kong, and outstanding debts in his native Nagasaki. After careful discussion with his Indian creditors, Nishiyama left for Singapore to collect unpaid debts from women he sold into brothels there.[46]

In transactions between the moneylender and Nishiyama, the women embodied the function of collateral for the sum advanced. The demographic imbalance between unmarried men and women meant there was a constant demand by single men for a wife or concubine. The customary desire to continue the patrilineal line in Asian societies produced the conditions in which, when Japanese traffickers could not repay their debt, the moneylender was able to regain his initial advance by claiming the women as his property due to the forfeit of payment and sell them to men willing to pay for a wife or concubine.

Cooperative credit associations founded on the savings of Japanese prostitutes also played a major role in the expansion of Japanese economic interests in the Malay Peninsula. As Christopher Nelson has shown, these societies played a dual role in the twentieth century. One role of the cooperatives was as *kyōsai kai* (mutual aid societies). Japanese women engaged in sex work joined these associations to have access to money in times of illness, to cover burial expenses and pay their medical fees for bimonthly examination for venereal disease. From the late 1880s, Japanese brothels began to contract either Japanese doctors or the colonial surgeon to carry out venereal examinations.[47] The cooperatives also functioned as credit societies (*tonomashiko*). The more speculative character of the *tonomashiko* provided an important source of credit to the participants. The best example of this in action is the rubber boom at the turn of the twentieth century. The boom was the result of technical innovations in rubber manufacturing, the growth of the electric industry and the increased use of pneumatic tyres for bicycles and later automobiles. Seeking to take advantage of rising prices in rubber, the British colonial authorities encouraged rubber planting in Malaya by offering subsidies to all planters.[48] Many Japanese living in Singapore utilized the cooperative credit associations to invest in rubber plantations. According to Shimizu and Hirakawa, in 1902, Kasada Noakichi and Nakagawa Kikuzo, both allegedly involved in the procuring and trafficking of Japanese women to and from Singapore, became joint owners of a 150-acre rubber plantation in the Malay Peninsula. They were the first Japanese investors in rubber. As rubber prices soared to unprecedented heights in 1909–10, many Japanese women engaged in sex work in Singapore, along with brothel owners and petty traders, invested in small-sized rubber estates in Johore and other locations on the Malay Peninsula.[49] The importance of cooperative credit associations in providing financing for Japanese investments in small-scale agricultural production in this area cannot be underestimated. In 1911, 106 individual Japanese owned rubber plantations in British Malaya. The number of Japanese-owned plantations rose to 221 in 1917 and peaked in 1920 with 226 owners.[50] Moreover, in 1920, on the eve of the abolition of licensed Japanese prostitutes from Singapore and the Federated Malay States, there were 28 active *tonomashiko*. The total monthly contributions to these cooperative credit associations came to $26,000, of which Japanese sex workers contributed $10,000.[51]

By the time of the outbreak of the First World War, however, the centrality of Japanese prostitutes to the Japanese community in Singapore came under attack from several directions. One stand of attack was European campaigns to abolish licensed prostitution in the colonies in South-East Asia.[52] Moral reformers, newspaper editors and politicians challenged the Straits Settlements authorities' insistence on the necessity of licensed prostitution in Singapore. The reformers' arguments had evolved over time. Moral campaigns to overthrow the CDO in the 1870s focused on the fact that state-legislated brothels not only encouraged prostitution, but also gave the state absolute police power over women via the compulsory medical examinations by (male) doctors. In the 1880s, social purity campaigns against vice increased in visibility and strength. The crusades initially focused on the 'widespread' child prostitution among the poor. In the 1890s, the focus of the abolitionist campaign fell on prostitution in the empire. The basic claim of advocates was that regulated prostitution in the imperial domains was a form of state-sanctioned sexual slavery that also encouraged vice among the military. In the early 1900s, the campaign to prevent the trafficking of women and girls became a transnational movement, which coalesced around efforts to suppress 'White Slave Traffic'.[53] In 1904 an International Agreement for the Suppression of the 'White Slave Traffic' was signed in Paris. Six years later, in 1910, thirteen countries signed the International Convention for the Suppression of the White Slave Trade. There was a subtle shift between the two agreements. That of 1904 emphasized the control and repatriation of migrant women and girls. The focus of the 1910 Convention, however, fell on the criminalization of trafficking. As a consequence, in the 1910s intense public pressure was placed on the Straits Settlements and other British dominions to end state-regulated prostitution on the grounds that licensed prostitution tacitly promoted international trafficking in women and children. The abolitionist debate was fuelled by sensationalist publications such as *The White Slave Market*, printed in 1912, which made special reference to the horrors that awaited innocent white maidens in Singapore.[54] The Singapore colonial authorities first attempted to deal with the problem of trafficking of women and children by banishing or imprisoning European *souteneurs* under an emergency amendment made to the Women and Girls Protection Ordinance in 1912. In May 1913, the colonial government adopted a policy of prohibiting European women from obtaining a licence to work in brothel.[55]

The outbreak of the First World War brought changes in colonial policy regarding prostitution. The control of venereal disease among British troops deployed from the empire quickly became a matter of patriotic duty. In Singapore, the issue of prostitution also merged with the question of race.[56] The outbreak of the war made Indian soldiers crucial to the operation of British empire. British faith in the suitability and loyalty of sepoys in Singapore was tested in February 1915 when 850 Indian soldiers mutinied, killing 47 British soldiers and civilians, including women. In the wake of the mutiny, the indiscriminate mixing of races in brothels became a sensitive issue. Consequently, to assert the supremacy of British rule and civilization, the colonial authorities used their emergency powers to extradite European prostitutes in the region. The authorities repatriated 26 women to other locations at their expense. The women were informed not to return as there was to be a ban on European prostitution in the colony effective from July 1916. Six remained in Singapore, most likely as concubines.[57]

The strongest move to banish Japanese prostitutes from the Straits Settlements came from the Japanese community, however. The commencement of the First World War was the beginning of a transitional period for the Japanese community in Singapore and Malaya. The war proved to be a boon for Japanese investment in South-East Asia as it curtailed trade between Europe and the region. Bereft of competition, Japanese industry became the dominant exporter of manufactured goods to South-East Asian markets. Japanese exports to Singapore in cotton textiles, matches, ceramics and other sundry items increased from $11,503,000 in 1913 to $44,530,000 in 1918.[58] By 1917, Japanese shipping firms, trading houses, investment banks and general stores were established and thriving in Singapore. Out of the 50 leading Japanese enterprises in Singapore in 1919, 35 had opened a branch at the colony since 1916.[59] During this time, Singapore witnessed a rapid increase in the number of Japanese, male white-collar workers: employees of trading firms, banks and shipping companies. Japanese consular population surveys capture the rapid change in the composition of the Japanese community. At the end of June 1914, there were 45 Japanese men listed as working in white-collar professions. A year later the number had doubled, with 106 white-collar professionals listed. In 1920, this number had reached 1,136.[60] The years 1916–20 saw the Japanese merchant community – constituted predominately by petty merchants and crystallized around the finance opportunities created by Japanese prostitutes – replaced by a community invested in the systematic advance of Japanese capitalism in South-East Asia and united by the shared commitment to expand Japanese industrial and financial sectors in the area. Paradoxically, it was during the years of the First World War that Japanese brothels started taking Japanese men as clients.

The changes in the Japanese community coalesced with the transformation in the Japanese state's interest in South-East Asia. Prior to the First World War, because of the fiscal complexities of imperial expansion into Korea and the added expenditure of building naval armament and battleships to counter US naval advances, Japanese policymakers opted for prudence and downplayed territorial ambitions in the Pacific, preferring to emphasize economic expansion into South-East Asia. However, this policy changed after October 1914. Japan seized the German Pacific possessions – the Mariana Islands, Marshall Islands and the East and West Caroline Islands – under the justification that it was fulfilling its defence obligations of the Anglo-Japanese alliance. The capture of the chain of islands in Micronesia provided policymakers an opportunity to reassess Japan's position in South-East Asia. The control of the former Germany colony effectively gave Japan a territorial foothold in the Pacific for imperial expansion.

As a result, the Japanese state initiated policy to incorporate the Japanese communities in South-East Asia into an autarkic vision of economic self-sufficiency. The goal of Japanese policymakers was to establish Japanese associations in South-East Asia that would work in tandem with the state, thus intersecting Japanese competition and expansion in the global market with national security and empire-building. By subsuming these issues Japanese policymakers hoped to mimic the success of overseas Chinese guilds, mutual aid associations and merchant societies that cultivated relations of solidarity, economically and politically, throughout Asia. Japanese policymakers saw the necessity of fostering similar models of associations among and between Japanese communities in South-East Asia in order to compete successfully with Chinese merchants. Primary resources and food staples via Japanese economic expansion in the region were to be funnelled to the industrial needs of Japan to enhance the economic and military might of the empire.

This policy shift by the Japanese government affected the Japanese community in Singapore in concrete ways. First, the consul allied with the newly arrived business class and began to organize the local Japanese community in their shared image of what constituted a patriotic and socially useful Japanese subject. The first action of this alliance was the establishment of the Japanese Association (*nihonjin kai*) in September 1915; the inauguration was a solemn patriotic affair, dedicated to the enthronement of the Taisho emperor.[61] The association, which comprised individuals from the newly arrived Japanese professional community, was a self-governing body given the task of freeing the Japanese community from the undesirable stigma of bygone days.[62] Working in tandem with the Japanese consul, one of the first moves of the Japanese Association was to undermine the influence of the mutual aid society (*kyōsai kai*), whose membership was comprised mostly of Japanese women engaged in prostitution, by taking over the management of the Japanese cemetery.[63] The Japanese Association also quickly established new institutions to cater to the patriotic and social needs of the newly arrived middle-class members: such as a Japanese Chamber of Commerce, elementary school and Young Men's Association.[64] A major function of these organizations was to cultivate a sense of solidarity and cooperation among the Japanese community as subjects of a larger imperial design.

The Japanese Association and the Japanese consul worked in tandem to integrate and regularize the Japanese workforce in the Straits Settlements. Both agreed that the abolition of Japanese prostitution in Singapore was a necessity. This proved a protracted task, however, and took several years. The outcry of British public opinion deeming licensed prostitution as sowing the seeds of international trafficking had the desired effect of pressuring colonial authorities to take pro-active, and if necessary draconian, measures against Japanese prostitution too. This policy shift was felt by the Japanese community on 31 March 1914, when the colonial authorities informed the Japanese consul in Singapore, Fujii Minoru, of their plan to banish 37 Japanese men suspected of running brothels and trafficking in Japanese women. Although the consul was in favour of such action, he was apprehensive about possible anti-Japanese sentiment and the potential negative economic repercussions for Japanese trading companies investing in Singapore. After protracted negotiations with the colonial government, Fujii was able to defer any arrests by the Chinese protectorate in return for his word that all 37 men would leave Singapore 'voluntarily'. The men were extradited on 21 May, under the expediency of Fujii's office.[65]

Fujii quickly seized upon the colonial authorities' desire to end the 'trafficking in women and children' and gained the Chinese protectorate's cooperation to implement procedures to regulate the entry of Japanese women into Singapore. In January 1915, he used the Japanese-language newspapers to inform the community of new procedures coming into effect. All Japanese women travelling steerage to Singapore were to be interviewed by the Chinese protectorate on alighting to ascertain if they were victims of trafficking. Moreover, from February Japanese hoteliers and boarding houses were to report daily to the consul on the arrival and departure of all Japanese guests. To ensure fidelity, hotel and boarding house ledgers recording the arrival and departure dates of guest were to be scrutinized by consul officials every Friday. The consul warned that any proprietor failing to comply with the new procedures or falsifying entries faced severe fines without exception. Fujii justified the strict procedures as necessary to prevent 'trafficking in women' (*mikkō fujin yūkai*) and the emigration of undesirables to the Straits Settlements and Federated Malay States.[66] The new procedures were the opening gambit by Fujii to eradicate Japanese prostitution from Singapore.

Fujii, however, was reluctant to take draconian measures to abolish Japanese prostitution overnight. He saw the purging of 'undesirables' as a protracted process. He was afraid that many of the women would become destitute, without means to make a living or recourse to money for return passage to Japan, forcing them to turn to 'sly prostitution' in the crooks and crannies of Singapore's streets, and thus staining the Japanese flag further. Moreover, Fujii was also aware that many of the small Japanese business in Singapore, such as drapers and haberdashers, centred most of their business on the needs of the women, and relied on the access to money invested in the local credit associations to finance the purchase of small-scale rubber plantations on the Malay Peninsula. The credit associations were financially buoyant by the considerable sums advanced by women who worked as prostitutes. Fujii feared that forcefully uprooting the women from Singapore would erase the gains the Japanese community had made in the region.[67]

To avoid agitation and a blow to Japanese prosperity, Fujii chose to give the Japanese community time to adjust to the eventual demise of Japanese prostitution in Singapore. The Japanese Association aided the consul by orchestrating a campaign via public gatherings and articles in the local Japanese-language newspapers to prepare Japanese business for the inevitable cessation of Japanese licensed prostitutes in the Straits Settlements. The campaign had two objectives. One aim was forewarning and forearming the community for the 'inevitable' end to Japanese prostitution in the region. Numerous articles appeared in the Japanese-language newspapers cautioning Japanese businesses that depended on the women for trade to liquidate their investments in the local credit associations, settle any outstanding debt and to start preparations for relocation to other regions more conducive to their line of work. Japanese women working as licensed prostitutes were given another set of directions. The women were warned that cessation of their work was imminent. They were directed to liquidate their investments in the credit associations and pay any outstanding debts. On cessation, they were to be repatriated to Japan. The newspapers announced that it was to be the woman's responsibility to meet the costs of repatriation. Therefore, in this period of grace, it was their duty to prepare earnestly for that moment by securing the necessary money to pay for their return to Japan.[68]

Another feature of the public campaign was the emphasis on the belief that the eradication of Japanese prostitution from the region was for the greater good and appropriate for Japan's newly found standing as a world power. The monies that the women made did not add to national prosperity. Because the women were no more than 'playthings [*ganrōbutsu*] for foreign men', their activities sullied the reputation of Japanese merchants and diminished the 'greatness of the Japanese empire'. It was time for the Japanese community to rid itself of sentiments that the women were the pioneers of a Japanese presence in the region, and to sacrifice short-term prosperity for the dignity, pride and long-term interests of Japan.[69]

The final decision to 'eradicate' Japanese licensed prostitutes from Singapore came quickly, albeit not painlessly. In December 1919, acting Consul-General Yamazaki Heikichi, fortified by instructions from Tokyo and with the support of the British colonial authorities, implemented an agenda for the abolition of Japanese prostitution from Singapore and the Federated Malay States. On New

Year's Day 1920, Yamazaki summoned the presidents of the Japanese Associations in Singapore and various regions of British Malaya to a two-day conference. The agenda of the conference was to coordinate the timetable for the repatriation of the Japanese prostitutes. In the meeting, Yamazaki reiterated that the banishment of Japanese prostitutes was beneficial to Japanese interests. Prostitution was not conducive to good business, he claimed, because most of the women were in debt, and the Japanese who lived off them were idle, lacked initiative and carried out their business in slovenly half measures. Yamazaki thought it best to compel most of the women to abandon their trade by December 1921, rather than give them a longer period of grace to sort out their financial obligations and raise funds for the return fare. Rather than postpone the inevitable, argued Yamazaki, a tight timetable was best, as it would 'wake up the businesses connected with the women to the frivolousness [*fumajime*] of their ways'. Yamazaki went on to point out what he considered was the obvious: the presence of many Japanese women of ill fame in foreign countries was a 'blot to the honour and reputation of Japan, and adversely affected the sound development of Japanese interest abroad'. Yamazaki considered the time ripe to replace the cooperative credit associations that ran on the membership of Japanese prostitutes with small-scale banks or credit and saving associations, whose securities would be guaranteed by the Yokohama Specie Bank and Bank of Taiwan. According to Yamazaki, such an arrangement was favourable for it allowed Japanese investors access to larger amounts of credit to invest in large-scale coffee and rubber plantations.[70]

To this end, the Japanese consulate issued to Japanese prostitutes who 'voluntarily' ceased working a certificate confirming that they no longer were engaged in the sex trade. Women who wanted to remain in Singapore or the Federated Malay States were required to present themselves to the consulate along with their guarantors, either their employers or common-law husband of reputable standing in the community. If the consul deemed the women suitable on screening, they were allowed to remain in the British colony albeit under constant surveillance. The Japanese *geisha* who entertained the male employees of Japanese companies and the eighteen Japanese restaurants also came under closer scrutiny by the Japanese consul and colonial police. Moreover, in June 1920 the Japanese Association formed a morals committee to keep vigil over the Japanese residents and restaurants in the Hylam-Malay section of the city.[71]

The abolition of Japanese prostitution in Singapore and the Federated Malay States was dramatic, but not unique. Japanese economic penetration into South-East Asia involved intense social integration and normalization of the Japanese communities in the region to the designs of empire. The new professional middle class that led the way, glad of their liberty to pursue their interests in commerce and trade, were only too eager to impose new codes of conduct on overseas Japanese communities to turn them into subjects worthy of the emperor. The new codes of conduct instituted by the Japanese company and bank employees were a self-affirmation by a social class keen to prove its fidelity to imperial ambitions. It does not take much imagination to realize that to the Japanese bankers, managers and conglomerates, the Japanese poor not socialized into a schedule and rhythm of 'productive' work – the spendthrift, the idle, the destitute, the prostitute and the dispossessed – were an enemy to the goals of economic development and imperial splendour.

The hidden history of the eradication of Japanese prostitution in South-East Asia is how peasant women trying their best to escape rural poverty were stripped of all endowments attributed to fellow countrywomen and branded with the mark of miscreant. Let the words of officialdom testify the judgement it passed on the poor in its own tongue:

> As a result of urgent recommendations passed by [British] Parliament and by various charitable associations, the Japanese government ... took strict ... measures for repatriating Japanese prostitutes ... In the eyes of the Japanese people this is a question of national prestige. Public opinion is convinced that the good name of the Japanese can only be safeguarded if all races abroad of such moral degradation are obliterated. The following are a few instances selected at random to illustrate the attitude of the country.
>
> In May 1920 the Japanese consul at Rangoon summoned all keepers and inmates of brothels to a meeting. He advised them to change their profession within two years and to go back to Japan. Many then decided to leave at once and others followed, as soon as they were able to settle their debts to the natives ...
>
> In November 1918 more than 100 Japanese prostitutes were repatriated from Manila on the advice of the Japanese consul. The Society of Japanese Residents takes an active part in the work, in close co-operation with the consul and the American authorities.
>
> Singapore has for 25 years been the centre of Japanese prostitutes in this part of the world ... In 1915 the Japanese consul, with the assistance of the Governor repatriated a considerable number of brothel-keepers. They discontinued giving licenses for prostitution. With the support of the Japanese colony the consul in 1919 decided to eradicate this social evil and ordered all Japanese prostitutes to abandon their profession. Thanks to the efforts of the consul and Japanese residents almost all the women in Singapore gave up their profession and the majority of them were repatriated. A vice-consul was sent to the spot with express instructions to proceed to the interior of the country [Federated Malay States] and to search for any prostitutes who might be found living in the provinces.
>
> In 1920 the Japanese consul in Hong Kong conferred with the Governor and decided to refuse further licenses for prostitution. The number of prostitutes has been consistently reduced since then.[72]

The message to integrate socially and regularize Japanese labour to a pan-imperial design was reinforced in instructions sent by the Japanese foreign minister, Uchida Yasuya, to all Japanese diplomatic representatives in the *Nanyō* (South Seas) and South America on 15 June 1921. In the missive, the actions of Singapore Consul-General Yamazaki were the prototype for the policies the foreign ministry wanted implemented for 'the eradication of women of ill fame abroad'. The foreign ministry cautioned it was impossible to implement a uniform policy as the social and economic conditions varied markedly from region to region. If, as was the case in Singapore, the consuls found it impossible to eradicate the women in one clean sweep, then it was advisable to 'adopt a policy of gradual eradication'. Uchida referred to the recent measures taken by the Hong Kong consul Ōmori to eliminate Japanese prostitution from the British colony by ensuring no new applications would be processed. He closed his instructions in a didactic flourish. The problem of overseas prostitution had a long and vexing history. Testimony to this was the fact that 'Yamaji Kajiko and six-hundred other members of the JWCTU petition the government every year for the enactment of a law for the control of prostitutes in foreign countries'. The eradication of Japanese women of ill fame abroad was 'a matter of imperative necessity' (*kinyō naru*). Success, warned Uchida, lay in each consul 'establishing a definite policy and to pursue it at all times' so as to facilitate the 'sound development of our interests abroad' (*kenjitsu naru kaigai hatten*).[73]

The effectiveness of Yamazaki's action to rid Singapore and the Federated Malay States of all Japanese women engaged in sex work was overstated, however. After 1920, consul reports from Singapore made constant reference to the many Japanese women continuing to engage in sex work, albeit on 'the sly', or the suspicion that Japanese women were still being 'trafficked' into the region from ships departing from Kyushu.[74] In 1927, the Japanese consul reported how a number of Japanese women operating 'ice shops' were in fact running brothels. The consul pointed to the undesirable talk that these women were attracting. The consul also reported that around 30 Japanese-run shops were a front for brothels, employing 126 women.[75]

Around this time, the colonial government in Singapore decided to take the first steps to close tolerated brothels by amending the Women and Girls Protection Ordinance. The amendment made running a brothel an offence. On 9 August 1927, the Chinese protectorate arrested eleven Japanese for running brothels employing 46 women. The accused were arraigned on 18 August, whereupon the court gave them 30 days to close their premises. With the closure of the brothels, around half the women left Singapore to find work elsewhere. The women who remained faced numerous summonses by the Japanese Association and Chinese protectorate, who took turns pressuring them to return to Japan without further encumbrance. Women were allowed to remain in Singapore, provided that they find honest and legitimate employment. Whether the women who remained kept their word is open to debate. We do know that the consul thought they could not be trusted.

CONCLUSION: GLOBALIZATION AND THE POOR

> This is an anthology of existences. Lives of a few lines or a few pages, countless misfortunes and adventures, gathered together in a handful of words. Brief lives, chanced upon in books and documents ... [F]or such is the contraction of things said in these texts that one does not know whether the intensity which traverses them is due to the vividness of the words or the violence of the facts which jostle about in them.
>
> Michel Foucault, 'The Life of Infamous Men'[1]

Sex in Japan's Globalization focuses on a fundamental problem of Japan's first experience of globalization: namely, the contradiction between the validity of the existence of the Japanese poor who engaged in sex work overseas as one response to the rapid social and economic changes occurring in Japan, and the prevailing understanding of the same women as unworthy and degrading to the name of the country. In a very modest way, the preceding chapters have attempted to work around a regime of history in which the lives of these women were described in terms of prostitutes, stowaways or both.

The Response of the Poor

The rural poor women who went abroad to find work at the start of the 1870s were endowed with the capacity to act and actualize their aspirations. At the micro-level of the women's immediate communities, the poor who left the country to find work, get money and, if really lucky, strike it rich, were not stigmatized as morally flawed individuals or as a group found on the margins of local society. Rather, the movement of young Japanese women into sex work occupations abroad was one of many reactions by the rural poor to the radical social restructuring unfolding in Japan from the 1870s onward. The movement of young Japanese women was only possible because of the increase in mobility offered by Japan's incorporation into a colonial money economy that transcended national boundaries and borders. Young women from Kyushu made use of the contingencies produced by capitalist modernization to enter the global labour market as sex workers, a consideration absent in accounts seeking to convey a moral tale concerning the shame and exploitation the women 'felt' as prostitutes. Capitalist modernization supplied the rural poor women with the opportunity for both economic and social autonomy. Peasant women from Kyushu searched for work abroad in anonymity. Success in finding work rested on the ability of escaping government attempts to regulate and control their movements.

In Japan, capitalist modernization – another term for globalization – was the relocation of capital and labour to South-East and East Asia, and led to Japanese women entering the labour market as 'things' to be sold. What happens to women when they enter a money economy where their bodies have exchange value? Georg Simmel, an early diagnostician of capitalism and the urban life it spawned, saw a specific gendered phenomenon in capitalist development at the turn of the twentieth century. He diagnosed the rise of prostitution in the great European cities spawned by capitalist development as a product of the intensification and spread of commodity relations that transformed the outer and inner life of the individual. In his *Philosophy of Money*, Simmel locates a powerful internal contradiction in the modern money economy; namely, how it robs things of their innate value and distinction by making everything interchangeable with money: 'the more objects are produced for the sake of money and are valued in terms of money, the less can the value of distinction be realized in men and objects'. The contradiction found in capitalist relations has gendered consequences. Simmel argues that when personal exchanges such as affection and sex are offered for money, the pricing of these interactions trivializes the social relation involved in the exchange, which in turn degrades and cheapens the value of the woman. The dynamics of the exchange, the purchase of affection and sex by men, robs the women of all personal identity and attachment to social relations outside the exchange of money for sex.

> We experience in the nature of money itself the essence of prostitution. The indifference as to its use, the lack of attachment to any individual because it is unrelated to any of them, the objectivity inherent in money as a mere means, which excludes any emotional relationship – all this produces an ominous analogy between money and prostitution.[2]

Simmel's argument is that that money and prostitution share the same essential qualities: both are mere means, and, as such, unsatisfactory mediators of personal relationships. Moreover, money and prostitution are both inherently indifferent to personal relationships, and reject from the outset any association beyond the initial monetary transaction. In the same way as prostitution, money reduces all social relations to the generic content of the exchange. For Simmel, the rise of prostitution as a social problem in the modern world is a product of the intensification and spread of commodity relations. Coeval with urbanism, the increase in prostitution in the late nineteenth early twentieth centuries was an effect of development.

The Response of the State: Redefining Free Labour

Globalization, however, intensifies the processes of exploitation to the detriment of the poor. Japanese peasants were offered to the world market as free labour. Yet, once offered, it was up to the Japanese peasants to manage the best they could. However, the language of the market presupposes not only wealth in the hands of the heroes of industry but also a pool of workers with nothing but their labour to sell. The market, which promises infinite development and profit, does have inbuilt limits on what can sell as socially useful labour power. Significantly, the concept of globalization mystifies and conceals the violent 'bloody legislation' enacted by the state to produce useful workers in the process of giving birth to a new society. The work available to emigrant Japanese peasant women in the global economy was limited. Finding themselves with insufficient means to support themselves abroad, rather than return to the poverty they had emigrated to escape, rural poor women from Japan worked as beggars and prostitutes. Their exchange value included the selling of their sex as a thing for barter, a condition of exchange open to women but not readily available to men. It is this attribute of exchange made possible by the market that transformed the peasant women from emigrants to an 'unsightly' stain on the flag of Japan. The market made the selling of their sex possible. The moral economy of nation-building turned them into amoral prostitutes or the pitiful victims of evil men.

The early Meiji state sought to impose controls on the everyday conduct of rural women at the precise moment it was seeking to transform the political economy into a capitalist order. The peasant women who left the land, drawn by the opportunities opened to them by Japan's incorporation in the global world market, did not become 'free workers', but rather a disenfranchised poor who resorted to prostitution as much as they showed up at the textile mills established by the Meiji government. Encoded in the processes of capitalist development is a moral schema that inlays the virtues of diligence, frugality and industry into 'socially useful' work. The work that rural peasant women performed as prostitutes abroad did not fit the demands of industrialization and nation-building. Consequently, sex work offered no social recognition, no dignity, nor political recognition. The light of virtue bathes activities that comply with the unconditional requirement of all workers to fulfil their capacity as producers.[3] At the same time, those who cannot adapt themselves to the new conditions, by force of circumstance – and who eke out an existence as beggars and prostitutes – are bathed in the light of criminality: 'unsightly women'. The work of 'unsightly women' consists of acts without quality, performed by people who also lacked value, and who counted as naught because the tasks they did were not recognized as acts worthy of subjects of Japan. Work brings social recognition only if it is authorized by an official system of regulation. The employment of rural Japanese women as prostitutes marked them as miscreants, and signalled an arrangement that materially reinforced a social system which ensured that rural migrants either become wage slaves or be subject to harsh regimes of control and exclusion.

The Public Sphere: The Response of Upper-Class Women

In liberal theories of globalization, the emergence of a public sphere is a sign of progress. Advocates of a free market economy, and the virtues of globalization, see the freedom of the market as also leading to the formation of a public sphere and political reform which, in turn, will lead to enhanced freedoms: the market is an invisible hand functioning without state intervention. However, the role of the public sphere and public opinion do not always follow this scenario. In fact, public opinion played a very different role when it came to Japanese overseas prostitutes. From the 1880s, 'public opinion', forged out of the details supplied by the foreign ministry about Japanese prostitutes abroad, became part of a wider social imperative concerning the struggle for existence facing the Japanese race in a hostile and competitive world dominated by Western powers. The characteristic feature of the relation of public opinion to overseas Japanese sex workers was the open invitation for the Japanese state to cultivate a new species of Japanese to meet the requirements of the 'current situation', understood as a novel and historically definitive break from the past. Christian philanthropists, journalists and administrators used public opinion to interweave details pertaining to the Japanese poor abroad into the domain of moral arithmetic, where the women became a symptom of some deeper disorder.

This monograph challenges the widespread tendency in Japanese historiography of seeing one strand of modernization: the downward diffusion of patterns of domesticity and womanhood from the former samurai strata to the rest of Japanese society. The source of this challenge is an important methodological point. To argue that modern Japanese womanhood was obtained by a singular route, constructed on the basis of a general doctrine such as 'good wife and wise mother' (*ryōsai kenbo*), which was diffused across classes by example and the force of ideology, in effect silences the multiplicity of experience born out of class, age and place. *Sex in Japan's Globalization* puts forward a counter-argument. The JWCTU moral campaigns are best understood when we focus on the different class effects of the 'endogamy of the body and sex'.[4] The group's discovery of sex as a political issue – the shame and dangers of prostitution and the promotion of monogamous marriage for men and women of the upper strata – was historically a creation of upper-strata women concerned with the survival of their 'class-body'. One historical strand of the Japanese family arises from a complex set of disciplinary rules (monogamy/prohibition of prostitution) and practices (social promotion via education) invented by former samurai women in early Meiji to train, cultivate and experience their 'class-body' as distinct and superior from the immoderate body of the unwashed.

The effects of this transformation in the substance and function of family did not operate 'symmetrically with respect to social class'.[5] The marriage of sex with the 'exclusive' chaste body of upper-class women was an affirmation and investment of the privilege of that class to deal with their concerns over the menace of concubines and prostitutes to lines of inheritance, and the need to protect the family from male debauchery, drink and wantonness. The JWCTU also linked the conditions of reproduction with political order. The churchwomen identified prostitution and male debauchery as undermining the household, and the future of Japan, because they depleted the available talent of the next generation. The JWCTU's moral campaigns were an act of self-affirmation coeval with maintaining and improving human lineage. As such, their philanthropic work cannot be taken as innocent. As Donzelot in his important work *The Policing of Families* has shown, philanthropic projects were a political ordering of life via self-affirmation *and* a mode of exercising social control and political subjugation of the poor through moralization campaigns.[6]

The JWCTU was a modern institution in the sense that it used public opinion for social engineering. This is best seen in the emphasis the churchwomen placed on the family as the first social structure, and on the importance of the socialization of the child by a cultivated and morally sound mother to allow the Japanese race to 'evolve'. Progress centred on conjugality, the preparation for marriage as an end, and concern for descent. Moreover, via the politics of purity, the JWCTU introduced the beginnings of social eugenic thought in Japan. Bearers of the worthiest intent, Japanese Christian organizations believed that the introduction of social policies would improve the qualities of the Japanese race. The philanthropic zeal of the JWCTU aimed to regulate the behaviour of the poor and to introduce an ideal type of family based on chastity and monogamy for women and men of their social strata. In the conjugality envisaged by the JWCTU, we see a new social and moral code slowly imposed with the help of the state that had different repercussions for the upper middle class and the poor. The increase in the domestic power of the upper-middle-class women gave them an expansive role in the fields of educational and charitable work. The domain in which they exercised their newly found authority was the lives of women from the lower strata of Japanese society. All forms of female sexuality and adult–child relations exhibited by the lower classes that did not conform to the sensibilities of the churchwomen were identified as being injurious to the collective good of society, and targeted for reform. Ultimately, Japanese Christian philanthropic organizations saw the state as the organizing moment of society, and aimed to turn its power to their own aims by calling on it to introduce a new form of humanism to Japan based on Christian principles.

Capitalist Development and Globalization as 'Evolution': Fukuzawa Yukichi

During the Meiji period, capitalist-induced change was led by Japan's state-driven programmes of industrialization and was bathed in a more or less heroic light of national destiny and survival. Fukuzawa Yukichi and fellow advocates of civilization and enlightenment (*bunmei kaika*) sanctioned capitalist-induced change as progress, denoting capitalism's impulses to transform pre-existing apparatuses of production and consumption by freeing practice from fixed and established codes of custom and habit as a rational projection of the future.

Fukuzawa is an interesting historical figure as he couples economic principles with the theory of evolutionary, progressive history. The novelty in his work was the idea that society was not a static entity but one of motion; the development of new productive forces provided society with a forward momentum towards the apex of human experience. Fukuzawa, among others, introduced Japan to a form of moral science devoted to the discovery of the natural laws governing the development of Japanese society, which would guide the Japanese to the means by which they could satisfy both physical and moral needs. The union of 'free market' economic principles with the theory of civilization constructed a frame of reference that allowed comparisons between Japan and other nation-states. The aim of these comparisons was to judge how far Japan had, or had not, evolved as a modern nation, where an abstract notion of the West functioned as a universal referent. Just as importantly, this index of civilization allowed a newly emerging middle class (journalists, civil servants and educators), divorced from authority and personified by Fukuzawa, to make internal distinctions between themselves and the uneducated and unpropertied masses. Just like the JWCTU, this numerically small stratum affirmed itself as the spokesperson of the future, the embodiment of an advanced form of reason that would improve the manners and morals of the Japanese as a collective. The men, and it was mostly men, situated in this social stratum saw themselves at the forefront of progress and ordained to lead the rest of Japan to its future. The responsibility they claimed, more often than not, was articulated in cultural terms, emphasizing character formation and moral cultivation.

Upper-middle-class men such as Fukuzawa saw the Meiji oligarchy's inability to revise unequal treaties with European powers as symptomatic of a material backwardness that stemmed from a deeper spiritual bankruptcy, and as a justifiable reason to try to goad or shame the government into action. The advocates of adaptation such as Fukuzawa argued for nurturing mental habits among the Japanese people so that they could adjust to the necessities of the present environment, transmute outdated custom and thus alter the course of history and Japan's destiny. They pinpointed the changing of custom, the adaptation of the lived space of the present to the demands of progress, as the qualifying moment in the development of Japanese history. Fukuzawa saw the presence of Japanese women abroad engaged in prostitution as a transient but necessary stage in Japan's development; the first buds of a vital and necessary enterprising spirit that the Japanese race/nation required to overcome the inertia of a feudal mentality that was the result of 200 years of isolation.

Placed within this context, the public interest in and opinion of Japanese women engaged in sex work abroad was diagnostic in nature. Overseas prostitution became a symptom, an object for naming a hidden disorder within Japanese society. Intellectuals, reformers and philanthropic associations alike understood the rural poor as a product of existing custom that constrained the ability of the Japanese people to develop their capacities further. They scanned the details of the women's lives to isolate the cause of their pitiful existence, with the hope of developing and applying a cure to the social malaise that produced them. However, diagnosing the cause proved elusive. Intellectuals, reformers and philanthropic associations could not reach a consensus, because they could not agree whether natural adaptation or social engineering constituted the correct path to progress.

Evaluations of the Human Condition

Sex in Japan's Globalization dramatizes the degree to which claims made about overseas prostitution by interested parties disqualified the voices of the poor while simultaneously concealing what was experienced by the women working as overseas prostitutes. The drive behind such an analysis is a rarely asked reflexive question: what evaluations about the human condition come into play when 'prostitution' is reduced by policymakers, NGOs, and researchers to 'sexual slavery' and 'omnipresent violence'? Lest we think this concern is just an academic exercise, let us turn our attention to the present. In the early 1990s some radical feminists and the religious faith groups in the US joined resources to launch a major anti-prostitution campaign.[7] Central to this campaign was the goal to abolish sex trafficking and prostitution as an unqualified evil that 'exploits women, regardless of women's consent', and the view that 'prostitution affects all women, justifies the sale of any woman, and reduces all women to sex'.[8] By 2003, social reformers against sex trafficking had successfully transformed their agenda from a social movement to a policy priority for the US government. In September 2003, President Bush pledged in his address to the United Nations General Assembly $50 million to 'the good work of organizations that are rescuing women and children from exploitation, and giving them shelter and medical treatment and the hope of a new life'.[9] US government support for the fight against human trafficking did not end there, however. The Bush administration allocated further generous funding to anti-trafficking conferences throughout the world and to faith-based groups and NGOs to identify victims and report on trafficking. Many of the faith-based groups also promoted anti-abortion programmes, abstinence education and church-run social services both domestically and abroad.[10] What was novel about the alliance between the Christian right, the abolitionist feminists and the Bush administration was the shared vision of American global leadership as a righteous instrument, which would herald a new international order that would protect human dignity through the promotion of freedom and human rights.

The crusade against the global sex trade wedded US foreign humanitarian intervention to a binding moral obligation to prevent the 'evil in the abuse and exploitation of the most innocent and vulnerable'.[11] The attraction and influence the affirmation of human rights has on US international policy determined the way the campaigners and the Bush administration understood and recognized themselves. Yet, it is a limitation when it comes to understanding non-Western societies because the affirmation of human rights is an abstract form of thinking that unconsciously separates the lives of the 'innocent and vulnerable' (read the poor) from the effects of the policies implemented. While prostitutes are defined by the US trafficking czar as 'victims of bodies demeaned, of spirits trampled, and souls destroyed', the increasingly draconian legislation implemented by the Bush administration allowed traffickers 'to exert an undue amount of power and control' over migrants.[12] Recent research by critical feminists has highlighted the limitations of the abolitionist desire of the anti-trafficking legislation: the emphasis on prohibiting prostitution and restricting travel had the adverse affect of attracting organized crime and creating 'the possibilities of large profits, as well as creating the prostitute's need for protection and assistance'.[13] The configuration of US humanitarian action towards the 'most innocent and vulnerable' has had tragic consequences on the international stage in other areas too. As many critics of US foreign policy point out, the uncompromising pro-life stance of the Bush administration on reproductive health saw the withdrawal of most US financial support for the United Nations Population Fund, which, ironically and disastrously, led to more abortions and more mothers dying in undeveloped countries.[14]

How do faith-based groups, radical feminists and US policymakers continue to see the righteousness in their decisions in the face of such devastating evidence to the contrary? A partial explanation is the way the notion of the autonomous individual, which grounds the notions of 'sex slavery' and 'sexual coercion' of trafficking as an out-and-out (social) evil, is double-sided. The constitution of the individual is given in naturalistic terms as development of innate inward forces and disposition of human personality and character. Yet, at the same time, the notion of the individual is evaluative. The 'free individual' stands for the value and affirmation of certain distinct and superior moral qualities enjoyed by 'mature' societies (such as the US) that have mastered appropriate ways of being 'autonomous' agents. A serious political ramification of investing excessively in autonomy and freedom as eternal values and anthropological universals is that it fails to offer any assistance to the migrant poor whose principle tactic of survival is to avoid the spotlight and live in the shadows. To come into the spotlight involves harsh punishment and a life of close policing.[15]

Another serious political ramification is making trafficking a moral issue. Here, Gilles Deleuze's concept of morality is a useful conceptual tool for analysis.[16] For Deleuze, any moral system of good and evil consists of judging actions and intentions in relation to universal values. The signs that identify a good and devoted Christian – loving one's neighbour, heterosexual marriage, abstinence from premarital sex, the sanctity of life – become the measure by which judgements are made about which mode of existence is good and praiseworthy. Judgements of this type are reactive. Beneath a disingenuous objectivity are unconscious investments in a specific, located socio-political order, which replaces the real activities of life with demands and recriminations in the name of an immutable order. In short, moral judgements are an invested perspective that determine the social utility of actions, and only recognize social value of like quality. The socio-political consequence is that when the moralist comes across a mode of existence that does not share the same values, does not conform to the same measure of humanity, he/she imputes all blame on the 'sinner' who cares naught about the worldly goods on offer, accepts no shame or responsibility, due to his/her incorrigibility.[17]

What Deleuze lays bare is the fact that feeling guilt and accepting responsibility are not innate attributes, but the products of a history by which the human species is trained and cajoled into developing a consciousness that can feel shame and blame. To claim as the Bush administration did that the US embodies freedom, human dignity and all things righteous in this world is to insist on conceptualizing freedom, the good and the praiseworthy on a very specific investment of humanity that reduces difference to common measure. Protection and aid are only given to the innocent (children), to the vulnerable (women involved in prostitution against their own volition) and the worthy 'deserving poor'.[18] The logical operation of such investments is complex. The emphasis on innocence or victimhood of the targets of humanitarian intervention confers a subordinate status on children for their lack of mature mental faculties that can differentiate good from bad, and on third-world women for their lack of liberty, the most valuable of all inner capacities, by violent coercion. The sign of innocence or victimhood is passivity: the inability to act on one's will due to a lack of developed mental faculties or liberty. Such logical operations re-invoke and re-inscribe the view that the West, and in particular the US, is at the apex of the natural universal progression of human experience due to the virtues of an independent civil society that promotes individual self-determination.

However, in cases where children and women of the third world do show volition, albeit contrary to the aims of US policymakers – such as electing to engage in sex work or to abort an unwanted child – they lose the status of the innocent or the vulnerable and become recodified under the sign of the immorally evil or criminal beyond the scope of 'neighbourly love', and must be punished accordingly. The socio-political ramifications of such judgements are significant. The altruism of the first world masks the same unbalanced, non-reciprocal relationship that has traditionally informed the relations the West has had with peoples of colour. The high esteem the Bush administration, US Christian right and radical abolitionist feminists had of their identity as the agents of human progress and God's Providence, due to their ability to demarcate good from evil and to judge life accordingly, allowed the justification of the most inhumane interventions into the lives of third-world women and the poor.[19]

NOTES

The following abbreviations are used throughout the notes:

HFTKHZ *Honpōjin fuseigyō torishimari kankei hōki zassan*, 2 vols, Diplomatic Record Office, Gaikō shiryōkan, Tokyo, Code No. 4.2.2.34.

HFTKZ *Honpōjin fuseigyō torishimari kankei zakken*, 7 vols, Diplomatic Record Office, Gaikō shiryōkan, Tokyo, Code No. 4.2.2.27.

HKMKZ *Honpōjin kaigai e mikkō kankei zakken*, 7 vols, Diplomatic Record Office, Gaikō shiryōkan, Tokyo, Code No. 3.8.8.4.

Introduction

1. The term *karayuki-san* is derived from two words: *kara*, an archaic term referring generally to mainland China, and *yuki*, meaning 'going' or 'one who goes'. *San* is an honorific suffix attached to personal nouns or certain professions – such as *oishasan* (doctor) and *omawarisan* (policeman) – to show respect or courtesy.
2. Other terms used were *karayukidon* and *karakuniyuki*. See Morisaki K., *Karayuki-san* (Tokyo: Asahi shinbunsha, 1976), pp. 17–18.
3. Ibid.
4. This is the English title preferred and used by Mori Katsumi, who wrote the first academic work on this topic. See Mori K., *Jinshin baibai – kaigai dekasegi onna* (Tokyo: Shibundō, 1966).
5. The article was written by Morisaki Kazue, who participated in the project. Miyamoto T. et al. (eds), *Nihon zankoku monogatari*, 5 vols (Tokyo: Heibonsha, 1959–60), vol. 1: *Mazushiki hitobito no mure*, ed. Shimonaka K.
6. 'Asiatic' here refers to Indian and Chinese labourers. See L. Potts, *The World Labour Market: A History of Migration* (London: Zed Books, 1990), p. 70.
7. 'Nyonin no kuni – II', *Fukuoka nichinichi shinbun*, 8 September 1926; Nihon Kirisutokyō Fujin Kyōfūkai (ed.), *Kaigai shūgyōfu mondai: dai ichigō – Amakusa no bu* (Kyoto: Nihon Kirisutokyō Fujin Kyōfūkai, 1920), p. 46.
8. See Irie T., *Hōjin kaigai hatten shi*, 2 vols (Tokyo: Ida shoten, 1942), vol. 1, pp. 231–5, vol. 2, pp. 227–34, 445–53; Miyaoka K., *Shōfu-kaigai rurōki* (Tokyo: San-ichi shobō, 1968), pp. 15–16.
9. J. Halliday, *A Political History of Japanese Capitalism* (London: Monthly Review Press, 1975), p. 295.
10. Examples of the variety of critical responses to the state of Japanese–Asia relations can be found in the films of Imamura Shohei and Oshima Nagisa, the weekly magazine *Shūkan*

Ampo published by the anti-Vietnam organization *Beiheiren*, and in J. Halliday and G. McCormack, *Japanese Imperialism Today: Co-Prosperity and Greater East Asia* (Harmondsworth, Middlesex: Penguin Books, 1974).

11. The sex tours of Korea became known as *Kisaeng* tours. *Kisaeng* were government-licensed brothels in the Republic of Korea. The Japanese Woman's Christian Temperance Union vehemently opposed Japanese sex tours abroad on the grounds that they were blatantly sexist and imperialistic in nature. See S. Awanohara, 'Protesting the Sexual Imperialists', *Far Eastern Economic Review*, 14 March 1975, special tourist supplement, pp. 5–6.
12. Yamazaki T., *Sandakan hachiban shōkan – teihen joseishi joshō* (Tokyo: Chikuma shobō, 1972), pp. 21–2.
13. Morisaki appeals to the truthfulness of authorial biographical experiences. She grew up in pre-war Korea, when it was a colony of Japan; the mother of one of her friends was a *karayuki-san*. See *Karayuki-san*, ch. 1 and epilogue.
14. Yamazaki, *Sandakan hachiban shōkan*, p. 8.
15. Yamazaki T., *The Story of Yamada Waka: From Prostitute to Feminist Pioneer* (Tokyo: Kodansha International, 1985), p. 28.
16. L. M. Agustín, *Sex at the Margins: Migration, Labour Markets and the Rescue Industry* (London and New York: Zed Books, 2007).
17. For more on the Coalition see http://www.catwinternational.org/.
18. Commitment to radical equality means reading against the grain of a history that has assigned us our truths and our roles. To do such a history, the historian no longer places himself '"somewhat ahead and to the side" in order to express the stifled truth of the collectivity' but by becoming sensitized to the procedures and practices not of his own making that 'transform him into its object and instrument of power in the sphere of "knowledge", "truth", "consciousness", and "discourse"'. M. Foucault, 'Intellectuals and Power', in *Language, Counter-Memory, Practice*, ed. D. Bouchard, trans. D. Bouchard and S. Simon (Ithaca, NY: Cornell University Press, 1977), pp. 205–17, on p. 208.
19. M. Foucault, 'On Problematization', *History of the Present*, 4 (1988), pp. 16–17.
20. M. Foucault, 'Polemics, Politics, and Problematization: An Interview', in *The Foucault Reader*, ed. P. Rabinow (New York: Pantheon, 1988), pp. 381–90, on pp. 388–9; M. Foucault, 'Question of Method', in *The Foucault Effect: Studies in Governmentality*, ed. G. Burchell, C. Gordon and P. Miller (London: Harvester Wheatsheaf, 1991), pp. 73–86, on pp. 78–82; R. Castel, '"Problematization" as a Mode of Reading History', in J. Goldstein (ed.), *Foucault and the Writing of History* (Oxford: Basil Blackwell, 1994), pp. 237–52.
21. M. Foucault, '*Omnes et Singulatim*: Towards a Criticism of Political Reason', in *The Tanner Lectures on Human Values*, 2, ed. S. M. McMurrin (Cambridge: Cambridge University Press, 1981), pp. 225–54, on pp. 253–4.
22. K. Marx, *Capital*, trans. B. Fowkes, 3 vols (Harmondsworth, Middlesex: Penguin, 1976–81), vol. 1, p. 896.
23. I. Hacking, 'Making Up People', in T. C. Weller, M. Sosna and D. Wellbery (eds), *Reconstructing Individualism: Autonomy, Individuality, and the Self in Western Thought* (Stanford, CA: Stanford University Press, 1986), pp. 222–36.

1 Another Japan

1. Yamazaki, *Sandakan hachiban shōkan*, p. 22.
2. *Sandakan hachiban shōkan* has been translated into Korean, Thai, Chinese and English and has sold over one million copies. It was also made into a feature film, directed by Kumai Kei. The film was nominated for an Academy Award for best foreign film in 1975.

For research influenced by the claims made by Yamazaki in *Sandakan hachiban shōkan*, see J. F. Warren, *Ah Ku and Karayuki-san: Prostitution in Singapore 1870–1940* (Singapore: Oxford University Press, 1993), especially pp. 25–36; K. C. Taylor's introduction in her translation of *Sandakan Brothel No. 8: An Episode in the History of Lower-Class Japanese Women* (Armonk, NY: M. E. Sharpe, 1999), pp. xiii–xxxix; D. C. S. Sissons, 'Karayuki-san: Japanese Prostitutes in Australia, 1887–1916, I', *Historical Studies*, 17 (April 1977), pp. 323–41; D. C. S. Sissons, 'Karayuki-san: Japanese Prostitutes in Australia, 1887–1916, II', *Historical Studies*, 17 (October 1977), pp. 474–88; M. Hane, *Peasants, Rebels, and Outcastes: The Underside of Modern Japan* (New York: Pantheon, 1982), pp. 217–25.

3. Yamazaki, *Sandakan hachiban shōkan*, pp. 8, 13. Yamazaki's work echoes the views of Catherine Mackinnon and Andrea Dworkin.
4. See T. Moore and S. Richards, 'Sandakan No. 8 Brothel', *Bulletin of Concerned Asian Scholars*, 7 (October–December 1975), pp. 52–60, on p. 60.
5. Yamazaki, *Sandakan hachiban shōkan*, p. 13.
6. I am intellectually indebted to M. Gatens, *Imaginary Bodies: Ethics, Power, and Corporeality* (New York: Routledge, 1996), p. 83.
7. Yamazaki, *The Story of Yamada Waka*, p. 28.
8. N. X. M. Tadiar, *Things Fall Away: Philippine Historical Experience and the Makings of Globalization* (Durham, NC: Duke University Press, 2009), pp. 37, 54.
9. Examples of recent scholarship that use such analysis are M. Driscoll, *Absolute Erotic, Absolute Grotesque: The Living, Dead, and Undead in Japan's Imperialism, 1895–1945* (Durham, NC: Duke University Press, 2010), pp. 57–80; S. Hanochi, 'Constitutionalism in Modern Patriarchal State: Japan, the Sex Sector and Social Reproduction', in I. Bakker and S. Gill (eds), *Power, Production and Social Reproduction* (Basingstoke: Palgrave Macmillan, 2003), pp. 83–98, on pp. 87–9.
10. Tadiar, *Things Fall Away*, p. 55.
11. Ibid., p. 57.
12. According to the research carried out by Kurahashi Masanao, the 1910 Japanese Consular Population Survey of Expatriate Japanese by Occupation recorded 19,097 women working abroad in 'unsightly occupations'. Of these, 14,254, or 75 per cent, plied their trade on the informal frontier of the Japanese colonial empire; 7,928 (42 per cent) Japanese women engaged, directly or indirectly, in sex work in the Kwantung Leased Territory; and 4,275 women (22 per cent) worked in southern Manchuria. The consular survey indicated that 20 per cent, or 3,745 women, made a living in 'unsightly occupations' in South-East Asia. See Kurahashi M., *Kita no karayuki-san* (Tokyo: Kyōei shobō, 1989), p. 73.
13. Ōga Kamekichi to Komura Jutarō, Dispatch no. 85, 5 September 1902, 'Shingapōru kata ni honpō shūgyōfu torai no gi nitsuki gushin', *HFTKZ*, vol. 2.
14. S. Sugiyama, *Japan's Industrialisation in the World Economy, 1859–1899: Export Trade and Overseas Competition* (London: Athlone Press, 1988), pp. 30–3.
15. P. Levine, *Prostitution, Race and Politics: Policing Venereal Disease in the British Empire* (New York: Routledge, 2003), pp. 25, 28.
16. The examination of women working in Hong Kong house-brothels for venereal disease and the licensing of brothels by the register general was first introduced in 1857. A similar law was put into effect in Singapore in 1872. P. Levine, 'Modernity, Medicine, and Colonialism: The Contagious Disease Ordinances in Hong Kong and the Straits Settlements', *Positions*, 6:3 (1998), pp. 675–705, on pp. 676–8. In Singapore, compulsory

medical inspection for all licensed prostitutes was abolished along with Contagious Disease Ordinance in 1888.

17. The Contagious Disease Ordinance regulations prohibited men from running or owning a brothel.
18. Warren, *Ah Ku and Karayuki-san*, pp. 91–121; N. Miners, *Hong Kong under Imperial Rule, 1912–1941* (Hong Kong: Oxford University Press, 1987), pp. 191–206.
19. J. D. Kelly, 'Gaze and Grasp: Plantations, Desires, Indentured Indians, and Colonial Law in Fiji', in L. Manderson and M. Jolly (eds), *Sites of Desire, Economies of Pleasure: Sexualities in Asia and the Pacific* (Chicago, IL: University of Chicago Press, 1997), pp. 72–98, on pp. 74–5.
20. Mori, *Jinshin baibai*, ch. 2; Higaki M., 'Kinsei amakusa no jinkōmondai to sono haikei', *Kyūshū bunkashi kenkyūsho kiyō*, 2 (1951), pp. 1–12; Nakamura M., 'Tokugawaki amakusa ni okeru dekasegi no shosō', *Kumamoto daigaku kyōiku gakubu kiyō*, 5 (1957), pp. 38–49.
21. Nihon Kirisutokyō Fujin Kyōfūkai (ed.), *Kaigai shūgyōfu mondai*, p. 27.
22. Japan was connected to the network of submarine telegraphic communication in 1871, when a line was laid between Shanghai and Nagasaki by a Danish telegraphic company. See Tsunoyama S. (ed.), *Nihon ryōjihōkoku no kenkyū* (Tokyo: Dōbunkan shuppan, 1986), 'Introduction', p. 6.
23. Sugiyama, *Japan's Industrialisation*, pp. 172–3.
24. See Harry Parkes to Lord Stanley, 11 September 1867, 'Reports Received from Her Majesty's Secretaries of Embassy and Legation respecting Coal', in *British Parliamentary Papers*, 79 (1867–8), p. 1075; Sugiyama, *Japan's Industrialisation*, p. 171.
25. *Rising Sun and Nagasaki Press*, 6 July 1878.
26. Sugiyama, *Japan's Industrialisation*, p. 189.
27. Sumiya M., *Nihon sekitan sangyō bunseki* (Tokyo: Iwanami shoten, 1968), p. 245.
28. Ibid., pp. 226–7, 245–6.
29. Nagasaki ken henshū i-inkai (ed.), *Nagasaki ken keisatsushi*, 3 vols (Nagasaki: Nagasaki ken keisatsu honbu, 1976), vol. 1, p. 1361.
30. Miyagawa Kyūjirō to Aoki Shūzō, Confidential Dispatch no. 19, 27 November 1890, 'Nihon fujin mikkō bōatsu no ken nitsuki utagai', *HFTKZ*, vol. 1. Karatsu is located in Saga prefecture, Kyushu.
31. Edward Porter, Master of the British SS *Macduff*, before C. Q. S. Crawford, 10 February 1894. Porter also claimed innocence as he did not know that taking the women on board was a violation of any kind. *HKMKZ*, vol. 1.
32. In November 1885 there were 46 Japanese women licensed to work as prostitutes in the public brothels. Minami Sadatsuke to Inoue Kaoru, Confidential Dispatch no. 28, 17 September 1885, *HFTKHZ*, vol. 1; Minami Sadatsuke to Inoue Kaoru, Confidential Dispatch no. 31, 7 November 1885; J. H. Stewart Lochart to Fredrick Stewart, 2 November 1885, *HKMKZ*, vol. 1.
33. Lock hospitals were hospitals that specifically treated patients with venereal disease. Men were treated as outpatients. It was compulsory for licensed prostitutes who contracted venereal disease to enter the hospital as an inpatient. The women could only leave the hospital by official consent. The compulsory requirement and strict daily regime often made the women housed in the hospitals compare them to prisons. Levine, *Prostitution, Race and Politics*, pp. 70–2.
34. Under the family registration law (*kosekihō*) enacted in 1873 all details of family were registered under the name of the head of the household. The oldest male member of the family effectively became the sole legal entity of the household and exercised legal

control over all other members, especially women and children, who were not legally recognized persons and therefore had no access to rights.

35. Miyagawa Kyūjirō to Aoki Shūzō, Confidential Dispatch no. 19, 27 November 1890, 'Nihon fujin mikkō bōatsu no ken nitsuki utagai', *HFTKZ*, vol. 1.
36. Ibid.
37. Ibid. Singapore consul Nakagawa Tsunejirō made a similar statement to Aoki Shūzō, Confidential Dispatch no. 4, 25 March 1889, *HFTKZ*, vol. 1.
38. The Société des Messageries Maritimes began providing a regular service between Yokohama and Shanghai in 1865. Receipt no. 12758, 25 September 1892, Petition sent by Sasaki Shigetoshi along with the signatures of 36 Japanese labourers to the foreign minister of Japan, via the honorary Japanese consul in Australia, Alexander Marks. The petition is titled 'Shūgyōfu kuchiku no ken ni tsuki seigansho', *HFTKZ*, vol. 1.
39. Yamamuro G., *Shakai kakusei ron* (Tokyo: Chūō kōronsha, 1977), pp. 255–8; Yasui T., 'Kaigai ni oite nameta nigai keiken', *Kakusei*, 3:2 (1913), pp. 14–15.
40. Tanaka Tokichi to Hayashi Tadasu, Receipt no. 12571, 13 June 1906, 'Shūgyō tokō torishimari no ken', *HFTKZ*, vol. 2.
41. See Kawai Y., *Muraoka Iheiji jiden* (Tokyo: Nanpōsha, 1960). In a series of interviews compiled and edited by Kawai Yuzuru in 1960, Muraoka, a native of Shimabara, paints himself as being the boss of procurers (*zegen*) responsible for kidnapping young Japanese women and selling them to brothels abroad. Mark Driscoll relies heavily on Muraoka's biography to show the connection between Japanese imperial expansion and trafficking in women. See Driscoll, *Absolute Erotic, Absolute Grotesque.*
42. In 1901, Matsumoto Murakichi, a known procurer of women for overseas brothels, was reported roaming Fukuoka, Kurume and Nagasaki. See Fukano Kazumi to Katō Takaaki, Receipt no. 40008, 4 October 1901, *HFTKZ*, vol. 2.
43. Noma Seiichi to Komura Jutarō, Receipt no. 366, 2 July 1902, 'Mikkōsha torishimarikata rinshin no ken', *HFTKZ*, vol. 2.
44. Aburatani I., *Keiteki – kōkoku no jiki ni saishi tsutsushinde waga dōhō ni keikokusu* (Okayama: Okayamakoji-in kappan-bu, 1895), pp. 7–8; Mori, *Jinshin baibai*, pp. 95–6.
45. *Ryōriten* was the term commonly used to refer to lower-class, unlicensed brothels in the Japanese colonies.
46. In 1900 a day labourer earned 37 *sen* a day. There were 100 *sen* in ¥1. *Nihon chōki tōkei sōran*, ed. Nihon Tōkei Kyōkai, 5 vols (Tokyo: Nihon Tōkei Kyōkai, 1987–8), vol. 4, p. 230.
47. *Kyushu nichinichi shinbun*, 10 August 1909.
48. Imai Shinoburō to Uchida Yasunori, 29 February 1912, no. 75, Receipt no. 184, 'Honkon ni okeru honpō shūgyōfujin no jōtai hōkoku no ken'. The actual report is found in an attached letter entitled 'Honkon ni okeru honpō shūgyōfu no jōtai'. *Kaigai ni okeru honpō shūgyōfu no insū oyobi sono jōkyō nado nen nikai hōkoku kata kuntatsu ikken*, Diplomatic Record Office, Gaikō shiryōkan, Tokyo, Code No. 4.2.2.99.
49. Ibid.
50. Nihon Kirisutokyō Fujin Kyōfūkai (ed.), *Kaigai shūgyōfu mondai*, p. 39.
51. Imai to Uchida, 29 February 1912, no. 75, Receipt no. 184.
52. 'Fujin yūkai shūdan no ichirei', *Fukuoka nichinichi shinbun*, 29 October 1905.
53. (Copy) 21 March 1888, Register General Office, Hong Kong, *HKMKZ*, vol. 1.
54. Hattori Ichizō to Aoki Shūzō, Confidential Receipt no. 214, 6 August 1900, *HFTKZ*, vol. 1.
55. Inoue Kizaburō to Aoki Shūzō, Receipt no. 2572, 1 September 1900, *HFTKZ*, vol. 1.

56. Ibid. The Singapore-based Japanese-language weekly *Nanyō oyobi nihonjin* recounted, in a retrospective piece on the Japanese community in the area, that, on average, brothel owners in Hong Kong paid the procurers around $250 to obtain a newly arrived Japanese woman. The cost in Singapore was higher, with the asking price between $300 and $350. The newspaper goes on to report that after deducting all expenses, the procurer made a profit of around $200 per woman. Yashikoyama M., 'Kagai no omoide – [part] 1', *Nanyō oyobi nihonjin*, 1 January 1928, p. 46.
57. Ibid.
58. *Nihon chōki tōkei sōran*, vol. 4, p. 230.
59. Such was the case of a patrolman, Seki, from Nagasaki prefecture, who in January 1901 brought seventeen women to Hong Kong to sell into Japanese brothels. Katō Motoshirō to Katō Takaaki, Receipt no. 1561, 1 February 1901, *HFTKZ*, vol. 2.
60. Miyagawa Kyūjirō to Hayashi Tadasu, Confidential Dispatch no. 7, 28 December 1892, 'Honkon ryojin yado eigyō Nishiyama Yūzō shūgyōfu shūsen no gi torishirabe wo yōsuru ken ni tsuki tōshin', *HFTKZ*, vol. 1.
61. In 1890 the rate of a loan was at around 25 per cent per month interest, which was borrowed by the procurer but made liable to the women he or she brought to Hong Kong. Saitō Miki to Aoki Shūzō, Confidential Dispatch no. 9, 20 February 1890, *HKMKZ*, vol. 1; Miyagawa Kyūjirō to Hayashi Tadasu, Confidential Dispatch no. 7, 28 December 1892, 'Honkon ryojin yado eigyō Nishiyama Yuzō shūgyōfu shūsen no gi torishirabe wo yōsuru ken ni tsuki', *HFTKZ*, vol. 1.
62. H. Satō to A. Marks, 10 August 1888, *HKMKZ*, vol. 1.
63. Miyagawa Kyūjirō to Hayashi Tadasu, 28 December 1892. Japanese procurers used Singapore as a clearing house from which to sell women to prospective buyers in the Malay Peninsula and Dutch East Indies. Ōga Kamekichi to Komura Jutarō, Dispatch no. 85, 5 September 1902, 'Singapōru kata ni honpō shūgyōfu torai no gi ni tsuki gushin', *HFTKZ*, vol. 2.
64. T. C. Smith, *Native Sources of Japanese Industrialization, 1750–1920* (Berkeley and Los Angeles, CA: University of California Press, 1988), pp. 206, 215–16, 218.
65. I would like to express my gratitude to the Miyazaki family for access and permission to use the interview.
66. Malay Street was also the heart of the Japanese community in Singapore until the start of the First World War.
67. My informant was convinced that K-san had engaged in sex work while abroad. Personally, I thought my informant might be jumping to preconceived conclusions. My aim in interviewing K-san was to try to gain insights into the motivations and logic of women undertaking migration abroad. The subject of sex work was not brought up.
68. C. Henriot, '"Little Japan" in Shanghai: An Insulated Community, 1875–1945', in R. Bickers and C, Henriot (eds), *New Frontiers: Imperialism's New Communities in East Asia, 1842–1953* (Manchester: Manchester University Press, 2000), pp. 146–69, on pp. 151–7.
69. Miyamoto T., *Wasurerareta Nihonjin* (Tokyo: Iwanami bunko, 1987), pp. 211, 44–58, 305–6.
70. The number of people leaving the island to find work in other parts of Japan was 600. Inokawa S., 'Shimabara amakusa kenkyū', *Fujin shinpō*, October 1919, pp. 12–13; N. O. K., 'Shimabara amakusa shisatsu', *Fujin shinpō*, September 1919, p. 12.
71. Inokawa, 'Shimabara amakusa kenkyu', pp. 12–13.

72. Nihon Kirisutokyō Fujin Kyōfūkai (ed.), *Kaigai shūgyōfu mondai*, pp. 18, 39, 41. See also 'Nanyō no kusawake – Sandakan no Okunibaasan', *Nanyō nichinichi shinbun*, 13 August 1915.
73. Inokawa, 'Shimabara amakusa kenkyū', p. 13.
74. Cited from Kitano N., *Amakusa kaigai hattenshi* (Fukuoka: Ashishobō, 1985), p. 146.
75. 'Nyonin no kuni-III', *Fukuoka nichinichi shinbun*, 9 September 1926; Inokawa, 'Shimabara amakusa kenkyū', p. 13.
76. Sasaki Shigetoshi to Alexander Marks, 25 August 1892, 'Shūgyōfujo kuchiku no ken ni tsuki seigansho', *HFTKZ*, vol. 1.
77. Ibid.
78. Inokawa, 'Shimabara amakusa kenkyū', p. 14.
79. I am indebted to the work of H. D. Harootunian for these insights. See *Things Seen and Unseen: Discourse and Ideology in Tokugawa Nativism* (Chicago, IL: University of Chicago Press, 1988), pp. 242–72.
80. Smith, *Native Sources of Japanese Industrialization*, pp. 205–6.
81. Inokawa, 'Shimabara amakusa kenkyū', p. 13.
82. Nihon Kirisutokyō Fujin Kyōfūkai (ed.), *Kaigai shūgyōfu mondai*, pp. 18, 39, 41. This practice was not peculiar to Amakusa. Wiswell noted the presence of several married women who had children from different men living in Suye mura. R. Smith and E. L. Wiswell, *The Women of Suye Mura* (Chicago, IL: University of Chicago Press, 1982), pp. 152–3.
83. Nihon Kirisutokyō Fujin Kyōfūkai (ed.), *Kaigai shūgyōfu mondai*, p. 41. The women's names and amounts donated were written on pieces of paper called *kifukin keiji* (literally, donation notice). A notable example is the Daishidō temple in the town of Shimabara. Inside the temple's enclosure is a tower called tenshiyō, which was built exclusively from donations sent by karayuki-san. Surrounding this tower is a stone fence, with the name and amount donated by each woman. For the history of how the temple was built, see Kurahashi M., *Shimabara no karayuki-san: Kiso Hirota Gonshō to Daishidō* (Tokyo: Kyōei shobō, 1993).

2 Creating the Archive

1. Hayakawa N., *Kindai tennō kokka to jendā: seiritsuki no hitotsu no rojikku* (Tokyo: Aoki shoten, 1998), p. 195.
2. The revered Confucian scholar Ogyū Sorai (1666–1728) considered women of the pleasure quarters (*yūjo*) as a separate species of human being (*sujō*) and was against the practice of common people (*heijin*) selling their daughters to the houses of prostitution in Edo. He did acknowledge, however, that it was not unthinkable for the lowly classes (*gesen no mono*) to sell their daughters into prostitution in times of need. Here, 'lowly people' refers to peasants who owned little or no land and could not subsist by farming alone. See O. G. Lindin, *Ogyū Sorai's Discourse on Government (Seidan): An Annotated Translation* (Wiesbaden: Harrassowitz Verlag, 1999), pp. 106–7. On the economic decline and accompanying rural distress during the Tokugawa period, see S. Vlastos, *Peasant Protests and Uprisings in Tokugawa Japan* (Berkeley, CA: University of California Press, 1990).
3. In Confucian thought, virtues are the result of developing what is already in the heart, the sense of compassion, of shame, of respect, and of right and wrong. In developing and cultivating these senses, compassion becomes the virtue of humanness, the feeling of

shame becomes the virtue of righteousness, respect becomes the virtue of propriety, and the sense of right and wrong transforms into the virtue of wisdom. Yamamoto S., *Nihon kōshōshi* (Tokyo: Chūō hōki shuppan kabushiki gaisha, 1983), p. 38.

4. *Dajōkan fukoku* (Council of State Proclamation) no. 295, 2 October 1872, reproduced in *Nihon fujin mondai shiryō shūsei*, ed. Ichikawa F. et al., 10 vols (Tokyo: Domesu shuppan, 1980), vol. 1, p. 195.
5. On 2 October 1900, the home ministry implemented the Tokyo model for regulating licensed prostitution nationally under the ordinance for the Regulation for the Control of Prostitutes. There was no uniform, national ordinance for the regulation of licensed brothels, however. The administration of brothels remained a matter of local government until the enactment of the Anti-Prostitution Law in 1956.
6. *Daily News* (London), 2 July 1896, cited in S. Garon, *Moulding Japanese Minds: The State in Everyday Life* (Princeton, NJ: Princeton University Press, 1997), p. 102. Itō Hirobumi was Japan's first prime minister from December 1895 until April 1898 and architect of the Meiji Constitution. During his time as prime minister, Japanese Christians and abolitionists of licensed prostitution complained Itō was not fit for office as he was married to a former *geisha*. There is no evidence to suggest that the current importance placed in the United States concerning the moral righteousness of its leaders as a prerequisite for office is historically shaped by the actions of Japanese Christians 110 years ago.
7. Garon, *Moulding Japanese Minds*, pp. 98–104, and ch. 4.
8. Copies of travel documents issued are housed at the Nagasaki Prefectural Library. Travel documents were issued by prefectural authorities at ports where foreign ships were allowed to berth. Travel documents were issued to offer protection to Japanese subjects travelling overseas rather than regulating the composition of Japanese overseas migration. In 1883 the English-language *Rising Sun and Nagasaki Press* reported that for three preceding months 92 people were issued with travel documents by the prefectural government, of which 33 were women.
9. C. Howe, *The Origins of Japanese Trade Supremacy: Development and Technology in Asia from 1540 to the Pacific War* (Chicago, IL: University of Chicago Press, 1996), pp. 100–1. For a micro view of the effects of inflation and the dislocation of the feudal economy in rural Japan, see Vlastos, *Peasant Protests and Uprisings in Tokugawa Japan*, chs 6, 7.
10. The political showdown was with Saigō Takamori. In 1873, Saigō advocated a military expedition to Korea in the name of national security due to the rejection by Korean authorities of Japanese overtures to opening diplomatic ties and their refusal to acknowledge the legitimacy of the Meiji Emperor as the head of the Japanese state.
11. Shimizu H., 'Kindai nihon no kaigai tsūshō jōhō senryaku to tōnan ajia', in Suehiro A. (ed.), *Chiiki kenkyū to shite no Ajia*, Iwanami kōza. 'Teikoku Nihon' no gakuchi, 8 vols (Tokyo: Iwanami shoten, 2006), vol. 6, pp. 205–37, on p. 209; K. Sugihara, 'The Development of an Informational Infrastructure in Meiji Japan', in L. Bud-Frierman (ed.), *Information Acumen: The Understanding and Use of Knowledge in Modern Business* (London; New York, Routledge, 1994), pp. 75–97, on p. 85.
12. Ian Hacking touches on this process in his seminal essay 'Making Up People' when he describes how 'numerous kinds of human beings and human acts come into being hand in hand with our own invention of the categories labelling them'. Hacking points to the fact that each category is a historical construct, and that the objects that these categories come to name are a vector of power from above, from a community of government 'experts' who create a reality that enables experts and government agencies to target the conduct of others. Hacking, 'Making Up People', pp. 228, 236.

13. Takashima M., 'Ryōjihōkoku seido no hatten to 'ryōjihōkoku' no kankō – 'tsūshō ihen' kara 'tsūshō isan',' in Tsunoyama (ed.), *Nihon ryōjihōkoku no kenkyū*, pp. 71–117, on p. 74.
14. Fukutake T., *Japanese Rural Society*, trans. R. P. Dore (London: Oxford University Press, 1967), p. 10.
15. Ike N., 'Taxation and Land Ownership in the Westernization of Japan', *Journal of Economic History*, 7:2 (November 1947), pp. 160–82, on p. 175.
16. The land tax accounted for over half of the all government revenues until 1890. During this period, taxation of the agricultural sector was double other sectors. H. Rosovsky, *Capital Formation in Japan, 1868–1940* (Glencoe: Free Press, 1961), p. 85.
17. J. Dresner, 'Emigration and Local Development in Meiji Era Yamaguchi' (PhD dissertation, Harvard University, 2001), p. 79.
18. Fujita T., *Kaigai zaikin shihanseiki no kaiko* (Tokyo: Kyōbunkan, 1931), pp. 1–2.
19. Andō was Japanese consul in Shanghai from the summer of 1884 until he took up his post in Honolulu in February 1886. During his time in Shanghai, Andō, with the aid of the manager of the Mitsubishi Steam Navigation Company, Shanghai office, extradited around 200 Japanese women to Japan for unseemly public conduct. Andō Tarō to Yoshida Kyōnari, Dispatch no. 89, 15 August 1885, *HFTKHZ*, vol. 1; *Nihon fujin mondai shiryō shūsei*, vol. 10, p. 27.
20. Andō Tarō to Aoki Shūzō, 12 March 1886, *HFTKZ*, vol. 1.
21. Andō Tarō to Yoshida Kyōnari, Dispatch no. 89, 15 August 1885, *HFTKHZ*, vol. 1.
22. Andō Tarō to Aoki Shūzō, 12 March 1886, *HFTKZ*, vol. 1. Article 9 of the Convention between the Empire of Japan and the Kingdom of Hawaiian Islands reads: 'The well-being, happiness, and prosperity of the Japanese subjects emigrating to Hawaii being equally objects of solicitude to both the Contracting parties, His Imperial Majesty's Government consents that His Hawaiian Majesty's Government shall have the right to send back to Japan all evil disposed, vicious, or vagrant Japanese subjects in Hawaii, who may create trouble or disturbance, or encourage dissipation of any kind among the emigrants, or may become a charge upon the State.' Translation taken from H. Conroy, *The Japanese Frontier in Hawaii, 1868–1898* (Berkeley, CA: University of California Press, 1953), p. 150.
23. In fact, by 1888 the number of women accompanying their husbands to work the sugar plantations in Hawaii had declined considerably. The reason was that it was mutually conducive to both the Japanese government and the Hawaiian plantation owners. Labour discipline on the plantation was easier for the Japanese supervisors without the presence of large numbers of women. The sugar plantation owners were reluctant to allow women to accompany their husbands because it was uneconomical. The women were limited to domestic chores and light work on the plantations. Women did not harvest the sugar cane as it was thought they lacked the necessary physical strength. Moreover, it was also more expensive to house labourers accompanied by their wives, as each couple required individual living quarters. Labourers unaccompanied by any dependants, on the other hand, could be housed together in large dormitories that required less outlay to build.
24. Andō Tarō to Ōkuma Shigenobu, 28 June 1887, 'Waga dekasegibito fujin torishimarimuki nitsuki jōshin', *HFTKZ*, vol. 1.
25. Alexander Marks (1838–1919) established a business as a merchant in partnership with his brother in Hong Kong and Yokohama in 1858. He resided in Yokohama until 1872, when he returned to Melbourne. He was appointed honorary Japanese consul at the opening of the Melbourne consul in 1880.
26. A. Marks to Aoki Shūzō, 13 December 1887, *HFTKZ*, vol. 1.
27. A. Marks to Hayashi Tadasu, 11 October 1891, *HFTKZ*, vol. 1.

28. Chinda Sutemi to Aoki Shūzō, Confidential dispatch no 5, 10 March 1891, 'Sōkō ni okeru shūgyōsha ni kansuru hōkoku no ken', in Gaimushō (ed.), *Nihon gaikō bunsho*, 73 vols (Tokyo: Nihon kokusai rengō kyōkai, 1953), vol. 24, p. 461.
29. Chinda Sutemi to Aoki Shūzō, Confidential dispatch no. 6, 25 April 1891, 'Gasshūkoku yoyaku rōdōsha ijū kinshi jōrei: sen happyaku kyūjūichi nen sangatsu mikka gasshūkoku kaitei gaikokujin ijū jōrei', in ibid. vol. 24, p. 464.
30. Aoki Shūzō to Yamagata Aritomo, Dispatch no. 434, 15 July 1890, *HFTKHZ*, vol. 1.
31. Foreign ministry internal memo, 'Bai-in fujo no kaigai tokō ni kansuru hōritsu no seitei wo yōsuru riyū', 20 February 1891, *HFTKHZ*, vol. 1.
32. Saitō Miki to Aoki Shūzō, 20 February 1890, *HFTKHZ*, vol. 1.
33. Taguchi Ukichi (1855–1905), established the influential journal *Keizai Zasshi*. He was one of the most vocal Meiji thinkers who asserted that the regions south of mainland China were a separate and independent area, and that Japan was a maritime power that should advance its interests into the Pacific Rim region. See M. Peattie, *Nan'yō: The Rise and Fall of the Japanese in Micronesia, 1885–1945* (Honolulu, HI: University of Hawaii Press, 1988), pp. 15–20.
34. Saitō Miki to Hayashi Tadasu, Receipt no. 926, 28 September 1892, 'Penan ni okeru yūfu nihonfu shōgimenkyo shutsugan ni tsuki setsyu irai no ken', *HFTKZ*, vol. 1.
35. The British colonial government established the Chinese protectorate in 1877. The duties of the protectorate were to safeguard the Chinese communities and incoming coolie migrant labourers from extortion by Chinese secret societies, prevent the illegal traffic in Chinese women and girls sold to brothel owners in Singapore, and prevent the spread of venereal disease.
36. Saitō Miki to Protector of Chinese, 9 June 1893, *HFTKZ*, vol. 1.
37. Saitō Miki to Protector of Chinese, 12 June 1894, *HKMKZ*, vol. 1.
38. Undated memo by Asada Tokusoku in response to Shinagawa Tadamichi to Ueno Kakenori, Dispatch no. 19, 22 March 1882, *HFTKHZ*, vol. 1.
39. Foreign Minister Inoue Kaoru clearly states the position of the Japanese government regarding Japanese destitute overseas in his missive to J. Kennedy, British consul in Tokyo, 25 June 1880, Foreign Office: Embassy and Consulates, Japan: General Correspondence, 1859–1957, National Archives, Kew Gardens, FO/262/527.
40. Aoki Shūzō to Yamagata Aritomo, Dispatch no. 23, 1 December 1891, *HFTKHZ*, vol. 1.
41. Aoki Shūzō to Yamagata Aritomo, Dispatch no. 434, 15 July 1890, 'Bai-in no baikai oyobi bai-in onna no kaigai tokō torishimari ni kansuru hōritsu seitei no gi seigi', *HFTKHZ*, vol. 1.
42. Ibid. A translation of the text of the bill before it was submitted to the House of Peers for discussion appeared in the *Japan Weekly Mail*, 7 March 1891.
43. The article 'Eight Persons Suffocated on a Steamer; Horrible Fate of Decoyed Girls' was sent by acting Japanese Consul Saitō Miki to the foreign ministry as part of his report. Found in *HKMKZ*, vol. 1.
44. Session 11, 3 March 1891, reproduced in Sangi-in jimukyoku (ed.), *Kizoku-in himitsukai giji sokkiroku shū* (Tokyo: San-yūkai, 1995), p. 4.
45. Like all generalizations, the above statement needs to be followed with a disclaimer. Between the mid-1880s and mid-1900s the major type of Japanese migration abroad was in the form of male labourers indentured to three-year contracts, which guaranteed their return to Japan. The destination of the majority of Japanese migrants was Hawaii and the North American west coast. From the mid-1910s, however, the destinations for most Japanese migrant labourers became South America and the colonies of the Japanese

empire due to restrictions imposed on Japanese migration by Australia, the United States and Canada. Japanese migration to South America was novel in another way. Many of the migrants made the journey with their families with the intention of settling permanently abroad. From the early 1920s onward, the Japanese government particularly encouraged permanent settlement. Migration was put forward as a solution to the array of 'social problems' (*shakai mondai*) discovered by Japanese bureaucrats – such as chronic rural poverty, rural-urban migration, substandard housing and the rise of urban slums culminating in the deterioration of the collective health of Japanese cities. In addition, as Japan's colonial adventures gathered momentum, successive Japanese governments encouraged entire Japanese families to settle permanently in the colonies of the Japanese empire – Taiwan, Korea, South Pacific Mandate (*Nanyō guntō*) and, after 1931, Manchuria.

46. Testimony to the foreign ministry's concern about Japanese women working in pitiable occupations abroad appears in the seven files labelled 'Miscellaneous items concerning the regulation of improper vocations by Japanese', comprising *HFTKZ*, compiled over a fifty-year period from the early 1880s to the 1930s, and housed in the diplomatic record office.
47. Historically, Ozaki Miyoshi is seen as a progressive element within a very conservative Meiji administration. His son Ozaki Yukio (pen name Gakudō) was a member of the House of Representatives twenty-five times. Yukio achieved the unofficial title of the 'guardian of the constitution' for his uncompromising antimilitarist stance that culminated in his expulsion from the Imperial Diet in 1942 by the Tojo government.
48. 'Dai ikkai teikoku gikai: Gaikoku ni okeru nippon fujo hogo hōan', in Sangi-in jimukyoku (ed.), *Kizoku-in himitsukai giji sokkiroku shū*, pp. 4–5.
49. Ibid., p. 5.
50. No. 11, 3 March 1891, in Sangi-in jimukyoku (ed.), *Kizoku-in himitsukai giji sokkiroku shū*, p. 4.
51. 'Dai ikkai teikoku gikai', in Sangi-in jimukyoku (ed.), *Kizoku-in himitsukai giji sokkiroku shū*, p. 4.
52. Ibid., p. 6.
53. Konoe Atsumaro (1863–1904) was one of the most prominent voices during the Meiji period advocating the Japanese government to forge closer ties with China and Korea to curtail the encroachment of foreign powers in the Far East. He is also the father of Konoe Fumimaro, who, paradoxically, was prime minister in June 1937 when Japan declared full-scale war against China.
54. 'Dai ikkai teikoku gikai', in Sangi-in jimukyoku (ed.), *Kizoku-in himitsukai giji sokkiroku shū*, pp. 6, 10
55. The *Genrōin* was a quasi-legislative body established in April 1875 as part of an administrative reform by the Meiji oligarchy to address calls by the advocates of the Freedom and People's Rights movements for a national assembly with increased representative democracy. The members of the *Genrōin* were drawn from among the peerage, high-ranking bureaucrats and legal scholars. The role of the *Genrōin* was to review legislation passed down by the cabinet; it had no power to propose new bills. The *Genrōin* was disbanded in October 1890 with the formation of the Imperial Diet.
56. 'Dai ikkai teikoku gikai', in Sangi-in jimukyoku (ed.), *Kizoku-in himitsukai giji sokkiroku shū*, pp. 9–10.
57. In 1873, brothels in Tokyo (and other major cities in Japan) were operating a 'room rental' (*kashizashiki*) licensing system approved by the government. Under this system, the prostitute (*shōgi*) was a licensed 'independent contractor' and the brothel a

'room-letting service'. The agreement between the woman and the brothel owner was reformulated as a loan contract between equitable, interested parties. The advancement of a loan by a brothel owner was to be repaid by either the woman herself or her guarantor, which in most cases was her immediate family. The areas where women could 'rent a room' to ply their trade were limited to the sections of Tokyo that had long been designated as spaces where prostitution was officially or tacitly accepted: Yoshiwara, Shinagawa, Shinjuku, Itabashi and Senju. See T. Kurimoto to B. Johnson, 'Observation of the Imperial Government of Japan on the Report concerning Japan and the League of Nations Commission of Enquiry into the Traffic in Women and Children in the East', 15 November 1932, and S. Sawada to E. Ekstrand, League of Nations Commission of Enquiry into the Traffic in Women and Children in the East, League of Nations Archive, Geneva, 11B/39491/38154; Morizaki K., 'Sekushuariti no rekishi', in Kono N. and Tsurumi K. (eds), *Onna to otoko no jikū: nihon joseishi saikō, Semegiau onna to otoko: kindai* (Tokyo: Fujiwara-shoten, 1995), pp. 153–82, on p. 157; Kim I., *Nihon josei aishi – yūjo, jorō, karayuki, ianfu no keifu* (Tokyo: Gendai shuppankai, 1960), pp. 104–5; Takemura T., *Haishō undō: kuruwa no josei wa dō kaihōsareta ka* (Tokyo: Chūkō shinsho, 1982), pp. 6–7; and J. M. Ramseyer, 'Indentured Prostitution in Imperial Japan: Credible Commitments in the Commercial Sex Industry', *Journal of Law, Economics, and Organisation*, 7 (1991), pp. 89–116, on pp. 97–100.

58. 'Dai ikkai teikoku gikai', in Sangi-in jimukyoku (ed.), *Kizoku-in himitsukai giji sokkiroku shū*, p. 13.
59. Enomoto Takeaki to Yamagata Aritomo, Dispatch no. 712, 18 September 1891, 'Honnen teikoku gikai e teishutsu subeki gaimushō shokan hōritsuan teishutsu miai no ken tsūchi', *HFTKHZ*, vol. 1.
60. Undated memo, Head of the Cabinet Legislative Bureau to Cabinet, *HFTKHZ*, vol. 1. A copy of the same memo can be found in Aoki Shūzō to Yamagata Aritomo, Dispatch no. 57, 31 January 1891, *HFTKHZ*, vol. 1. Inoue Kowashi (1844–1895) was one of the most important contributors in the drafting of the Meiji Constitution.
61. Enomoto T. to Yamagata A., Dispatch no. 712, 18 September 1891, *HFTKHZ*, vol. 1.
62. Takamura S., 'Enomoto Takeaki no shokumin kōsō to nanyō guntō baishū kengi', *Kokushigaku*, 167 (1999), pp. 77–110, on p. 80.
63. Ibid., pp. 90–1. Quinine was the first effective treatment for malaria.
64. Ibid., pp. 90–2.
65. Ibid., pp. 87–92.
66. Tsunoyama Y., *Enomoto Takeaki to Mekishiko shokumin ijū* (Tokyo: Dōbunkan shuppan, 1986), p. 41. See also H. D. Harootunian, 'The Economic Rehabilitation of the Samurai in the Early Meiji Period', *Journal of Asian Studies*, 19:4 (August 1960), pp. 433–44.
67. The embarrassment came from the fact that Tsuda was one of several Shiga prefecture police officers chosen to escort and protect Nicholas.
68. Kusaka Yoshio to Asada Tokunori, 13 March, 1891, *HFTKZ*, vol. 1.
69. The Japanese government was very keen to ensure that Japanese subjects be exempted from the 1882 Chinese Exclusion Act because it would kill Japanese labour migration to the US. Aoki S. to Yamagata A., Dispatch no. 434, 15 July 1890, *HFTKHZ* vol. 1; 'Dai ikkai teikoku gikai', in Sangi-in jimukyoku (ed.), *Kizoku-in himitsukai giji sokkiroku shū*, p. 6.
70. See 'Viscount Enomoto and Colonization', *Japan Weekly Mail*, 15 August 1890, which asserts that Enomoto's plans to send large numbers of Japanese to settle in Mexico would surely be sabotaged by the United States government in its inception.

71. 'Gaimushō no kaikakuan', *Jiji shimpō*, 10 July 1891.
72. Y. Kimura, *Issei: Japanese Immigrants in Hawaii* (Honolulu, HI: University of Hawaii Press, 1988), p. 133.
73. 'Viscount Enomoto and Colonization'.
74. During the 1870s and 1880s this same landed social strata participated in the Freedom and People's Right Movement (*jiyū minken undo*), which called for the establishment of representative institutions, reduction in centralized tax and treaty revision for Japanese industries and commerce to achieve economic and political equity with foreign merchants trading in Japan.
75. 'Iminka secchi iken', *Yūbin hōchi*, 5 August 1891. See also 'Iminka secchi noriyū', *Jiji shimpō*, 6 August 1891.
76. Enomoto is referring to the US Immigration Act (1891).
77. 'Iminka secchi iken'.
78. Tsunoyama, *Enomoto Takeaki to Mekishiko shokumin ijū*, p. 41.
79. Enomoto T. to Yamagata A., Dispatch no. 712, 18 September 1891, *HFTKHZ*, vol. 1.
80. The suggested clause read: 'Persons enticing or assisting women to travel abroad for the purpose of prostitution were liable to imprisonment for a period no less than six months and up to three years in addition to a fine of no less than ¥10 and no more than ¥100. [Persons punished under the provision of this law were] also to be put under police supervision for a period no less than six months no more than two years.' Enomoto Takeaki to Tanaka Fujimaro, Dispatch no. 588, 3 August 1891, *HFTKHZ*, vol. 1.
81. Tanaka Fujimaro to Enomoto Takeaki, Confidential Receipt no. 641, 13 August 1891, *HFTKHZ*, vol. 1.
82. Enomoto Takeaki to consuls in Korea, China, Hong Kong, Singapore and San Francisco, Confidential Dispatch no. 208, 23 March 1892, 'Kaigai tokō bai-in fujo torishimari kata ni kansuru kuntatsu', *HFTKHZ*, vol. 1.
83. Foreign ministry memo circulated to foreign minister, vice-foreign minister, Commerce and Trade bureau, Police Affairs bureau, Emigration department, Research bureau, Political Affairs bureau and Home Minster, Dispatch no. 67, 2 February 1893, *HFTKHZ*, vol. 1.
84. *Gaimushō kunrei* no. 1, 3 February 1893, 'Fujo kaigai tokō ni kansuru torishimari kata'. The English title for the directive was 'Regulation Regarding Passage Abroad of Women: For the Suppression of Passage Abroad of Women under Temptation'. The directive read as follows: 'It is noticed of late that wicked men go around the country enticing with tempting promises women ignorant of conditions in foreign countries and inducing them to take passage abroad by various means. After sending the women abroad, instead of finding for them legitimate employment, these men coerce them with threats to take up immoral occupations or deliver them to the hands of other people in consideration of monetary recompenses. As a consequence, women suffering from indescribable difficulties in foreign countries are on the increase. Efforts are being put forth by our diplomatic representatives for the rescue of such unfortunate women, but it is impossible to find out whereabouts of many of them, as they live in remote places. There are also many [women] in difficulties that are unable to appeal to the authorities for help on account of various obstacles placed in their way. Accordingly, steps shall be taken to suppress passage of women going abroad under the temptation and also to restrain women from thoughtlessly attempting passage to foreign countries.'
85. Ibid., pp. 23–7.
86. Komura Jutarō to Hong Kong, Singapore, San Francisco, Vancouver, Tacoma consuls and Vladivostock trade secretariat, March 1897, 'Honpō shūgyōfu no shutsunyū oyobi jōkyō

nado hōkoku kata tsūtatsu'. Extra instructions were sent to consul general of Hawaii, Minister Resident in Siam and the consuls of Townsville, Sydney and Manila. See *Kaigai ni okeru honpō shūgyōfu no insū oyobi nado nen nikai hōkoku kata kuntatsu ikken.*

87. Shimizu H., 'Gaimushō 'kaigai zairyū honpōjin shokugyōbestsu jinkō chōsa ikken' no shiryō teki seikaku', *Ajia keizai*, 26:3 (1985), pp. 70–92.
88. A sample of articles reporting on the number of Japanese women abroad making a living as prostitutes during the last two decades of the nineteenth century can be found in Nishida M., 'Kaigai ni okeru nihon no baishōfu nitsuite: meiji nijūnendai no jōtai', *Nihon rekishi*, 62 (February 1954), pp. 47–59. The English-language press also participated in circulating information about Japanese prostitution abroad to its reading public. See 'Japanese Paphians', *Japan Echo*, 15 November 1890; 'Japanese Women Abroad', *Japan Weekly Mail*, 7 March and 6 June 1891, and 30 May 1896. Perhaps the most widely circulated information concerning Japanese prostitution abroad was published by Yamamuro Gunpei, the leader of the Japanese Salvation Army, in his *Shakai kakusei ron*, first published in October 1914.
89. K. Karatani, *Origins of Modern Japanese Literature* (Durham, NC: Duke University Press, 1993), pp. 83–96.

3 Sexuality and Class

1. I. Tyrrell, 'Women and Temperance in International Perspective: The World's WCTU, 1880–1920s', in S. Barrows and R. Room (eds), *Drinking: Behavior and Belief in Modern History* (Berkeley, CA: University of California Press, 1991), pp. 217–42.
2. M. Ogawa, 'American Women's Destiny, Asian Women's Dignity: Trans-Pacific Activism of the Woman's Christian Temperance Union, 1886–1945' (PhD dissertation, University of Hawaii, 2004), p. 44.
3. S. Garon, 'The World's Oldest Debate? Prostitution and the State in Imperial Japan, 1900–1945', *American Historical Review*, 98:3 (June 1993), pp. 710–32; Garon, *Moulding Japanese Minds*, pp. 88–114; E. Dorn, 'Crusading against Prostitution: The Woman's Christian Temperance Union in Meiji Japan', *Japanese Religions*, 29:1–2 (January 2004), pp. 29–43; Fujime Y., *Sei no rekishigaku: kōshō seido, dataizai taisei kara baishun bōshihō, yūsei hogohō taisei e* (Tokyo: Fuji shuppan, 1997), pp. 87–116.
4. Fujime, *Sei no rekishigaku*, pp. 103–10.
5. R. Yasutake, *Transnational Women's Activism: The United States, Japan, and Japanese Immigrant Communities in California, 1859–1920* (New York: New York University Press, 2004); Ogawa, 'American Women's Destiny'.
6. For example, Yasutake writes: 'Thus, under the influence of Christian Missionary teachers, some Japanese women learned how to be "strong willed" in their actions and perhaps even rebel against the orders of their parents, husbands, and teachers, as well as the social constraints of Japanese womanhood'. Yasutake, *Transnational Women's Activism*, p. 33.
7. N. Rose, *Powers of Freedom: Reframing Political Thought* (Cambridge: Cambridge University Press, 1999), pp. 73–4.
8. W. Benjamin, *Illuminations* (New York: Schocken Books, 1968), pp. 129–30.
9. See M. Foucault, *'Society Must Be Defended': Lectures at the Collège de France, 1975–76*, ed. M. Bertani and A. Fontana, trans. D. Macey (New York: Picador, 2003), pp. 276–81; M. Foucault, *The History of Sexuality*, trans. R. Hurley, 3 vols (New York: Vintage, 1985), vol. 1, pp. 120–2.

10. I. Scheiner, *Christian Converts and Social Protest in Meiji Japan* (Berkeley, CA: University of California Press, 1970); Karatani, *Origins of Modern Japanese Literature*, pp. 83–7; Fukuzawa Y., *An Outline of a Theory of Civilization*, trans. C. Dilworth and G. C. Hurst (Tokyo: Sophia University, 1973), p. 176. See also J. Sand, 'At Home in the Meiji Period', in S. Vlastos (ed.), *Mirror of Modernity: Invented Traditions of Modern Japan* (Berkeley, CA: University of California Press, 1998), pp. 191–207; K. B. Pyle, *The New Generation in Meiji Japan: Problems of Cultural Identity, 1885–1895* (Stanford, CA: Stanford University Press, 1969).
11. The overriding Confucian concern is that if virtuous men lead by moral example, good government will follow naturally. For example, Confucius said 'He who rules by moral force (*tê*) is like the pole-star, which remains in its place while all the lesser stars do homage to it' (Book 2:1) and 'If the ruler himself is upright, all will go well even though he does not give orders. But if he himself is not upright, even though he gives orders, they will not be obeyed' (Book 13:6). *The Analects of Confucius*, trans. A. Waley (New York: Vintage Books, 1989), pp. 88, 173.
12. The 'natural' social order articulated by neo-Confucians was based on a hierarchical model for the division of labour in which the samurai were the rulers, farmers were the principal producers, artisans were auxiliary producers, and the merchants were intermediaries of questionable value. Besides the four major occupation status differentiations, the Tokugawa status system included two ranks of privilege – court nobles (*kuge*) and religious persons (*sōni*) – and two ranks without station – the polluted (*eta*) and the nonhuman (*hinin*). For a detailed account of the status system (*mibunseido*) in action, see D. V. Botsman, *Punishment and Power in the Making of Modern Japan* (Princeton, NJ: Princeton University Press, 2005).
13. H. D. Harootunian, 'Late Tokugawa Culture and Thought', in *Cambridge History of Japan*, gen. ed. J. W. Hall et al., 6 vols (Cambridge: Cambridge University Press, 1989), vol. 5: Nineteenth Century, ed. M. B. Jansen, pp. 168–258, on pp. 171–2.
14. The Tokyo WCTU began with 51 members. 'Fujin Kyōfūkai', *Jogaku zasshi*, 44 (15 December 1886), pp. 75–6; Ogawa, 'American Women's Destiny', p. 72.
15. I refer to all Japanese unions as Japanese Woman's Christian Temperance Union (*Nihon kirisutokyō fujin kyōfūkai*; JWCTU) for the sake of clarity despite its historical inaccuracy. The exclusion of any reference to Christianity from the name of the organization appears to have been a strategic choice by its members to emphasize their agenda for social reform and to avoid the impression that they were involved in any form of evangelical missionary work. 'Christian' was added to the organization's name after the World Temperance Christian Union convention was held in Japan in 1897. Yasutake, *Transnational Women's Activism*, p. 169.
16. Yamamuro Gumpei, leader of the Japanese Salvation Army, records how a leader of the JWCTU explained her conversion to Christianity in the following way: 'When I first listened to the teachings of Christianity, I learnt that it instructed chastity in both men and women. This was the reason why I decided to convert to Christianity without delay.' Yamamuro, *Shakai kakusei ron*, p. 290.
17. J. Henning, *Outpost of Civilization: Race, Religion, and the Formative Years of American–Japanese Relations* (New York: New York University Press, 2000), pp. 55–6.
18. M. L. Nagata, 'Mistress or Wife? Fukui Sakuzaemon vs. Iwa, 1819–1833', *Continuity and Change*, 18:2 (August 2003), pp. 287–309, on p. 290.
19. Harald Fuess points out that population records for 1880 reveal that the ratio of concubines to male household heads was 4:10 for high nobility (*kazoku*), 4:1,000 for samurai

(*shizoku*) and 5:10,000 for commoners (*heimin*). H. Fuess, *Divorce in Japan: Family, Gender, and the State, 1600–2000* (Stanford, CA: Stanford University Press, 2004), p. 55.

20. Yasutake, *Transnational Women's Activism*, p. 31.
21. Nagata, 'Mistress or Wife?', pp. 294–5. The Civil Code of 1898 removed the concubine's legal status and disqualified children born to concubines from inheriting property ahead of children begat in matrimony. The code fell short of securing the wife's marital position, however. Following the precept set by the *Shinritsu Kōryō*, the Civil Code still allowed a man to sue for divorce if a wife committed adultery. On the other hand, a woman could not sue for divorce for any infidelities committed by her husband, faced imprisonment if she had sex with anyone but her husband (Article 813) and was prohibited from marrying her extramarital lover even after divorce (Article 768). See Hayakawa N., 'Sexuality and the State: The Early Meiji Debate on Concubinage and Prostitution', in V. Mackie (ed.), *Feminism and the State in Modern Japan* (Melbourne: Japanese Studies Centre, 1995), pp. 31–40.
22. Confucius comments on the difficulty of self-transformation through a commitment to virtue, 'I have never yet seen anyone whose desire to build up moral power was as strong as sexual desire' (Book 9:17). *The Analects*, p. 17.
23. Yamajima K., 'Tokyo fujin kyōfūkai shuisho', *Jogaku zasshi*, 70 (6 August 1887), pp. 191–2.
24. 'Fujin kyōfūkai shiritsu, yakuin oyobi kisoku', reproduced in *Nihon fujin mondai shiryō shūsei*, vol. 1, p. 206.
25. 'Tokyo fujin kyōfūkai no giketsu', *Jogaku zasshi*, 62 (30 April 1887), p. 38; Ogawa, 'American Women's Destiny', p. 74.
26. See the petition sent by Yuasa Hatsuko to the government, 27 June 1889, in Nihon Kirisutokyō Fujin Kyōfūkai (ed.), *Nihon Kirisutokyō Fujin Kyōfūkai hyakunenshi* (Tokyo: Domesu shuppan, 1986), p. 63.
27. L. S. Roberts, 'The Petition Box in Eighteenth-Century Tosa', *Journal of Japanese Studies*, 20 (1994), pp. 423–58.
28. See M. Patessio, 'The Creation of Public Spaces by Women in the Early Meiji Period and the Tōkyō Fujin Kyōfūkai', *International Journal of Asian Studies*, 3 (2006), pp. 155–82.
29. Nihon Kirisutokyō Fujin Kyōfūkai (ed.), *Nihon Kirisutokyō Fujin Kyōfūkai hyakunenshi*, p. 64. A similar petition with 800 signatures was sent in March 1890 to both houses of the Imperial Diet. The petition called for the government to amend the Japanese civil code, which gave the concubine the same legal status as wife to the entitlement of succession. The JWCTU requested that the concubine and her children be prohibited from inheriting the family name and property ahead of children conceived by the legally married wife. The petition continued with a plea for gender equality in the eyes of the law. The JWCTU demanded that the criminal code (Article 183) be amended to punish both men and women for adultery (not just married women), and that the reach of the law be extended to include liaisons by married men with prostitutes, *geisha* and concubines as acts of adultery. 'Keihō oyobi minpō narabi ni bai-infu torishimarihō seitei ni kansuru seigan', reproduced in *Nihon fujin mondai shiryō shūsei*, vol. 1, p. 230.
30. An example of prostitution presented as a threat to national vitality can be found in the petition sent by Asai Saku to both houses of the Imperial Diet: 'Teikoku shūgi-in kizokuin gi-in kakui ni seigan', *Tokyo fujin kyōfū zasshi*, 32 (20 December 1890), pp. 2–3.
31. See, e.g., the public talk given by Sasaki Toyoju, a pivotal founding member and inaugural secretary of the (Tokyo) JWCTU and a pioneering activist for women's (economic) rights, in May 1887, in which she addressed the lack of professional opportunities for

Japanese women and her concerns for the national prestige of Japan as a civilized country when prostitutes were exported abroad from every port of Japan. 'Fujin bunmei no hataraki', *Jogaku zasshi*, 65 (21 May 1887), pp. 86–8.

32. Ibid., p. 88.
33. On the US Chinese Exclusion Act (1882), the Immigration Act (1891) and regulations against the immigration of ethnic groups regarded as impure, unclean, dim-witted, non-white or not having the mental or cultural faculties to understand the principles of republicanism, see J. Torpey, *The Invention of the Passport: Surveillance, Citizenship, and the State* (Cambridge: University of Cambridge Press, 2000), pp. 96–103.
34. Chinda Sutemi to Aoki Shūzū, 25 April 1891, in Gaimushō (ed.), *Nihon gaikō bunsho*, vol. 24, p. 464.
35. Aoki Shūzū to Yamagata Aritomo, 15 July 1890, *HFTKHZ*, vol. 1.
36. 'Kashizashiki hikite-jaya oyobi shōgi dekasegi no eigyō wo kinshi seraretaki no seigan', reproduced in Nihon Kirisutokyō Fujin Kyōfūkai (ed.), *Nihon Kirisutokyō Fujin Kyōfūkai hyakunenshi*, pp. 71–4.
37. In 1873, brothels in Tokyo (and other major cities in Japan) began operating a 'room rental' (*kashizashiki*) licensing system approved by the government. Under this system, the prostitute (*shōgi*) was a licensed 'independent contractor', and the brothel a 'room letting service'. It took the Japanese government until 1900 to implement the 'room-rental' system nationwide. One of the stipulations for women obtaining a licence was that they would undergo mandatory medical inspections for venereal diseases.
38. 'Keihō oyobi minpō narabi ni bai-infu torishimarihō seitei ni kansuru seigan', reproduced in *Nihon fujin mondai shiryō shūsei*, vol. 1, p. 230.
39. Aburatani, *Keiteki*, p. 7.
40. Ibid., pp. 7–8.
41. S. Nolte and S. Hastings, 'The Meiji State's Policy Toward Women, 1890–1910', in G. L. Bernstein (ed.), *Recreating Japanese Women, 1600–1945* (Berkeley, CA: University of California Press, 1991), pp. 151–74, on p. 158.
42. Sheldon Garon has put forth the explanation that Japanese Protestant Christians were readily co-opted by the state because they shared the same backgrounds, experiences and aspirations as state bureaucrats. S. Garon, 'Rethinking Modernization and Modernity in Japanese History: A Focus on State–Society Relations', *Journal of Asian Studies*, 53:2 (May 1994), pp. 346–66, on p. 351. Rumi Yasutake, however, offers a different explanation. Her view is that because of the conservative tide in the late Meiji period, the JWCTU accommodated itself to Japanese imperial aspirations. The reason for this was in part to ensure its survival, and in part because the JWCTU had the ambition to become a mass woman's movement of vital significance for the cause of the Japanese empire. See Yasutake, *Transnational Women's Activism*, pp. 5, 95–103.
43. H. D. Harootunian, *Overcome by Modernity: History, Culture and Community in Interwar Japan* (Princeton, NJ: Princeton University Press, 2000), pp. 95–201.
44. Maeda, A., *Text and the City: Essays on Japanese Modernity*, ed. J. A. Fuji (Durham, NC: Duke University Press, 2004), pp. 21–64.
45. In April 1918, the Home Ministry under the leadership of Gotō Shimpei established a formal group (*Toshi kenkyūkai*) to study urban planning, with Gotō serving as chair. In 1919, in direct response to the 1918 rice riots, the Tokyo municipal government established a Bureau of Social Affairs (*Shakai Kyoku*) to deal specifically with the chronic poverty and social unrest that plagued the country's capital. The Home Ministry fol-

lowed suit in August 1920 when it too established a Bureau of Social Affairs to deal specifically with declining living standards in the urban centres of Japan.
46. Garon, *Moulding Japanese Minds*, p. 16.
47. J. Donzelot, *The Policing of Families*, trans. R. Hurley (Baltimore, MD: Johns Hopkins University Press, 1997).
48. The JWCTU argued that licensed prostitution undermined the principle of equality fundamental to democracy because it allowed the trade and enslavement of women. See Onozawa A., 'Dai-ichiji seikai taisengo ni okeru haishō undō no kakudai – Nihon Kirisutokyō Fujin Kyūfūkai no katsudō wo chūshin toshite', *Kokusai kankei gaku kenkyū*, 26 (1999), pp. 55–68.
49. Takemura, *Haishō undō*, pp. 35–8.
50. Onozawa, 'Dai-ichiji seikai taisengo ni okeru haishō undō no kakudai', p. 57; Garon, *Moulding Japanese Minds*, pp. 98–100, 112. The JWCTU intensified its attempts to abolish all forms of prostitution in Japan when *geisha* performed in the coronation ceremony of the Taisho emperor. The leaders of the JWCTU announced in their 23rd annual conference held in Doshisha Academy, Kyoto, that the primary goal of the organization was to abolish all prostitution by 1921.
51. Onozawa, 'Dai-ichiji seikai taisengo ni okeru haishō undō no kakudai', p. 58.
52. The pledging of monies for rescue and moral education was known as *go-sen bukuro undō* (literally: five-*sen* envelope movement). For details on the *go-sen bukuro undō*, see Yang S., '*Nihon Kirisutokyō Fujin Kyōfūkai* to *haishō undo*' (PhD dissertation, Tokyo University of Foreign Studies, 2005), pp. 91–6.
53. The relatively large islands of Amakusa are situated just off the west coast of Kyushu, Japan's southernmost island. The islands nestle between the jutting Shimabara Peninsula (Nagasaki prefecture) and the coastline of Kumamoto prefecture.
54. Miyagawa S., 'Shiberia shisatsu no shirushi', *Fujin shinpō*, 13 April 1919, pp. 10–15.
55. Ibid.; Kurahashi K., '"Karayuki" to Fujin Kyōfūkai (1): Kyūshū no ichi chiiki joseishi no shikaku kara', *Kirisutokyō shakai mondai kenkyūkai*, 51 (December 2002), pp. 1–62, on p. 40.
56. Takemura, *Haishō undō*, p. 84.
57. Miyagawa, 'Shiberia shisatsu no shirushi'; Nunokawa S., 'Nihon fujin no tsura yogoshi', reproduced in *Nihon fujin mondai shiryō shūsei*, vol. 1, pp. 330–6; Kurahashi M., *Karayuki-san no uta* (Tokyo: Kyōei shobō, 1990), pp. 215–16.
58. Miyagawa, 'Shiberia shisatsu no shirushi'.
59. 'Shiberiya shūgyōfu mondai enzetsukai', *Fujin shinpō*, 13 April 1919, pp. 27–8.
60. 'Shiberiya i'inkai', *Fujin shinpō*, 15 July 1919, p. 32.
61. For example, in 1916–17 Nunokawa was commissioned by the Ministry of Agriculture and Commerce to investigate the possible markets for sending Japanese goods and Japanese labour to South Africa. K. Kitagawa, 'Japan's Economic Relations with Africa between the Wars: A Study of Japanese Consular Reports', *African Study Monographs*, 11:3 (December 1990), pp. 125–41, on p. 131.
62. 'Shiberiya kakuchi ni aru nihon shyūgyōfu', *Fujin shinpō*, 10 February 1919, p. 13.
63. He wrote the article using the pen name Shizubuchi.
64. 'Shiberiya kakuchi ni aru nihon shyūgyōfu', p. 13.
65. Nunokawa, 'Nihon fujin no tsura yogoshi', p. 330; Kurahashi, *Karayuki-san no uta*, pp. 219–20.
66. Nihon Kirisutokyō Fujin Kyōfūkai (ed.), *Kaigai shūgyōfu mondai*.

67. Ibid., pp. 51, 55–6. For the connection between marriage customs and leaving the island for work, see 'Ranryō e mikkō no tochu- kanken nite toriosaerare sōkan', *Nanyō nichinichi shinbun*, 27 April 1915.
68. See M. Asano Tamanoi, 'Japanese Nationalism and the Female Body: A Critical Reassessment of the Discourse of Social Reformers on Factory Women', in H. Tonomura, A. Walthall and H. Wakita (eds), *Women and Class in Japanese History*, Michigan Monograph Series in Japanese Studies, 25 (Ann Arbor, MI: Center for Japanese Studies, University of Michigan, 1999), pp. 275–98. On how sexuality with its regulatory devices was imported into the sphere of work, see Foucault, *The History of Sexuality*, vol. 1, pp. 125–7.
69. 'Kyushubukai no taikai no ketsugi', *Fujin shinpō*, 15 December 1919, pp. 26–8.
70. 'Kaitō ni shitagatte, shinshū kara kyūshū made yon shūkan no tabi', *Fujin shinpō*, 20 January 1920, p. 24.
71. G. Kasza, 'War and Welfare Policy in Japan', *Journal of Asian Studies*, 61:2 (May 2002), pp. 417–35.
72. M. Ogawa, '"Hull House" in Downtown Tokyo: The Transplantation of a Settlement House from the United States into Japan and the North American Missionary Woman, 1919–1945', *Journal of World History*, 15:3 (September 2004), pp. 359–87, on p. 371.
73. Foucault, *The History of Sexuality*, vol. 1, p. 123.

4 Sex as Progress

1. Fukuzawa Y., *An Encouragement of Learning*, trans. D. Dilwirth and U. Hirano (Tokyo: Sophia University, 1969), p. 16.
2. Fukuzawa Y., 'Jinmin no ijū to shōfu no dekasegi', in *Fukuzawa Yukichi zenshū*, ed. Keiō Gijuku, 22 vols (Tokyo: Iwanami shoten, 1960), vol. 15, pp. 362–4, on p. 364.
3. N. Hiraishi, 'The Formation of Maruyama Masao's Image of Japanese Intellectual History during the War Period', *Social Science Japan Journal*, 6:2 (2003), pp. 241–54, on p. 252.
4. A. Schad-Seifert, 'Constructing National Identities: Asia, Japan and Europe in Fukuzawa Yukichi's Theory of Civilization', in D. Stegewerns (ed.), *Nationalism and Internationalism in Imperial Japan: Autonomy, Asian Brotherhood, or World Citizenship?* (London: Routledge Curzon, 2003), pp. 45–68, on pp. 55–6.
5. Fukuzawa, *An Outline of a Theory of Civilization*, p. 15.
6. Fukuzawa Y, *Gakumon no susume*, in *Fukuzawa Yukichi senshū*, ed. Tomida M., 14 vols (Tokyo: Iwanami shoten, 1980), vol. 3, pp. 53–176, on p. 72. Albert Craig analyses this theme in *Civilization and Enlightenment: The Early Thought of Fukuzawa Yukichi* (Cambridge, MA: Harvard University Press, 2009).
7. For research that puts Maruyama Masao and his political project in historical context, see R. Kersten, *Democracy in Japan: Maruyama Masao and the Search for Autonomy* (London; Routledge, 1996); J. V. Koschmann, *Revolution and Subjectivity in Postwar Japan* (Chicago, IL: University of Chicago Press, 1996).
8. D. R. Howland, *Translating the West: Language and Political Reason in Nineteenth-Century Japan* (Honolulu, HI: University of Hawaii Press, 2002), pp. 22–3; E. H. Kinmonth, 'Fukuzawa Reconsidered: *Gakumon no susume* and its Audience', *Journal of Asian Studies*, 37:4 (August 1978), pp. 677–96.
9. See Banno J., *Meiji shisō no jitsuzō* (Tokyo: Sōbonsha, 1977). Fukuzawa first published his essay 'Datsu-a ron' on 16 March 1885 in the *Jiji shimpō*. In this essay Fukuzawa turns his back on efforts to promote pan-Asian political associations (under Japanese tutelage) in Korea and China with the aim of gaining power and implementing modernization

reforms, and urges the government to follow the example of Western imperial powers and engage in gunboat diplomacy.

10. See Yoshimi K., 'Baishun no jittai to haishō undō', reproduced in *Nihon joseishi – dai 4 kan, kindai*, ed. Joseishi sōgō kenkyūkai, 5 vols (Tokyo: Tokyo daigaku shuppankai, 1982), vol. 4, pp. 223–58, on p. 236. This five-volume collection of essays on Japanese women's history from antiquity to the post-war period announced the study of women's history and gender relations as a legitimate area of historical investigation to the Japanese academic community.
11. The general custom was that the eldest son inherited property and status. In 1872 the Meiji government introduced the household registry system (*koseki*). Its initial function was as a census from which to calculate taxation. However, it quickly evolved to institute the continuity of patriarchal lineage as the foundation of the state. The household registry gave power to the family head and emphasized the superiority of the eldest son in their relations with other family members.
12. Fukuzawa, *An Outline of a Theory of Civilization*, p. 1; Fukuzawa Y., *Bunmeiron no gairyaku*, in *Fukuzawa Yukichi senshū*, vol. 4, pp. 5–254, on p. 6; Fukuzawa, *Gakumon no susume*, vol. 3, p. 138; Fukuzawa, *An Encouragement of Learning*, p. 79.
13. Fukuzawa had compared the penetration of Western colonial powers into Asia to the spread of measles in his famous essay 'Datsu-a ron' ('Disassociating from Asia'). Fukuzawa Y., 'Datsu-a ron', in *Fukuzawa Yukichi zenshū*, vol. 10, pp. 238–40.
14. This sentence echoes the title of the prize-winning work by J. Diamond, *Guns, Germs, and Steel: The Fates of Human societies* (New York: W. W. Norton & Co., 1997).
15. Fukuzawa Y., 'On Japanese Women', in *Fukuzawa Yukichi on Japanese Women: Selected Works*, ed. and trans. E. Kiyooka (Tokyo: University of Tokyo; 1988), pp. 6–36, on pp. 8, 11–13, 27.
16. Fukuzawa Y., 'On Japanese Women, Part Two', in ibid., pp. 37–69, on p. 54.
17. Fukuzawa, 'On Japanese Women', pp. 6, 24.
18. Fukuzawa, 'On Japanese Women, Part Two', pp. 42–5. *The Greater Learning for Women* was a treatise on the proper roles for women and was widely influential in the later Edo period. The treatise is commonly attributed to the Confucian scholar Kaibara Ekken (1630–1714). Some researchers argue that the work may be written by his wife, Kaibara Tōken (1652–1713), who was a renowned scholar of Confucian thought in her own right.
19. Fukuzawa, 'On Japanese Women', pp. 24–5, 21.
20. Ibid., pp. 35, 27, 36.
21. S. Sekiguchi, 'Confucian Morals and the Making of a "Good Wife and Wise Mother": From "Between Husband and Wife there is Distinction" to "As Husbands and Wives be Harmonious"', *Social Science Japan Journal*, 13:1 (January 2010), pp. 95–113, on pp. 98–100.
22. Fukuzawa, 'On Japanese Women, Part Two', pp. 64–5.
23. Fukuzawa Y., 'On Morality', in *Fukuzawa Yukichi on Japanese Women*, pp. 70–102, on pp. 70–1, 86.
24. Ibid., pp. 83–6.
25. Ibid., pp. 90, 95–6, 100–1.
26. Ibid., pp. 79, 87, 88–9.
27. Treaty revision is frequently argued to have been the motivation for the Meiji legal reforms based on Western legal principles. See R. Ishii, *A History of Political Institutions in Japan* (Tokyo: Tokyo University Press, 1980), p. 92; F. C. Jones, *Extraterritoriality in*

Japan and the Diplomatic Relations Resulting in Its Abolition 1853–1899 (New York: Ams Press, 1970), pp. 1–2, 61–3, 71.

28. Fukuzawa, *Bunmeiron no gairyaku*, vol. 4, p. 227; Howland, *Translating the West*, p. 148.
29. Fukuzawa, *Bunmeiron no gairyaku*, vol. 4, pp. 231–2.
30. Fukuzawa Y., 'Refuting Nishi's Discussion on Travel by Foreigners in the Country', in *Meiroku Zasshi: Journal of the Japanese Enlightenment*, trans. W. R. Braisted (Tokyo: University of Tokyo Press, 1976), pp. 319–24.
31. See Fukuzawa, *An Encouragement of Learning*, pp. 27–8; Fukuzawa, *Gakumon no susume*, vol. 3, p. 84.
32. Fukuzawa Y., *The Autobiography of Fukuzawa Yukichi*, trans. E. Kiyooka (New York: Columbia University Press, 1966), pp. 313–15.
33. The *goyōshonin* mediated in the financial affairs of the shogunate and daimyo as money lenders and financial advisors. Due to their virtual monopoly of trade and finance to these groups, many of the *goyōshonin* assumed positions of power despite their status as commoners. Few of the *goyōshonin* survived the fall of the Tokugawa shogunate during the Meiji Restoration (1867–8).
34. Fukuzawa, *An Encouragement of Learning*, p. 19; Fukuzawa, *Gakumon no susume*, vol. 3, pp. 74–5.
35. Fukuzawa, *An Encouragement of Learning*, p. 22; Fukuzawa, *Gakumon no susume*, vol. 3, p. 78.
36. Fukuzawa Y., 'Bunkenron', in *Fukuzawa Yukichi zenshū*, vol. 4, pp. 231–98, on pp. 270–3.
37. Howland, *Translating the West*, pp. 148–9.
38. Ibid., p. 28.
39. N. Sakai, 'Equality, Hierarchy, and Identity in Modern Japan: Reflections on the Nationalist Ethics of Fukuzawa Yukichi', in S. Y. S. Chien and J. Fitzgerald (eds), *The Dignity of Nations: Equality, Competition, and Honor in East Asian Nationalism* (Hong Kong: Hong Kong University Press, 2006), pp. 23–31, on p. 27.
40. Ibid., p. 29.
41. Howland, *Translating the West*, pp. 146–52.
42. Fukuzawa Y., 'Gaikokujin no naichi zakkyo yurusu bekarazu no ron', in *Fukuzawa Yukichi zenshū*, vol. 19, pp. 518–24, on p. 519.
43. Schad-Seifert, 'Constructing National Identities', pp. 51–5.
44. Fukuzawa, *An Encouragement of Learning*, p. 32; Fukuzawa, *Gakumon no susume*, vol. 3, pp. 89–90.
45. Fukuzawa, *An Encouragement of Learning*, p. 33; Fukuzawa, *Gakumon no susume*, vol. 3, p. 91.
46. N. Tamaki, '"Learn and Earn, Earn and Learn": British Influence and Fukuzawa Yukichi's Creation of the First Japanese Business Elite', in C. Hosoya and I. Nish (gen. eds), *The History of Anglo-Japanese Relations, 1600–2000*, 5 vols (Houndsmills, Basingstoke, and New York: Palgrave, 2000–3), vol. 4: 'Economic and Business Relations', ed. J. E. Hunter and S. Sugiyama, pp. 133–55, on pp. 138–45.
47. Translation by Kinmonth, 'Fukuzawa Reconsidered', p. 685; Fukuzawa, *Gakumon no susume*, vol. 3, p. 57.
48. Ibid.
49. Fukuzawa, *An Encouragement of Learning*, p. 5; Fukuzawa, *Gakumon no susume*, vol. 3, pp. 59–60.

50. J. Yasukawa, 'Fukuzawa Yukichi', in B. C. Duke (ed.), *Ten Great Educators of Modern Japan: A Japanese Perspective* (Tokyo: University of Tokyo Press, 1989), pp. 17–37, on pp. 29–30.
51. Fukuzawa Y., 'Go Abroad', in *The Speeches of Fukuzawa: A Translation and Critical Study*, ed. W. H. Oxford (Tokyo: Hokuseido, 1973), pp. 216–18.
52. Fukuzawa Y., 'Aete kokyō wo sare', in *Fukuzawa Yukichi zenshū*, vol. 9, pp. 525–8, on pp. 525–6; E. Azuma, *Between Two Empires: Race, History, and Transnationalism in Japanese America* (New York: Oxford University Press, 2005), p. 21.
53. Banno J., *The Establishment of the Japanese Constitution System*, trans. A. A. Stockwin (London and New York: Routledge, 1992), pp. 39–51.
54. W. D. Wray, *Mitsubishi and the N.Y.K., 1870–1914*, Council on East Asian Studies, Harvard East Asian monographs, 108 (Cambridge, MA: Harvard University Press, 1984), pp. 263–4.
55. Tsunoyama, *Enomoto Takeaki to Mekishiko shokumin ijū*, pp. 57–67; Irie, *Hōjin kaigai hatten shi*, vol. 1, p. 104.
56. 'The "*Jiji Shimpo*" on Emigration', 12 May, 1891, *Japan Weekly Mail*. Other articles by the *Jiji shimpō* in favour of overseas emigration covered by the *Japan Weekly Mail* during this period are found on 18 April and 19 September 1891, and 12 March and 21 May 1892.
57. 'Japanese Reputation Abroad', *Japan Weekly Mail*, 3 October 1891.
58. Ibid.
59. Gaimushō (ed.), *Nihon gaikō nenpyō narabini shuyō bunsho*, 2 vols (Tokyo: Nihon kokusai rengō kyōkai, 1955), vol. 1, pp. 143–4; N. Bennett, 'Bitter Fruit: Japanese Migration and Anglo-Saxon Obstacles, 1890–1924', *Transactions of the Asiatic Society of Japan*, 4th series, 8 (1993), pp. 67–83, on pp. 68–9.
60. G. C. Allen, *A Short History of Modern Japan* (London and Basingstoke: Macmillan Press, 1981), pp. 54–5, K. Ishii, 'Japanese Foreign Trade and the Yokohama Specie Bank, 1880–1913', in O. Checkland, Nishimura S. and Tamaki N., *Pacific Banking, 1859–1959: East Meets West* (Basingstoke: Macmillan Press, 1994), pp. 1–23.
61. *Imin hogokisoku*, 12 April 1894, reproduced in Naikaku kampōkyoku (ed.), *Hōrei zensho* [1894], 2 (Tokyo: Hara shobō, 1974), pp. 112–15; *Imin hogohō*, 7 April 1896, reproduced in *Hōrei zensho* [1896], 2 (Tokyo: Hara shobō, 1974), pp. 116–20.
62. The revised overseas passport ordinance transferred the responsibility for issuing passports to the prefectures, who were directed to review all requests for labour emigration other than China and Korea. Japan had extra-territoriality privileges in both countries which vested Japanese consuls with the authority forcibly to repatriate an individual deemed as harming the prevailing social mores. Proclamation no. 337, 8 October 1873, *Shinkoku zairyū nihon kokujin kokoroe kata kisoku*, reproduced in Naikaku kampōkyoku (ed.), *Hōrei zensho* [1873] (Tokyo: Hara shobō, 1974), p. 517; M. Sawada, 'Culprits and Gentlemen: Meiji Japan's Restrictions of Emigrants to the United States, 1891–1909', *Pacific Historical Review*, 60:3 (August 1991), pp. 339–59, on pp. 345–7; A. T. Moriyama, *Imingaisha: Japanese Emigration Companies and Hawaii, 1894–1908* (Honolulu, HI: Hawaii University Press, 1985), pp. 33–42.
63. The Japanese population increased by nearly 16 million between the years of 1868 to 1912, a growth rate of almost 50 per cent.
64. Fukuzawa Y., 'Jinkō no hanshoku', *Jiji shimpō*, 3 January 1896, reproduced in *Fukuzawa Yukichi senshū*, vol. 7, pp. 274–7.
65. Fukuzawa Y., 'Jinmin no ishoku', 4 January 1896, in *Fukuzawa Yukichi senshū*, vol. 7, pp. 277–80.

66. Fukuzawa Y., 'Nihonjin wa ishoku ni tekisuruya inaya', 7 January 1896, in *Fukuzawa Yukichi senshū*, vol. 7, p. 282.
67. See 'Imin to shūkyō', in *Fukuzawa Yukichi senshū*, vol. 7, pp. 361–2.
68. Fukuzawa Y., 'The Equal Numbers of Men and Women', in *Meiroku Zasshi*, pp. 385–6.
69. Fukuzawa, 'Jinmin no ijū to shōfu no dekasegi', in *Fukuzawa Yukichi zenshū*, vol. 15, p. 364.
70. Ibid.
71. See Fukuzawa Y., 'Imin no kōkai', 25 January 1896 and 'Imin no hogo', 26 January 1896, in *Fukuzawa Yukichi zenshū*, vol. 15, pp. 371–3, 373–5.
72. M. Hane, 'Fukuzawa Yukichi and Women's Right', in P. Kornicki (ed.), *Meiji Japan; Political, Economic and Social History 1868–1912*, 4 vols (London: Routledge, 1998), vol. 2, pp. 200–16, on p. 205.

5 Disciplining Globalizing

1. The 'freedom to abode'; 'freedom from arrest, detention, trial, and punishment except in accordance of law'; the 'right to judicial trial'; and 'the freedom from unlawful entry and searches' were fundamental rights protected by the 1889 Meiji Constitution, ch. II, articles 22–5.
2. I. Brown, 'The British Merchant Community in Singapore and Japanese Commercial Expansion in the 1930s', in S. Sugiyama and M. C. Guerrero (eds), *International Commercial Rivalry in Southeast Asia in the Interwar Period* (New Haven, CT: Yale Southeast Asian Studies, 1994), pp. 111–32.
3. Levine, *Prostitution, Race and Politics*, p. 24.
4. Ibid., p. 25.
5. Shimizu H. and Hirakawa H., *Japan and Singapore in the World Economy: Japan's Economic Advance into Singapore 1870–1965* (London: Routledge, 1999), p. 12.
6. Levine, *Prostitution, Race and Politics*, p. 25.
7. See 30 July 1870, Newton to Terajima, Foreign Office: Embassy and Consulates, Japan: General Correspondence, 1859–1957, National Archives, Kew Gardens, FO/262/203.
8. For the detailed working of the Contagious Disease Ordinance (CDO) in Singapore, see Levine, *Prostitution, Race and Politics*, ch. 2; Warren, *Ah Ku and Karayuki-san*, ch. 3.
9. In 1881, the newly established Chinese protectorate was given the brief of preventing the spread of sexually transmitted diseases and infiltrating and destroying the secret societies that engaged in the human trafficking of women and children. The office of the Protectorate saw the CDO as an important legislation in its fight to regulate prostitution and maintain stringent health measures to prevent the spread of primarily gonorrhoea, which was endemic in the Straits Settlements. The CDO was replaced by the Protection of Women and Girls Protection Ordinance in 1888, which eased the requirement of compulsory venereal examinations. Warren, *Ah Ku and Karayuki-san*, pp. 91–5.
10. As Levine points out, the reality of the registration processes was that the women remained anonymous to the colonial bureaucrats because the Chinese protectorate did not deal directly with them. The registration process required the brothel keeper to pay the registration and medical fees on the women's behalf, and to police their movements at all times. Levine, *Prostitution, Race and Politics*, pp. 53, 93.
11. Miyagawa Kyūjirō to Aoki Shūzō, Confidential Dispatch no. 19, 27 November 1890, 'Nihon fujin mikkō bōatsu no ken nitsuki utagai', *HFTKZ*, vol. 1. Until the Alien Act of 1905, the British government hardly restricted the movement of people entering and

leaving its domains due to its commitment to economic liberalism and 'open trade' as the surest recipe for prosperity. See Torpey, *The Invention of the Passport*, pp. 69–70, 91.

12. Miyagawa Kyūjirō to Aoki Shūzō, Confidential Dispatch no. 19, 27 November 1890, *HFTKZ*, vol. 1.
13. Nanyō oyobi Nihonjinsha, *Nanyō no gojūnen – Singapōru wo chūshin ni dōhō katsuyaku*, ed. Nomura T. (Singapore: Hokuto shobō, 1938), p. 523.
14. Fujita Toshirō to Hara Takashi, Confidential Dispatch no. 14, 16 November 1895, *HFTKZ*, vol. 1.
15. Ibid.
16. The Kanagawa treaty of 1876 negotiated between Japan and Korea promoted Japanese trade in Korea by securing the freedom of Japanese subjects under international law to pursue their interests freely. The treaty reconfirmed the right of Japanese to continue trade in Korea (article 4), and stipulated the grounds of Japanese extraterritorial jurisdiction (article 10). Japanese Foreign Office, *Treaties and Conventions between the Empire of Japan and other Powers Together with Universal Conventions, Regulations and Communications, since March 1854* (Tokyo: Kokubunsha Printing Office, 1884), pp. 171–4. The Tientsin Treaty (1871) gave Japan the right to appoint consuls to each of the Chinese 'open ports for the control of their respective subject' (article 3). The consuls' authority over Japanese subjects was codified in 1873 with the 'Rules and Regulations for Japanese resident in China'. The last of thirteen items in the regulations stated that: '[Japanese] women should not engage in occupations that were wanton and could be mistaken for prostitution'. Proclamation no. 337, 8 October 1873, *Shinkoku zairyū nihonkokujin kokoroe kata kisoku*, in Naikaku kampōkyoku (ed.), *Hōrei zensho* [1873], p. 517.
17. Edict 26, 15 August 1885, in Naikaku kampōkyoku (ed.), *Hōrei zensho* [1885], 1 (Tokyo: Hara shobō, 1974), p. 53. Persons extradited could not return to Korea and China for up to three years. In certain circumstances, the three-year ban could be waived if monies were deposited with the consul as security against further offences to public order and morality.
18. *Nihon fujin mondai shiryō shūsei*, vol. 10, p. 27; Andō Tarō to Yoshida Kyōnari, Dispatch no. 89, 15 August 1885, *HFTKHZ*, vol. 1.
19. Ibid.
20. Asada Tokunori to Okimori Motoyori, 6 August 1883, in Gaimushō (ed.), *Nihon gaikō bunsho*, vol. 16, p. 440.
21. Andō T. to Yoshida K., 15 August 1885.
22. Okimori Takashi to Inuoe Kaoru, Confidential Dispatch no. 135, 25 June 1885, 'Honpōfujin kaigai yuki torishimari no gi ni tsuki jōshin', *HFTKHZ*, vol. 1.
23. Tōjō Ichirō to Kiyoura Keigo, 29 January 1890, *HFTKHZ*, vol. 1.
24. Asada Tokunori to Machida Tsuneichi, Personal Correspondence no. 16, 15 May 1885, *HFTKHZ*, vol. 1.
25. Inoue Kaoru to Minami Sadatsuke, Confidential Dispatch no. 21, 19 August 1885, *HFTKHZ*, vol. 1.
26. 'Dai ikkai teikoku gikai', in Sangi-in jimukyoku (ed.), *Kizoku-in himitsukai giji sokkiroku shū*, p. 5.
27. In 1885, the CDO was still in effect in Hong Kong.
28. In November 1885, there were 46 Japanese women licensed to work as prostitutes in Hong Kong's licensed brothels. Minami Sadatsuke to Inoue Kaoru, Confidential Dispatch no. 28, 17 September 1885, *HFTKHZ*, vol. 1; Minami Sadatsuke to Inoue Kaoru,

Confidential Dispatch no. 31, 7 November 1885; J. H. Stewart Lochart to Fredrick Stewart, 2 November 1885, *HKMKZ*, vol. 1.

29. Minami Sadatsuke to Aoki Shūzō, Dispatch no. 36, 16 September 1887, *HFTKHZ*, vol. 1.
30. Minami Sadatsuke to Itō Hirobumi, Confidential Dispatch no. 1, 27 January 1888, *HFTKHZ*, vol. 1; Saitō Miki to Aoki Shūzō, Confidential Dispatch no. 9, 20 February 1890, *HFTKZ*, vol. 1.
31. Miyagawa Kyūjirō to Aoki Shūzō, Confidential Dispatch no. 19, 27 November 1890, 'Nihon fujin mikkō bōatsu no ken nitsuki utagai', *HFTKZ*, vol. 1.
32. Minami Sadatsuke to Inoue Kaoru, Dispatch no. 74, 25 October 1886, *HFTKZ*, vol. 1.
33. Saitō Miki to Aoki Shūzō, Confidential Dispatch no. 9, 20 February 1890, *HFTKZ*, vol. 1.
34. Miyagawa K. to Aoki S., 27 November 1890. See also 'Dai ikkai teikoku gikai', in Sangi-in jimukyoku (ed.), *Kizoku-in himitsukai giji sokkiroku shū*, p. 5.
35. In 1891, there were eight registered brothels run by Japanese in Hong Kong, with 80 women working them.
36. Yagishita H., 'Senzenki no ryoken no hensen', *Gaikōshiryōkanpō*, 12 (June 1998), pp. 36–7.
37. Fujita Toshirō to Minister Hara Takashi, Confidential Dispatch no. 14, 16 November 1895, *HKMKZ*, vol. 1.
38. Yano T., *Nanshin no keifu* (Tokyo: Chūō kōronsha, 1985), pp. 124–9; Warren, *Ah-Ku and Karyuki-san*, p. 49.
39. Mori, *Jinshin baibai*, pp. 175–6.
40. Shingaporu Nihonjinkai, *Singaporu nihonjin bochi: shashin to kiroku* (Singapore: Japan Association, 1983), pp. 8–9; 'Seipōru hōjin no konjaku – II', *Nanyō nichinichi shinbun*, 21 September 1914.
41. Kee Y. S., 'The Japanese in Malaya before 1942', *Journal of the South Seas*, 20:1–2 (1965), pp. 48–88, on p. 67. For the detailed workings of cooperative credit associations, see J. Embree, *A Japanese Village: Suye Mura* (London: Kegan Paul, Trench Trubner & Co., 1946), pp. 103–13.
42. Irie, *Hōjin kaigai hatten shi*, vol. 1, p. 237.
43. 'Hōjin yōshigun no bikyo', *Nanyō nichinichi shinbun*, 5 February 1915.
44. Shimizu and Hirakawa, *Japan and Singapore in the World Economy*, pp. 61–6.
45. Ibid., p. 39.
46. Miyakawa Kyūjirō to Hayashi Tadasu, Confidential Dispatch no. 7, 28 December 1892, 'Honkon ryojin yado eigyō Nishiyama Yūzō shūgyōfu shūsen no gi torishirabe wo yō suru ken ni tsuki tōshin', *HFTKZ*, vol. 1.
47. Levine, *Prostitution, Race and Politics*, p. 131.
48. Kee, 'The Japanese in Malaya before 1942', p. 53. Restrictions to land ownership took effect in July 1917 when the colonial government promulgated the Rubber Lands Restriction Enactment. The provisions prohibited the selling of rubber plantations over 50 acres to persons who were not British subjects. See Shimizu H., 'The Pattern of Japanese Economic Penetration of Prewar Singapore and Malaya', in S. Shiraishi and T. Shiraishi (eds), *The Japanese in Colonial Southeast Asia*, Translation of Contemporary Japanese Scholarship on Southeast Asia Series, 3 (Ithaca, NY: Cornell University Press, 1993), pp. 63–87, on p. 85.
49. Shimizu and Hirakawa, *Japan and Singapore in the World Economy*, p. 39.

50. Hara F., *Eiryō Maraya no Nihonjin* (Tokyo: Ajia keizai kenkyūsho, 1986), table 4, p. 222.
51. The details are in a series by the foreign ministry summarizing the abolition of Japanese prostitutes residing in Singapore and the Federated Malay States, part of a report sent by the Singapore consul, 27 January 1920, *HFTKZ*, vol. 5.
52. Shimizu and Hirakawa, *Japan and Singapore in the World Economy*, pp. 41–2.
53. The international trafficking of women came to the fore in European with national crusades against white slavery; the procurement – by use of force, deceit or drugs – of a white woman or a girl against her will for prostitution.
54. Warren, *Ah-Ku and Karyuki-san*, pp. 153–5; O. C. M. MacKirdy and W. N. Willis, *The White Slave Market* (London: S. Paul & Co., 1912).
55. Warren, *Ah-Ku and Karyuki-san*, p. 155.
56. Levine, *Prostitution, Race and Politics*, pp. 146–7.
57. Governor Young to Colonial Secretary Long, 13 June 1917, Colonial Office: Straits Settlements Original Correspondence, 1838–1946, National Archives, Kew Gardens, CO 273/457.
58. Nanyō oyobi Nihonjinsha, *Nanyō no gojūnen*, p. 235.
59. Warren, *Ah-Ku and Karyuki-san*, p. 163.
60. Shimizu, 'The Pattern of Japanese Economic Penetration of Prewar Singapore and Malaya', p. 69.
61. 'Jūrai no Seipōru ryōji', *Nanyō nichinichi shinbun*, 8 January, 1917.
62. Ibid.; Nanyō oyobi Nihonjinsha, *Nanyō no gojūnen*, pp. 496–502; Kee, 'The Japanese in Malaya before 1942', p. 64. For a sample of the debate amongst the local Japanese community over who should be included in the Japanese Association, see the two-part series by Fuchitoki Satoru, 'Zairyūmin no igi', *Nanyō nichinichi shinbun*, 8 and 9 June, 1915.
63. Mori, *Jinshin baibai*, p. 232.
64. Yuen C. L., 'The Japanese Community in Malaya before the Pacific War: Its Genesis and Growth', *Journal of Southeast Asian Studies*, 9:2 (September 1978), pp. 163–80, on p. 172.
65. The details were in a report sent by the Singapore consul Fujii Minoru dated 30 May 1914, *HFTKZ*, vol. 5; Shimizu and Hirakawa, *Japan and Singapore in the World Economy*, p. 43; Nanyō oyobi Nihonjinsha, *Nanyō no gojūnen*, pp. 147–9. In this account however, the number of Japanese 'pimps' banished is put at 72.
66. 'Mikkō torishimari to hōjin ryōkan', *Nanyō nichinichi shinbun*, 26 January 1916; 'Mikkō fujin yūkai torishimari iyoiyo kaishi', *Nanyō nichinichi shinbun*, 27 January 1916.
67. 'Nihon shōgi sōkan zehi', *Nanyō nichinichi shinbun*, 26 May, 1916. It was estimated that there were around 30 credit associations in the region with a total investment of $45,000.
68. Ibid.; 'Iwayuru seigyōsha to shūgyōsha gawa', *Nanyō nichinichi shinbun*, 21 June 1917; 'Suteretsu ni taisuru – ryōjisan no kun-yu', *Nanyō nichinichi shinbun*, 18 September 1919.
69. 'Nihon shōgi sōkan zehi'.
70. The details were in a report sent by the consul-general Yamazaki Heikichi dated 27 January 1920, *HFTKZ*, vol. 5; 'Fūki mondai wa mottomo kokka taimen ni kansuru koto jūdai de aru', *Nanyō nichinichi shinbun*, 1 January 1920.
71. Ibid; Shimizu and Hirakawa, *Japan and Singapore in the World Economy*, p. 45.
72. Report Concerning Japan Presented by Mr Sugimura, Member of the Advisory Committee on Traffic in Women and Children, Geneva, 6 April 1924, C.T.F.E. 215, League of Nations Archive, Geneva, 11B/39491/38154.
73. Uchida Yasuya to all diplomatic representatives in *Nanyō* and South America, Dispatch no. 291, 15 June 1921, 'Shūgyōfu torishimari kata ni kansuru ken', *HFTKHZ*, vol. 2.

74. Ukita Kyōji to Uchida Yasuya, Dispatch no. 265, 21 December 1922, 'Shūgyō oyobi shūgyō ruiji fujoshi narabini sono yūkaisha nado no tokō torishimari kata ni kan suru ken', *HFTKZ*, vol. 7; Ukita Kyōji to Matsui Keishirō, Dispatch no. 32, 'Shingapōru ni okeru hōjin shūgyōfu no jyōkyō', enclosed in 'Shingapōru ni okeru hōjin shūgyōfu fukkatsu mondai ni kansuru ken', 24 January 1924.
75. Shimizu, 'The Pattern of Japanese Economic Penetration of Prewar Singapore and Malaya', p. 68.

Conclusion

1. M. Foucault, 'The Life of Infamous Men', in *Power, Truth, Strategy*, ed. M. Morris and P. Patton (Sydney: Feral Publications, 1979), pp. 76–91, on p. 76.
2. G. Simmel, *Philosophy of Money* (London: Routledge, 1990), p. 391.
3. See E. Faison, *Managing Women: Disciplining Labor in Modern Japan* (Berkeley, CA: University of California Press, 2007).
4. Foucault, *The History of Sexuality*, vol. 1, p. 124. Class formation according to Foucault follows a key materialist thesis in Nietzsche's *On the Genealogy of Morals*: namely, the assertion that the superiority of the soul stems from claims to political superiority.
5. Foucault, *The History of Sexuality*, vol. 1, p. 127.
6. Donzelot, *The Policing of Families*.
7. The alliance was formed among faith groups and non-governmental organizations. On the religious right: Focus of the Family, National Association of Evangelicals, Catholic Bishops Conference, Traditional Values Coalition, Concerned Women for America, Salvation Army, Shared Hope International, and Religious Freedom Coalition among others. The major abolitionist feminist organization is Coalition Against Trafficking in Women (CATW). R. Weitzer, 'The Social Construction of Sex Trafficking: Ideology and Institutionalization of a Moral Crusade', *Politics and Society*, 35:3 (September 2007), pp. 447–75, on p. 449.
8. CATW's website, 'An Introduction to CATW', at http://www.catwinternational.org/about/index.php.
9. President Bush Addresses United Nations General Assembly, 23 September 2003, at http://www.whitehouse.gov/news/releases/2003/09/20030923-4.html.
10. Weitzer, 'The Social Construction of Sex Trafficking', p. 460.
11. President Bush Addresses United Nations General Assembly, 23 September 2003; T. Eastland, 'Bush's Gospel', *Weekly Standard*, 1 March 2004, pp. 16–22. The idea of freedom as the God-given right of men and women everywhere was made the founding principle of foreign policy by Ronald Reagan during his tenure as US president.
12. The quote is from John Miller's testimony at the Congressional Hearing on Trafficking in Women in Children in East Asia and Beyond, April 2003. The reauthorization of the Victims of Trafficking and Violence Protection Act in 2003 and 2005 got rid of the distinction between 'sex trafficking' – which may be voluntary – and 'severe trafficking' – which involves fraud or coercion of persons underage. The Acts of 2003 and 2005 include provisions targeting domestic traffickers, link prostitution to trafficking, and open the possibility of mandatory sanctions against nations with poor records in suppressing trafficking. See Weitzer, 'The Social Construction of Sex Trafficking', pp. 461–2.
13. A. Murray, 'Debt-Bondage and Trafficking: Don't Believe the Hype', in K. Kempadoo and J. Doezema (eds), *Global Sex Workers: Rights, Resistance, and Redefinition* (New York: Routledge, 1998), pp. 51–64, on p. 60. See also the essays by V. Munro and S. A.

Fitzgerald in V. E. Munro and M. D. Giusta (eds), *Demanding Sex: Critical Reflections on the Regulation of Prostitution* (Aldershot, Hampshire: Ashgate, 2008).

14. On the issue of the 'sanctity of life' and its apparent contradictions, see P. Singer, *The President of Good and Evil: The Ethics of George W. Bush* (New York: Dutton, 2004).
15. For an illuminating example of how the limitations of Western practices of human rights play out in contemporary China, see M. Dutton *Streetlife China* (Cambridge: Cambridge University Press, 1998).
16. G. Deleuze, *Nietzsche and Philosophy* (London: Continuum, 1992).
17. Singer, *The President of Good and Evil*, pp. 111–46.
18. The Evangelical Christian lobby played a major role gaining support for US intervention in the Sudan civil war in order to protect the ethnic and religious minorities from being victims of further atrocities by the brutal Khartoum regime.
19. See the J. Doezema, 'Loose Women or Lost Women? The Re-emergence of the Myth of "White Slavery" in Contemporary Discourse in "Trafficking in Women"', *Gender Issues*, 18 (Winter 2000), pp. 23–50; J. Doezema, 'Ouch! Western Feminists' "Wounded Attachment" to the "Third World Prostitute"', *Feminist Review*, 67 (Spring 2001), pp. 16–38.

WORKS CITED

Archival Material

Colonial Office: Straits Settlements Original Correspondence, 1838–1946, National Archives, Kew Gardens, CO 273.

Foreign Office: Embassy and Consulates, Japan: General Correspondence, 1859–1957, National Archives, Kew Gardens, FO/262.

Honpōjin fuseigyō torishimari kankei hōki zassan, 2 vols, Diplomatic Record Office, Gaikō shiryōkan, Tokyo, Code No. 4.2.2.34.

Honpōjin fuseigyō torishimari kankei zakken, 7 vols, Diplomatic Record Office, Gaikō shiryōkan, Tokyo, Code No. 4.2.2.27.

Honpōjin kaigai e mikkō kankei zakken, 7 vols, Diplomatic Record Office, Gaikō shiryōkan, Tokyo, Code No. 3.8.8.4.

Kaigai ni okeru honpō shūgyōfu no insū oyobi sono jōkyō nado nen nikai hōkoku kata kuntatsu ikken, Diplomatic Record Office, Gaikō shiryōkan, Tokyo, Code No. 4.2.2.99.

League of Nations Commission of Enquiry into the Traffic in Women and Children in the East, League of Nations Archive, Geneva, 11B/39491/38154.

Official Publications

British Parliamentary Papers, 79 (1867–8).

Gaimushō (ed.), *Nihon gaikō bunsho*, 73 vols (Tokyo: Nihon kokusai rengō kyōkai, 1953).

— (ed.), *Nihon gaikō nenpyō narabini shuyō bunsho*, 2 vols (Tokyo: Nihon kokusai rengō kyōkai, 1955).

Japanese Foreign Office, *Treaties and Conventions between the Empire of Japan and other Powers together with Universal Conventions, Regulations and Communications, since March 1854* (Tokyo; Kokubunsha Printing Office, 1884).

Naikaku kampōkyoku (ed.), *Hōrei zensho* [1873] (Tokyo: Hara shobō, 1974).

—, *Hōrei zensho* [1885] (Tokyo: Hara shobō, 1974).

—, *Hōrei zensho* [1894] (Tokyo: Hara shobō, 1974).

—, *Hōrei zensho* [1896] (Tokyo: Hara shobō, 1974).

Sangi-in jimukyoku (ed.), *Kizoku-in himitsukai giji sokkiroku shū* (Tokyo; San-yūkai, 1995).

Newspapers

Fujin shinpō.

Fukuoka nichinichi shinbun.

Japan Echo.

Japan Weekly Mail.

Jiji shimpō.

Kyushu nichinichi shinbun.

Nanyō nichinichi shinbun.

Rising Sun and Nagasaki Press.

Yūbin hōchi.

Published Sources

Aburatani I., *Keiteki – kōkoku no jiki ni saishi tsutsushinde waga dōhō ni keikokusu* (Okayama: Okayamakoji-in kappan-bu, 1895).

Agustín, L. M., *Sex at the Margins: Migration, Labour Markets and the Rescue Industry* (London and New York: Zed Books, 2007).

Allen, G. C., *A Short History of Modern Japan* (London and Basingstoke: Macmillan Press, 1981).

Asano Tamanoi, M., 'Japanese Nationalism and the Female Body: A Critical Reassessment of the Discourse of Social Reformers on Factory Women', in H. Tonomura, A. Walthall and H. Wakita (eds), *Women and Class in Japanese History*, Michigan Monograph Series in Japanese Studies, 25 (Ann Arbor, MI: Center for Japanese Studies, University of Michigan, 1999), pp. 275–98.

Awanohara, S., 'Protesting the Sexual Imperialists', *Far Eastern Economic Review*, 14 March 1975, special tourist supplement, pp. 5–6.

Azuma, E., *Between Two Empires: Race, History, and Transnationalism in Japanese America* (New York: Oxford University Press, 2005).

Banno J., *Meiji shisō no jitsuzō* (Tokyo: Sōbonsha, 1977).

—, *The Establishment of the Japanese Constitution System*, trans. A. A. Stockwin (London and New York: Routledge, 1992).

Benjamin, W., *Illuminations* (New York: Schocken Books, 1968).

Bennett, N., 'Bitter Fruit: Japanese Migration and Anglo-Saxon Obstacles, 1890–1924', *Transactions of the Asiatic Society of Japan*, 4th series, 8 (1993), pp. 67–83.

Botsman, D. V., *Punishment and Power in the Making of Modern Japan* (Princeton, NJ: Princeton University Press, 2005).

Brown, I., 'The British Merchant Community in Singapore and Japanese Commercial Expansion in the 1930s', in S. Sugiyama and M. C. Guerrero (eds), *International Commercial*

Rivalry in Southeast Asia in the Interwar Period (New Haven, CT: Yale Southeast Asian Studies, 1994), pp. 111–132.

Castel, R., '"Problematization" as a Mode of Reading History', in J. Goldstein (ed.), *Foucault and the Writing of History* (Oxford: Basil Blackwell, 1994), pp. 237–52.

Confucius, *The Analects of Confucius*, trans. A. Waley (New York: Vintage Books, 1989).

Conroy, H., *The Japanese Frontier in Hawaii, 1868–1898* (Berkeley, CA: University of California Press, 1953).

Craig, A., *Civilization and Enlightenment: The Early Thought of Fukuzawa Yukichi* (Cambridge, MA: Harvard University Press, 2009).

Deleuze, G., *Nietzsche and Philosophy* (London: Continuum, 1992).

Diamond, J., *Guns, Germs, and Steel: The Fates of Human societies* (New York: W. W. Norton & Co., 1997).

Doezema, J., 'Loose Women or Lost Women? The Re-emergence of the Myth of "White Slavery" in Contemporary Discourse in "Trafficking in Women"', *Gender Issues*, 18 (Winter 2000), pp. 23–50.

—, 'Ouch! Western Feminists' "Wounded Attachment" to the "Third World Prostitute"', *Feminist Review*, 67 (Spring 2001), pp. 16–38.

Dorn, E., 'Crusading against Prostitution: The Woman's Christian Temperance Union in Meiji Japan', *Japanese Religions*, 29:1–2 (January 2004), pp. 29–43.

Dresner, J., 'Emigration and Local Development in Meiji Era Yamaguchi' (PhD dissertation, Harvard University, 2001).

Driscoll, M., *Absolute Erotic, Absolute Grotesque: The Living, Dead, and Undead in Japan's Imperialism, 1895–1945* (Durham, NC: Duke University Press, 2010).

Donzelot, J., *The Policing of Families*, trans. R. Hurley (Baltimore, MD: Johns Hopkins University Press, 1997).

Dutton, M., *Streetlife China* (Cambridge: Cambridge University Press, 1998).

Eastland, T., 'Bush's Gospel', *Weekly Standard*, 1 March 2004, pp. 16–22.

Embree, J., *A Japanese Village: Suye Mura* (London: Kegan Paul, Trench Trubner & Co., 1946).

Faison, E., *Managing Women: Disciplining Labor in Modern Japan* (Berkeley, CA: University of California Press, 2007).

Foucault, M., 'Intellectuals and Power', in *Language, Counter-Memory, Practice*, ed. D. Bouchard, trans. D. Bouchard and S. Simon (Ithaca, NY: Cornell University Press, 1977), pp. 205–17.

—, 'The Life of Infamous Men', in *Power, Truth, Strategy*, ed. M. Morris and P. Patton (Sydney: Feral Publications, 1979), pp. 76–91.

—, '*Omnes et Singulatim*: Towards a Criticism of Political Reason', *The Tanner Lectures on Human Values*, 2, ed. S. M. McMurrin (Cambridge: Cambridge University Press, 1981), pp. 225–54.

—, *The History of Sexuality*, trans. R. Hurley, 3 vols (New York: Vintage, 1985).

—, 'On Problematization', *History of the Present*, 4 (1988), pp. 16–17.

—, 'Polemics, Politics, and Problematization: An Interview', in *The Foucault Reader*, ed. P. Rabinow (New York: Pantheon, 1988), pp. 381–90.

—, 'Question of Method', in *The Foucault Effect: Studies in Governmentality*, ed. G. Burchell, C. Gordon and P. Miller (London: Harvester Wheatsheaf, 1991), pp. 73–86.

—, *'Society Must Be Defended': Lectures at the Collège de France, 1975–76*, ed. M. Bertani and A. Fontana, trans. D. Macey (New York: Picador, 2003).

Fuess, H., *Divorce in Japan: Family, Gender, and the State, 1600–2000* (Stanford, CA: Stanford University Press, 2004).

Fujime Y., *Sei no rekishigaku: kōshō seido, dataizai taisei kara baishun bōshihō, yūsei hogohō taisei e* (Tokyo: Fuji shuppan, 1997).

'Fujin Kyōfūkai', *Jogaku zasshi*, 44 (15 December 1886), pp. 75–6.

Fujin shinpō, 56 vols (Tokyo: Fuji shuppan, 1985–6).

Fujita T., *Kaigai zaikin shihanseiki no kaiko* (Tokyo: Kyōbunkan, 1931).

Fukutake, T., *Japanese Rural Society*, trans. R. P. Dore (London: Oxford University Press, 1967).

Fukuzawa Y., *Fukuzawa Yukichi zenshū*, ed. Keiō Gijuku, 22 vols (Tokyo: Iwanami shoten, 1960).

—, *The Autobiography of Fukuzawa Yukichi*, trans. E. Kiyooka (New York: Columbia University Press, 1966).

—, *An Encouragement of Learning*, trans. D. Dilwirth and U. Hirano (Tokyo: Sophia University, 1969).

—, *An Outline of a Theory of Civilization*, trans. C. Dilworth and G. C. Hurst (Tokyo: Sophia University, 1973).

—, *The Speeches of Fukuzawa: A Translation and Critical Study*, ed. W. H. Oxford (Tokyo: Hokuseido, 1973).

—, 'Refuting Nishi's Discussion on Travel by Foreigners in the Country', in *Meiroku Zasshi*, pp. 319–24.

—, 'The Equal Numbers of Men and Women', in *Meiroku Zasshi*, pp. 385–6.

—, *Fukuzawa Yukichi senshū*, ed. Tomida M., 14 vols (Tokyo: Iwanami shoten, 1980).

—, *Fukuzawa Yukichi on Japanese Women: Selected Works*, ed. and trans. E. Kiyooka (Tokyo: University of Tokyo, 1988).

Garon, S., 'The World's Oldest Debate? Prostitution and the State in Imperial Japan, 1900–1945', *American Historical Review*, 98:3 (June 1993), pp. 710–32.

—, Rethinking Modernization and Modernity in Japanese History: A Focus on State–Society Relations', *Journal of Asian Studies*, 53:2 (May 1994), pp. 346–66.

—, *Moulding Japanese Minds: The State in Everyday Life* (Princeton, NJ: Princeton University Press, 1997).

Gatens, M., *Imaginary Bodies: Ethics, Power, and Corporeality* (New York: Routledge, 1996).

Hacking, I., 'Making Up People', in T. C. Heller, M. Sosna and D. E. Wellberry (eds), *Reconstructing Individualism: Autonomy, Individuality, and the Self in Western Thought* (Stanford, CA: Stanford University Press, 1986), pp. 222–36.

Halliday, J., *A Political History of Japanese Capitalism* (London: Monthly Review Press, 1975).

Halliday, J., and G. McCormack, *Japanese Imperialism Today: Co-Prosperity and Greater East Asia* (Harmondsworth, Middlesex: Penguin Books, 1974).

Hane, M., *Peasants, Rebels, and Outcastes: The Underside of Modern Japan* (New York: Pantheon, 1982).

—, 'Fukuzawa Yukichi and Women's Right', in P. Kornicki (ed.), *Meiji Japan; Political, Economic and Social History 1868–1912*, 4 vols (London: Routledge, 1998), vol. 2, pp. 200–16.

Hanochi S., 'Constitutionalism in Modern Patriarchal State: Japan, the Sex Sector and Social Reproduction', in I. Bakker and S. Gill (eds), *Power, Production and Social Reproduction* (Basingstoke: Palgrave Macmillan, 2003), pp. 83–98.

Hara F., *Eiryō Maraya no Nihonjin* (Tokyo: Ajia keizai kenkyūsho, 1986).

Harootunian, H. D., 'The Economic Rehabilitation of the Samurai in the Early Meiji Period', *Journal of Asian Studies*, 19:4 (August 1960), pp. 433–44.

—, *Things Seen and Unseen: Discourse and Ideology in Tokugawa Nativism* (Chicago, IL: University of Chicago Press, 1988).

—, 'Late Tokugawa Culture and Thought', in *Cambridge History of Japan*, gen. ed. J. W. Hall et al., 6 vols (Cambridge: Cambridge University Press, 1989), vol. 5: Nineteenth Century, ed. M. B. Jansen, pp. 168–258.

—, *Overcome by Modernity: History, Culture and Community in Interwar Japan* (Princeton, NJ: Princeton University Press, 2000).

Hayakawa N., 'Sexuality and the State: The Early Meiji Debate on Concubinage and Prostitution', in V. Mackie (ed.), *Feminism and the State in Modern Japan* (Melbourne: Japanese Studies Centre, 1995), pp. 31–40.

—, *Kindai tennō kokka to jendā: seiritsuki no hitotsu no rojikku* (Tokyo: Aoki shoten, 1998).

Henning, J., *Outpost of Civilization: Race, Religion, and the Formative Years of American–Japanese Relations* (New York: New York University Press, 2000).

Henriot C., '"Little Japan" in Shanghai: An Insulated Community, 1875–1945', in R. Bickers and C. Henriot (eds), *New Frontiers: Imperialism's New Communities in East Asia, 1842–1953* (Manchester: Manchester University Press, 2000), pp. 146–69.

Higaki M., 'Kinsei amakusa no jinkōmondai to sono haikei', *Kyūshū bunkashi kenkyūsho kiyō*, 2 (1951), pp. 1–12.

Hiraishi, N., 'The Formation of Maruyama Masao's Image of Japanese Intellectual History during the War Period', *Social Science Japan Journal*, 6:2 (2003), pp. 241–54.

Howe, C., *The Origins of Japanese Trade Supremacy: Development and Technology in Asia from 1540 to the Pacific War* (Chicago, IL: University of Chicago Press, 1996).

Howland, D. R., *Translating the West: Language and Political Reason in Nineteenth-Century Japan* (Honolulu, HI: University of Hawaii Press, 2002).

Ike N., 'Taxation and Land Ownership in the Westernization of Japan', *Journal of Economic History*, 7:2 (November 1947), pp. 160–82.

Irie T., *Hōjin kaigai hatten shi*, 2 vols (Tokyo: Ida shoten, 1942).

Ishii, K., 'Japanese Foreign Trade and the Yokohama Specie Bank, 1880–1913', in O. Checkland, Nishimura S. and Tamaki N., *Pacific Banking, 1859–1959: East Meets West* (Basingstoke: Macmillan Press, 1994), pp. 1–23.

Ishii, R., *A History of Political Institutions in Japan* (Tokyo: Tokyo University Press, 1980).

Jogaku zasshi, nos 1–526 (1885–1904) (Kyoto: Rinsen shoten, 1966–7).

Jones, F. C., *Extraterritoriality in Japan and the Diplomatic Relations Resulting in Its Abolition 1853–1899* (New York: Ams Press, 1970).

Karatani, K., *Origins of Modern Japanese Literature* (Durham, NC: Duke University Press, 1993).

Kasza, G., 'War and Welfare Policy in Japan', *Journal of Asian Studies*, 61:2 (May 2002), pp. 417–35.

Kawai Y., *Muraoka Iheiji jiden* (Tokyo: Nanpōsha, 1960).

Kee Y. S., 'The Japanese in Malaya before 1942', *Journal of the South Seas*, 20:1–2 (1965), pp. 48–88.

Kelly, J. D., 'Gaze and Grasp: Plantations, Desires, Indentured Indians, and Colonial Law in Fiji', in L. Manderson and M. Jolly (eds), *Sites of Desire, Economies of Pleasure: Sexualities in Asia and the Pacific* (Chicago, IL: University of Chicago Press, 1997), pp. 72–98.

Kersten, R., *Democracy in Japan: Maruyama Masao and the Search for Autonomy* (London; Routledge, 1996).

Kim I., *Nihon josei aishi – yūjo, jorō, karayuki, ianfu no keifu* (Tokyo: Gendai shuppankai, 1960).

Kimura, Y., *Issei: Japanese Immigrants in Hawaii* (Honolulu, HI: University of Hawaii Press, 1988).

Kinmonth, E. H., 'Fukuzawa Reconsidered: *Gakumon no susume* and its Audience', *Journal of Asian Studies*, 37:4 (August 1978), pp. 677–96.

Kitagawa, K., 'Japan's Economic Relations with Africa between the Wars: A Study of Japanese Consular Reports', *African Study Monographs*, 11:3 (December 1990), pp. 125–41.

Kitano N., *Amakusa kaigai hattenshi* (Fukuoka: Ashishobō, 1985).

Koschmann, J. V., *Revolution and Subjectivity in Postwar Japan* (Chicago, IL: University of Chicago Press, 1996).

Kurahashi K., '"Karayuki" to Fujin Kyōfūkai (1): Kyūshū no ichi chiiki joseishi no shikaku kara', *Kirisutokyō shakai mondai kenkyūkai*, 51 (December 2002), pp. 1–62.

Kurahashi M., *Kita no karayuki-san* (Tokyo: Kyōei shobō, 1989).

—, *Karayuki-san no uta* (Tokyo: Kyōei shobō, 1990).

—, *Shimabara no karayuki-san: Kiso Hirota Gonshō to Daishidō* (Tokyo: Kyōei shobō, 1993).

Levine, P., 'Modernity, Medicine, and Colonialism: The Contagious Disease Ordinances in Hong Kong and the Straits Settlements', *Positions*, 6:3 (1998), pp. 675–705.

—, *Prostitution, Race and Politics: Policing Venereal Disease in the British Empire* (New York: Routledge, 2003).

Lindin, O. G., *Ogyū Sorai's Discourse on Government (Seidan): An Annotated Translation* (Wiesbaden: Harrassowitz Verlag, 1999).

MacKirdy, O. C. M. and W. N. Willis, *The White Slave Market* (London: S. Paul & Co., 1912).

Maeda, A., *Text and the City: Essays on Japanese Modernity*, ed. J. A. Fuji (Durham, NC: Duke University Press, 2004).

Marx, K., *Capital*, trans. B. Fowkes, 3 vols (Harmondsworth, Middlesex: Penguin, 1976–81).

Meiroku Zasshi: Journal of the Japanese Enlightenment, trans. W. R. Braisted (Tokyo: University of Tokyo Press, 1976).

Miners, N., *Hong Kong under Imperial Rule, 1912–1941* (Hong Kong: Oxford University Press, 1987).

Miyamoto T., *Wasurerareta Nihonjin* (Tokyo: Iwanami bunko, 1987).

Miyamoto T. et al. (eds), *Nihon zankoku monogatari*, 5 vols (Tokyo: Heibonsha, 1959–60).

Miyaoka K., *Shōfu-kaigai rurōki* (Tokyo: San-ichi shobō, 1968).

Moore, T., and S. Richards, 'Sandakan No. 8 Brothel', *Bulletin of Concerned Asian Scholars*, 7 (October–December 1975), pp. 52–60.

Mori K., *Jinshin baibai – kaigai dekasegi onna* (Tokyo: Shibundō, 1966).

Morisaki K., *Karayuki-san* (Tokyo: Asahi shinbunsha, 1976).

Moriyama, A. T., *Imingaisha: Japanese Emigration Companies and Hawaii, 1894–1908* (Honolulu, HI: University of Hawaii Press, 1985).

Morizaki K., 'Sekushuariti no rekishi', in Kono N. and Tsurumi K. (eds), *Onna to otoko no jikū: nihon joseishi saikō, Semegiau onna to otoko: kindai* (Tokyo: Fujiwara-shoten, 1995), pp. 153–82.

Munro, V. E., and M. D. Giusta (eds), *Demanding Sex: Critical Reflections on the Regulation of Prostitution* (Aldershot, Hampshire: Ashgate, 2008).

Murray, A., 'Debt-Bondage and Trafficking: Don't Believe the Hype', in K. Kempadoo and J. Doezema (eds), *Global Sex Workers: Rights, Resistance, and Redefinition* (New York: Routledge, 1998), pp. 51–64.

Nagasaki ken henshū i-inkai (ed.), *Nagasaki ken keisatsushi*, 3 vols (Nagasaki: Nagasaki ken keisatsu honbu, 1976).

Nagata, M. L., 'Mistress or Wife? Fukui Sakuzaemon vs. Iwa, 1819–1833', *Continuity and Change*, 18:2 (August 2003), pp. 287–309.

Nakamura M., 'Tokugawaki amakusa ni okeru dekasegi no shosō', *Kumamoto daigaku kyōiku gakubu kiyō*, 5 (1957), pp. 38–49.

Nanyō oyobi Nihonjinsha, *Nanyō no gojūnen – Singapōru wo chūshin ni dōhō katsuyaku*, ed. Nomura T. (Singapore: Hokuto shobō, 1938).

Nihon chōki tōkei sōran, ed. Nihon Tōkei Kyōkai, 5 vols (Tokyo: Nihon Tōkei Kyōkai, 1987–8).

Nihon fujin mondai shiryō shūsei, ed. Ichikawa F. et al., 10 vols (Tokyo: Domesu shuppan, 1980).

Nihon joseishi – dai 4 kan, kindai, ed. Joseishi sōgō kenkyūkai, 5 vols (Tokyo: Tokyo daigaku shuppankai, 1982).

Nihon Kirisutokyō Fujin Kyōfūkai (ed.), *Kaigai shūgyōfu mondai: dai ichigō – Amakusa no bun* (Kyoto: Nihon Kirisutokyō Fujin Kyōfūkai, 1920).

— (ed.), *Nihon Kirisutokyō Fujin Kyōfūkai hyakunenshi* (Tokyo: Domesu shuppan, 1986).

Nishida M., 'Kaigai ni okeru nihon no baishōfu nitsuite: meiji nijūnendai no jōtai', *Nihon rekishi*, 62 (February 1954), pp. 47–59.

Nolte, S., and S. Hastings, 'The Meiji State's Policy Toward Women, 1890–1910', in G. L. Bernstein (ed.), *Recreating Japanese Women, 1600–1945* (Berkeley, CA: University of California Press, 1991), pp. 151–74.

Ogawa, M., 'American Women's Destiny, Asian Women's Dignity: Trans-Pacific Activism of the Woman's Christian Temperance Union, 1886–1945' (PhD dissertation, University of Hawaii, 2004).

—, '"Hull House" in Downtown Tokyo: The Transplantation of a Settlement House from the United States into Japan and the North American Missionary Woman, 1919–1945', *Journal of World History*, 15:3 (September 2004), pp. 359–87.

Onozawa A., 'Dai-ichiji seikai taisengo ni okeru haishō undō no kakudai – Nihon Kirisutokyō Fujin Kyūfūkai no katsudō wo chūshin toshite', *Kokusai kankei gaku kenkyū*, 26 (1999), pp. 55–68.

Patessio, M., 'The Creation of Public Spaces by Women in the Early Meiji Period and the Tōkyō Fujin Kyōfōkai', *International Journal of Asian Studies*, 3 (2006), pp. 155–82.

Peattie M., *Nan'yō: The Rise and Fall of the Japanese in Micronesia, 1885–1945* (Honolulu, HI: University of Hawaii Press, 1988).

Potts, L., *The World Labour Market: A History of Migration* (London: Zed Books, 1990).

Pyle, K. B., *The New Generation in Meiji Japan: Problems of Cultural Identity, 1885–1895* (Stanford, CA: Stanford University Press, 1969).

Ramseyer, J. M., 'Indentured Prostitution in Imperial Japan: Credible Commitments in the Commercial Sex Industry', *Journal of Law, Economics, and Organisation*, 7 (1991), pp. 89–116.

Roberts, L. S., 'The Petition Box in Eighteenth-Century Tosa', *Journal of Japanese Studies*, 20 (1994), pp. 423–58.

Rose, N., *Powers of Freedom: Reframing Political Thought* (Cambridge: Cambridge University Press, 1999).

Rosovsky, H., *Capital Formation in Japan, 1868–1940* (Glencoe: Free Press, 1961).

Sakai, N., 'Equality, Hierarchy, and Identity in Modern Japan: Reflections on the Nationalist Ethics of Fukuzawa Yukichi', in S. Y. S. Chien and J. Fitzgerald (eds), *The Dignity of Nations: Equality, Competition, and Honor in East Asian Nationalism* (Hong Kong: Hong Kong University Press, 2006), pp. 23–31.

Sand, J., 'At Home in the Meiji Period', in S. Vlastos (ed.), *Mirror of Modernity: Invented Traditions of Modern Japan* (Berkeley, CA: University of California Press, 1998), pp. 191–207.

Sasaki T., 'Fujin bunmei no hataraki', *Jogaku zasshi*, 65 (21 May 1887), pp. 86–8.

Sawada, M., 'Culprits and Gentlemen: Meiji Japan's Restrictions of Emigrants to the United States, 1891–1909', *Pacific Historical Review*, 60:3 (August 1991), pp. 339–59.

Schad-Seifert, A., 'Constructing National Identities: Asia, Japan and Europe in Fukuzawa Yukichi's Theory of Civilization', in D. Stegewerns (ed.), *Nationalism and Internationalism in Imperial Japan: Autonomy, Asian Brotherhood, or World Citizenship?* (London: Routledge Curzon, 2003), pp. 45–68.

Scheiner, I., *Christian Converts and Social Protest in Meiji Japan* (Berkeley, CA: University of California Press, 1970).

Sekiguchi, S., 'Confucian Morals and the Making of a "Good Wife and Wise Mother": From "Between Husband and Wife there is Distinction" to "As Husbands and Wives be Harmonious"', *Social Science Japan Journal*, 13:1 (January 2010), pp. 95–113.

Shimizu H., 'Gaimushō 'kaigai zairyū honpōjin shokugyōbestsu jinkō chōsa ikken' no shiryō teki seikaku', *Ajia keizai*, 26:3 (1985), pp. 70–92.

—, 'The Pattern of Japanese Economic Penetration of Prewar Singapore and Malaya', in S. Shiraishi and T. Shiraishi (eds), *The Japanese in Colonial Southeast Asia*, Translation of Contemporary Japanese Scholarship on Southeast Asia Series, 3 (Ithaca, NY: Cornell University Press, 1993), pp. 63–87.

—, 'Kindai nihon no kaigai tsūshō jōhō senryaku to tōnan ajia', in Suehiro A. (ed.), *Chiike kenkyū to shite no Ajia*, Iwanami kōza. 'Teikoku Nihon' no gakuchi, 8 vols (Tokyo: Iwanami shoten, 2006), vol. 6, pp. 205–37.

Shimizu H. and Hirakawa H., *Japan and Singapore in the World Economy: Japan's Economic Advance into Singapore 1870–1965* (London: Routledge, 1999).

Shingaporu Nihonjinkai (ed.), *Singaporu nihonjin bochi: shashin to kiroku* (Singapore: Japan Association, 1983).

Simmel, G., *Philosophy of Money* (London: Routledge, 1990).

Singer. P., *The President of Good and Evil: The Ethics of George W. Bush* (New York: Dutton, 2004).

Sissons, D. C. S, 'Karayuki-san: Japanese Prostitutes in Australia, 1887–1916, I', *Historical Studies*, 17 (April 1977), pp. 323–41.

—, 'Karayuki-san: Japanese Prostitutes in Australia, 1887–1916, II', *Historical Studies*, 17 (October 1977), pp. 474–88.

Smith, R., and E. L. Wiswell, *The Women of Suye Mura* (Chicago, IL: University of Chicago Press, 1982).

Smith, T. C, *Native Sources of Japanese Industrialization, 1750–1920* (Berkeley and Los Angeles, CA: University of California Press, 1988).

Sugihara, K., 'The Development of an Informational Infrastructure in Meiji Japan', in L. Bud-Frierman (ed.), *Information Acumen: The Understanding and Use of Knowledge in Modern Business* (London; New York, Routledge, 1994), pp. 75–97.

Sugiyama, S., *Japan's Industrialisation in the World Economy, 1859–1899: Export Trade and Overseas Competition* (London: Athlone Press, 1988).

Sumiya M., *Nihon sekitan sangyō bunseki* (Tokyo: Iwanami shoten, 1968).

Tadiar, N. X. M., *Things Fall Away: Philippine Historical Experience and the Makings of Globalization* (Durham, NC: Duke University Press, 2009).

Takashima M., 'Ryōjihōkoku seido no hatten to 'ryōjihōkoku' no kankō – 'tsūshō ihen' kara 'tsūshō isan',' in Tsunoyama (ed.) *Nihon ryōjihōkoku no kenkyū*, pp. 71–117.

Takamura S., 'Enomoto Takeaki no shokumin kōsō to nanyō guntō baishū kengi', *Kokushigaku*, 167 (1999), pp. 77–110.

Takemura T., *Haishō undō: kuruwa no josei wa dō kaihōsareta ka* (Tokyo: Chūkō shinso, 1982).

Tamaki, N., '"Learn and Earn, Earn and Learn": British Influence and Fukuzawa Yukichi's Creation of the First Japanese Business Elite', in in C. Hosoya and I. Nish (gen. eds), *The History of Anglo-Japanese Relations, 1600–2000*, 5 vols (Houndsmills, Basingstoke, and New York: Palgrave, 2000–3), vol. 4: 'Economic and Business Relations', ed. J. E. Hunter and S. Sugiyama, pp. 133–55.

'Teikoku shūgi-in kizokuin gi-in kakui ni seigan', *Tōkyō fujin kyōfū zasshi*, 32 (20 December 1890), pp. 2–3.

Tōkyō fujin kyōfū zasshi, 3 vols (Tokyo: Fuji shuppan, 1985).

'Tokyo fujin kyōfūkai no giketsu', *Jogaku zasshi*, 62 (30 April 1887), p. 38.

Torpey, J., *The Invention of the Passport: Surveillance, Citizenship, and the State* (Cambridge: University of Cambridge Press, 2000).

Tsunoyama S. (ed.), *Nihon ryōjihōkoku no kenkyū* (Tokyo: Dōbunkan shuppan, 1986).

Tsunoyama Y., *Enomoto Takeaki to Mekishiko shokumin ijū* (Tokyo: Dōbunkan shuppan, 1986).

Tyrrell, I., 'Women and Temperance in International Perspective: The World's WCTU, 1880–1920s', in S. Barrows and R. Room (eds), *Drinking: Behavior and Belief in Modern History* (Berkeley, CA: University of California Press, 1991), pp. 217–42.

Vlastos, S., *Peasant Protests and Uprisings in Tokugawa Japan* (Berkeley, CA: University of California Press, 1990).

Warren, J. F., *Ah Ku and Karayuki-san: Prostitution in Singapore 1870–1940* (Singapore: Oxford University Press, 1993).

Weitzer, R., 'The Social Construction of Sex Trafficking: Ideology and Institutionalization of a Moral Crusade', *Politics and Society*, 35:3 (September 2007), pp. 447–75.

Wray, W. D., *Mitsubishi and the N.Y.K., 1870–1914*, Council on East Asian Studies, Harvard East Asian Monographs, 108 (Cambridge, MA: Harvard University Press, 1984).

Yagishita H., 'Senzenki no ryoken no hensen', *Gaikōshiryōkanpō*, 12 (June 1998), pp. 36–7.

Yamajima K., 'Tokyo fujin kyōfūkai shuisho', *Jogaku zasshi*, 70 (6 August 1887), pp. 191–2.

Yamamoto S., *Nihon kōshōshi* (Tokyo: Chūō hōki shuppan kabushiki gaisha, 1983).

Yamamuro G., *Shakai kakusei ron* (Tokyo: Chūō kōronsha, 1977).

Yamazaki T., *Sandakan hachiban shōkan – teihen joseishi joshō* (Tokyo: Chikuma shobō, 1972).

—, *The Story of Yamada Waka: From Prostitute to Feminist Pioneer* (Tokyo: Kodansha International, 1985).

—, *Sandakan Brothel No. 8: An Episode in the History of Lower-Class Japanese Women*, trans. K. C. Taylor (Armonk, NY: M. E. Sharpe, 1999).

Yang S., '*Nihon Kirisutokyō Fujin Kyōfūkai* to *haishō undo*' (PhD dissertation, Tokyo University of Foreign Studies, 2005).

Yano T., *Nanshin no keifu* (Tokyo: Chūō kōronsha, 1985).

Yasui T., 'Kaigai ni oite nameta nigai keiken', *Kakusei*, 3:2 (1913), pp. 14–15.

Yasukawa, J., 'Fukuzawa Yukichi', in B. C. Duke (ed.), *Ten Great Educators of Modern Japan: A Japanese Perspective* (Tokyo: University of Tokyo Press, 1989), pp. 17–37.

Yasutake, R., *Transnational Women's Activism: The United States, Japan, and Japanese Immigrant Communities in California, 1859–1920* (New York: New York University Press, 2004).

Yuen C. L., 'The Japanese Community in Malaya before the Pacific War: Its Genesis and Growth', *Journal of Southeast Asian Studies*, 9:2 (September 1978), pp. 163–80.

INDEX

abortions, 132
agriculture, 51–3, 91, 116
  settlements, 39, 53, 54–6, 57, 59, 98, 100
Agustín, Laura María, 7–8
Amakusa Islands, 3, 6, 11, 15–16, 20, 31, 32–6, 76, 77
  marriage, 32
  studies of women migrating from, 32, 78–9
American Protestantism, 64, 65–6, 80, 104
Andō Tarō, 42–3, 53–4, 110–11
Anglo-Japanese Treaty of Commerce and Navigation, 99, 119
Anti-Prostitution Law (1958), 67–8
Aoki Shu-zō, 43, 51, 53
Asada Tokunori, 111
Asai Saku, 70–1
associations, 13, 93–4, 96, 103, 104, 116, 119
Australia, 1, 29, 43–4, 48, 53, 59, 70
autonomy, 90–6, 103, 133
  see also freedom

Bank of Taiwan, 115, 122
Banno Junji, 85
Barry, Kathy, 8
Batavia, 51
Bolsheviks, 76
Bonin Islands, 52
Britain
  and colonies, 19–20, 43, 59, 97, 106, 111
  trade, 93
British Columbia, 44, 54
British empire, 117–18
British forces, 117–18
  in Hong Kong, 19, 102
  in Singapore, 19, 108
brothels, 2, 5, 15, 19–20
  Hong Kong, 19–20, 23–4, 28
  house-, 2
  owners, 27, 28–9, 33, 34
  Queensland, 33–4
  Singapore, 18, 19–20, 31, 105, 108, 112, 113–17, 118, 123, 124
Buddhism, 65
  missionaries, 100–1
bureaucracy, 12, 39–41, 45, 74, 79–80

California, 44, 54
capitalism, 17, 125–8, 130–1
Caroline Islands, 52, 119
Chikuhō, 22
child labour, 30
child prostitution, 117
children
  of concubines, 66, 73
  of prostitutes, 35
  protection, 133–4
  socializing, 129
  trafficking, 108
  of wives, 66
China, 110
  labourers from, 3, 19, 43, 53, 70, 96, 107
  ports, 47
  see also Hong Kong
Chinda Sutemi, 44
Chinese Exclusion Act, 53
Chinese protectorate, 18, 45, 107–9, 120, 124
Christianity, 60, 64
Christians, 4, 38, 60, 73–4, 75, 79–81, 129, 131–2, 133, 134
  see also Protestants
CIA, 8

Civil Code
1882, 66
1898, 73
class, social, 65–9, 128–9
middle classes, 9, 13, 60, 74, 81, 87, 102, 130
coal exports, 11, 17, 21–2, 24–5, 47
Coalition Against Trafficking in Women, 8
colonial rule, 3, 10, 19–20, 43, 59, 96, 106, 111
Colonization Society, 97–8
competition, 91, 92, 94–5
concubines, 38, 63, 65–6, 68, 83, 89
legal status, 66, 73, 89
Confucianism, 65, 84, 86, 87, 92–3, 104
consuls, 4, 42, 43, 44–6, 48, 56–7, 58–9, 91, 105–6, 110, 112, 124
authority, 106, 108–9, 111
Hong Kong, 23, 39, 40–1, 124
reports, 39, 40–1
Singapore, 45–6, 105, 112, 113, 120–1, 123, 124
and trade, 39–41
Contagious Disease Ordinance, 108, 117
cooperative credit associations, 116–17, 121, 122

Deleuze, Gilles, 133
Diamond Jubilee Year, 114–15
Diplomatic Record Office, 8–9
Donzelot, Jacques, 74, 129
Dorn, Elizabeth, 62
Dutch East Indies, 1, 51

Edo, 20, 21, 51
education, 48–9, 64–5, 74, 75, 79, 95
and talent, 95
women's, 73
emigration
clandestine, 4, 22–3, 24–5, 26, 48–9
control, 46–51, 53–4, 56–7, 70, 109, 112, 120
passports, 28, 112–13
encouraged, 96–9
labour force, 4, 32, 41–3, 54–6, 96–8, 125
contracts, 110–11
made possible, 17–18
societies for, 97–8
studies of women from Amakusa, 32, 78–9
Emigration Protection Ordinance/Law, 99
empire
British, 117–18
Japanese, 4–5, 67, 81, 119
see also colonial rule; imperialism
Enomoto Takeaki, 51–7, 96, 98
equality, 5, 8, 63, 67, 68, 85, 88, 93–4, 104
Evans, William, 18
exchange, 16–17, 91, 126–7
exports, 5, 39–40
coal, 21–2, 24, 25
extradition, 110–11, 118, 120

family, 31–2, 63, 67–9, 71–2, 73, 74, 128–9
Confucian, 92–3
daughters sold, 15, 28, 32, 37
gender relations, 86–8
see also fathers; households; mothers
fathers, 31–2, 68–9, 74
feminists, 5–6, 8, 9–10, 25, 61–2, 64, 80, 85, 86, 131, 132, 134
Formosa, 100
Foucault, Michel, 10, 81, 125
free market, 60, 128, 130
freedom, 1, 59, 85, 88, 94–5, 103, 106, 128, 133
autonomy, 90–6, 103, 133
Freedom and Popular Rights Movement, 68, 91
Fujii Minoru, 120–1
Fujime Yuki, 62
Sei no Rekishigaku, 9
Fujin Kōron, 77
Fujin shinpō, 76
Fujita Toshirō, 109–10, 113
Fukuoka, 21, 22
Fukuoka nichinichi, 27
Fukuzawa Yukichi, 12–13, 83–104, 130–1
fuseigyō, 47
Fushiki-maru, 47, 112

Garon, Sheldon, 62, 74
geisha, 68, 89–90, 122
gender hierarchies and roles, 5, 10–11, 18, 68
in family, 86–8
see also women

global market, 1, 39–41, 59, 86, 91, 93, 97, 106
globalization, 1, 3, 7, 11, 105–7
  and the poor, 125–34
government, good, 13, 88–90
Griffith, Samuel, 43
Guam, 52

Hacking, Ian, 11–12
Hakodate, 21
harbour authorities, 22–3, 48
  US, 70
Hawaii, 1, 41, 42–3, 51, 54, 59, 97, 97, 100, 109
Hayashi Utako, 76–7
Hiraishi Nao'aki, 84
Hirawaka Hitoshi, 115, 116
Hiroshima, 54
Hokkaida, 52, 54
Hong Kong, 18–20, 26, 29, 45, 102, 111–12
  arrival of *Fushiki-maru*, 47
  British troops, 102
  brothels, 19–20, 23–4, 28
  consulate, 22, 23–4, 28, 113, 123, 124
  gambling, 115
  harbour, 22–3, 27–8, 47
  market, 21, 22
House of Peers, 46, 48, 49, 50, 61
House of Representatives, 97
households, 12, 30, 59, 63, 64, 66, 68, 71–2, 129
  authority, 31–2
  economy, 11, 30, 34–5
  peasant, 30, 37
  as property, 68
  samurai, 66
  see also family
Howland, Douglas, 91
humanism, 80–1, 129
Hyogo, 21

Imai Shinoburō, 27
immigration control
  Singapore, 22–3, 120
  US, 44, 70
Imperial Army, 5
imperialism
  European, 3, 86
  Japanese, 5, 17, 119
  see also empire

India
  labourers from, 3, 19, 43, 107
  soldiers, 118
individuals, 6, 10, 63, 84–6, 92, 93–6, 102, 132–3
industrialization, 3, 39, 41, 91–3, 127, 130
  expense, 92, 99
inheritance, 66, 68–9, 73
Inoue Kaoru, 41–2, 51, 89, 109, 111
Inuoe Kizaburō, 28–9
Inoue Kowashi, 50
intervention, 10
Itagaki Taisuke, 91
Itōirobumi, 38, 89
Iwakura Tomomi, 54, 96

Janes, L. L., 64
Japan Weekly Mail, 98–9
Japanese Association (in Singapore), 119–20, 121, 122, 124
Japanese Woman's Christian Temperance Union (JWCTU), 61–81, 83, 90, 103–4, 124, 128, 129, 130
  field study of Amakusa, 32
  pledging, 67
Jiji shimpō, 85–6, 94, 98–9

kaigai shu-gyo-fu, 3–4
Kanagawa, 21
kara, 2
Karatini Ko-jin, 64
Karatsu, 22
karayuki-san, 2–13, 14
  dictionary definition, 15
  Yamazaki writes of, 15–16
Kasada Noatkichi, 116
Keio University, 83
Kinmouth, Earl, 95
Kitazawa Shinjirō, 77
Kobe, 25
Kodansha Encyclopedia of Japan, 15
Komura Jutarō, 57–8
Konoe Atsumaro, 49
Korea, 4, 48, 85, 110, 118
K-san, 31
Kubushiro Naokatsu, 77
Kubushiro Ochimi, 77, 79
kuchi-ireya, 27
Kuchinotsu, 17, 21–2, 23, 25, 31

Kumamoto, 18, 21, 54
Kurino Shinichirō, 56
Kyōoka Takamoto, 49–50
Kyushu, 2–3, 20
  coal mines, 11, 17, 21–2, 24
  JWCTU chapters, 79
  women's migration from, 3, 15–16, 17–18, 22, 24, 124, 125–6
  see also Amakusa Islands; Shimbara Peninsula

labour
  child, 30
  control, 59
  free, 1, 11, 127
  Marx on, 17
  migration, 4, 30, 32, 41–5, 54–6, 96–8, 125
Law for the Protection of Japanese Women in Foreign Countries, 46–50, 61, 98–9
League of Nations, 69
Leavitt, Mary Clement, 62
Levine, Phillipa, 108

Macduff, SS, 22–3
Malay Peninsula, 45, 57, 116, 118, 121, 122, 123, 124
Manchuria, 76
Manila, 123
Mariana Islands, 52, 119
Marks, Alexander, 43–4
marriage, 35, 63, 64, 65, 66–7, 68–9, 73, 80, 88, 101, 128–9
  Amakusa, 32, 78
  dowry, 32
  and status, 66–7
  wives, status of, 66–7, 68, 73, 75
Maruya Trading, 94
Maruyama Masao, 84–5
Marx, Karl, 10, 17
Matsukata Masayoshi, 41, 57, 96, 97
Meiji rule, 1, 2, 15, 21, 37–40, 50, 52–3, 58–60, 65, 66, 83, 84, 89, 96, 102–3, 127, 129, 130
  opposition to, 90–1, 97
Mexico, 7, 57, 98
Micronesia, 119
middle class, 9, 13, 60, 74, 87, 102, 130
  sexuality, 81
Miike, 21, 22
mikko-fu, 4
Minami Sadatsuke, 23, 111, 112
missionaries
  American Protestant, 65–6
  Shinto and Buddhist, 100–1
Mitsubishi, 22
Miyagawa Kyūjirō, 22, 29, 112–13
Miyagawa Shizue, 76–7
Miyamoto, Tsuneichi, *Wasurerareta Nihojin*, 31–2
Miyazaki Kōhei, 30
modernization, 1–2, 10–13, 18, 36, 39, 60, 63, 64, 65, 84, 85, 125–6, 128
  expense, 92
Moji, 17, 22, 25, 26
money economy, 11, 30, 125–6
moral judgements, 11, 64, 67, 69–70, 78–9, 90, 128, 129, 133–4
morality, 60, 73–81, 133
Mori Katsumi, *Jinshin baibai*, 2–3
Morisaki Kazue, 5–6, 7
Moriya Asuma, 79
mothers, 61–2, 63, 68–9, 73, 74, 86, 87, 129
Muraoke Iheji, 25
Murata Tatomutsu, 50

Nagasaki, 17, 18, 20, 21, 22–3, 25, 26–7, 28, 31, 38
Nagasaki kaisho, 20
Nagata, Mary Louise, 66
Nakagawa Kikuzo, 116
Nakagawa Tsunejirō, 109
Nakano Goichi, 41
Naoki Sakai, 92–3
nation-building, 10, 11, 13, 21, 35, 38–40, 46, 69–73, 75, 84–5, 92–4, 97, 98, 103, 106, 127
nationality, 93
Nelson, Christopher, 116
Netherlands, 51, 91
NGOs, 7–8, 131
Nihon zankoku monogatari, 2–3
Niigata, 21
Nippon Yūen Kaisha, 97
Nishiyama Yūzō, 115–16
Noma Seiichi, 26
Nunokawa Magoichi, 77–8

Ōga Kamekichi, 18
Ogawa, Manako, 62
Ōkubo Toshimichi, 40
Ōkuma Shigenobu, 96
Ōmori, 124
Ōmuta, 21
Onio, 27–8
Ordinance for the Emancipation of Prostitutes, 37
Origukuchi Shinobu, 2
Osaka, 21, 29, 31
  slums, 74, 79
Osaki, 15–16
Outline of a New Criminal Code, 66
Ozaki Miyoshi, 48–9

Pacific islands, 52–3
Pacific War, 2
passports, 28, 112–13
patriarchy, 15, 16–17, 29, 30, 31, 32, 65, 66, 68, 73
patriotism, 102
petitions, 61, 68, 69, 70–1, 124
philanthropy, 73–6, 79–80, 128
Philippines, 112
Ping Yang, Princess, 4–5
'pleasure quarter', 37
Police Offences, 50
population
  rise in, 100, 103
  surveys, 59
Porter, Edward, 23
power, 8, 10
problematization, 10
procurers *see* traffickers
progress, 84
prostitutes
  repatriation, 117, 121–3
  returning home, 26, 32, 36, 72
  see also brothels; concubines; *geisha*; *karayuki-san*
prostitution
  Anti-Prostitution Law (1958), 67–8
  child, 117
  clandestine, 37
  eradication, 120–4
  Fukazawa on, 89–90, 99–104
  licensed, 9, 18, 19, 37–8, 56, 70, 90, 103–4
  prohibition, 9–10, 56, 67–8, 117
  punishment, 48–50
  and race, 117–18
  see also trafficking, human
Protestants, 64, 65, 73, 75–6, 79, 80–1, 104
  missionaries, 65–6
public opinion, 38, 61, 83, 91–2, 128, 129
Purity Society, 75

race, 1, 59, 117–18
railways, 22, 26
Rangoon, 123
representation, 10
Rokumeikan, 89
Rose, Nikolas, 63
rōshigun, 4
rubber plantations, 19, 116, 121, 122
Russia, 53
Russo-Japanese War, 25, 74

Saigō Takamori, 90
Saitō Miki, 45–6, 112
Salvation Army, 75, 79
samurai strata, 1, 63, 65, 66
  former, 52–3, 55, 64, 85–6, 64, 90–1
  women, 86–7, 128–9
Sasaki Shigetoshi, 24, 33–5
Sasaki Toyoju, 66
Satsuma rebellion, 53, 90
Scheiner, Irwin, 64
settlements, agricultural, 39, 53, 54–6, 57, 59, 98, 100
  and prostitutes, 86–7, 101–2, 103
sexuality, 81, 128–9
shame, 11, 63–4, 70, 71, 80–1, 108, 133
Shanghai, 21, 31, 40, 42, 110
Shimbara Peninsula, 6, 15, 20, 21, 30, 32, 76, 77
Shimizu Hajime, 105
Shimizu Hiroshi, 115, 116
Shimonaka Kunihiko, 2
Shinto missionaries, 100–1
Siberia, 76–8
Simmel, Georg, 126

Singapore, 13, 18–20, 21, 22, 24–5, 45, 105–24
  brothels, 18, 19–20, 31, 105, 108, 112, 113–17, 118, 123, 124
  consulate, 45–6, 105, 112, 113, 120–1, 123, 124
  finance, 115–16
  immigration control, 120
  Japanese Association, 119–20, 121, 122, 124
  Japanese cemetery, 114, 119
  market, 21
  prostitution eradicated, 120–4
  trade, 106–7, 118
  World War I, 117–18
Sino-Japanese War, 71
slavery, 8, 25, 64, 108, 112, 117
social work, 73–81
South Korea, 5
S-san, 30–1
status *see* class
Straits Settlements, 18–19, 28, 29, 45, 105, 107–8, 115, 117–18, 120–1
  see also Malay Peninsula; Singapore

Tadir, Neferti, 16–17
Taguchi Ukichi, 45
Taisho period, 2, 119
Taiwan, 5, 26
Takada Tokijirō, 29
Takashima, 21
Tanaka Fujimaro, 56
Tanaka Tokichi, 24–5
Tang Dynasty, 4
Tetartos, SS, 27–8
Thailand, 5
Thursday Island, 24, 33, 43, 115
Tokugawa shogunate, 20–1, 37, 38, 52, 54, 92, 93, 102
Tokyo, 4, 42, 43, 79
  Kanda district, 77
  Metropolitan Police, 38
  slums, 74
  Yoshiwara quarter, 75, 89
Tokyo Fujin Kyo-fu-kai zasshi, 61
tour groups, 5
trade, 38–41, 58, 91, 92, 106–7, 115, 118
  Anglo-Japanese Treaty of Commerce and Navigation, 99
  exports, 5, 21–2, 24, 25, 39–40, 97, 118
  free, 93
  imports, 38–9
  and national security, 96–7
  and prostitution, 20–5, 99–104
  routes, 3, 18–19, 20–1, 39, 44
  in World War I, 118
  see also global market
traffickers (procurers), 15, 25–7, 28–31, 71, 109–10, 111–12
trafficking, human, 8, 57, 69, 71, 108–10
  Coalition Against Trafficking in Women, 8
  finance, 115
  opposition, 117, 120, 131–3
  purchase price, 28–9
Tsuda Sanzō, 53

Uchida Yasuya, 123–4
United Nations Population Fund, 132
urbanism, 74, 126
USA, 1, 5, 48, 118, 133, 134
  anti-trafficking measures, 131–2
  immigration control, 70
  immigration to, 44–5, 70, 96
  trade, 5, 21
  see also California; Hawaii
Ushibukai, 31

value, exchange, 17, 126–7
value judgements, 11
venereal disease, 70, 108, 116, 117
victimization, 7, 8, 16–17, 113
Vietnam War, 5
Vladivostock, 102

war, 91
  see also Russo-Japanese War; Vietnam War; World War I
Wakamatsu, 22
'Warning Bell', 72–3
White Slave Market, The, 117
White Slave Traffic, 117
Willard, Frances E., 62
wives, status of, 66–7, 68, 73, 75
women
  education, 73
  equality, 5–6, 61–2, 67, 68, 85, 88, 104
  see also concubines; *geisha*; Japanese Woman's Christian Temperance Union; mothers; prostitutes; wives

Women and Girls Protection Ordinance, 117, 124
Women's Reform Society, Kyoto branch, 72
World War I, 13, 117–18

Yajima, Kajiko, 67, 75
Yamaguchi, 41, 54
Yamaji Kajiko, 124
Yamazaki Heikichi, 121–2, 124
Yamazaki Tomoko, 5–7, 15–16, 25
  Sandakan hachiban sho-kan, 15–16
  Sandakan No. 8 Brothel, 7, 16
Yasutake, Rumi, 62–3
Yokohama Specie Bank, 94, 99, 122
Yokoyama Kikuno, 26–7
Young Men's Moral Reform Association, 72
Yuasa Hatsuko, 68

For Product Safety Concerns and Information please contact our EU
representative GPSR@taylorandfrancis.com
Taylor & Francis Verlag GmbH, Kaufingerstraße 24, 80331 München, Germany

www.ingramcontent.com/pod-product-compliance
Ingram Content Group UK Ltd.
Pitfield, Milton Keynes, MK11 3LW, UK
UKHW022127190926
475702UK00013B/1685